Differentiated SCHOOL LEADERSHIP

North Carolina Wesleyan College

WISDOM AND COURAGE THROUGH CHRISTIAN EDUCATION

1956

ROCKY MOUNT, N.C.

*To all school leaders who are
engaged in the ongoing,
complex struggle of helping all
students succeed academically*

Differentiated SCHOOL LEADERSHIP

Effective Collaboration, Communication, and
Change Through Personality Type

Jane A.G. Kise   🍁   Beth Russell

CORWIN PRESS
A SAGE Publications Company
Thousand Oaks, CA 91320

For information:

Corwin Press
A Sage Publications Company
2455 Teller Road
Thousand Oaks, California 91320
www.corwinpress.com

Sage Publications Ltd.
1 Oliver's Yard
55 City Road
London EC1Y 1SP
United Kingdom

Sage Publications India Pvt. Ltd.
B 1/I 1 Mohan Cooperative Industrial Area
Mathura Road, New Delhi
India 110 044

Sage Publications Asia-Pacific Pte. Ltd.
33 Pekin Street #02-01
Far East Square
Singapore 048763

Printed in the United States of America.

Library of Congress Cataloging-in-Publication Data

Kise, Jane A. G.
Differentiated school leadership: effective collaboration, communication, and change through personality type/Jane A. G. Kise, Beth Russell.
    p. cm.
Includes bibliographical references and index.
ISBN 978-1-4129-1772-8 (cloth)
ISBN 978-1-4129-1773-5 (pbk.)
    1. Educational leadership. 2. School supervision. 3. School management and organization. I. Title.

LB2805.K524 2008
371.2′01—dc22   2007014591

This book is printed on acid-free paper.

07   08   09   10   11   10   9   8   7   6   5   4   3   2   1

Acquisitions Editor:	Rachel Livsey
Managing Editor:	Dan Alpert
Editorial Assistants:	Phyllis Cappello and Tatiana Richards
Production Editor:	Jenn Reese
Copy Editor:	Paula L. Fleming
Typesetter:	C&M Digitals (P) Ltd.
Proofreader:	Charlotte J. Waisner
Indexer:	Ellen Slavitz
Cover Designer:	Monique Hahn
Graphic Designer:	Lisa Miller

Contents

Table of Professional Development Activities

A Note From the Authors

Beth: In my first school administration position, while working with a committee to plan a career day for our middle school students, one of the parents introduced Jane Kise to me as an expert on personality differences. The committee wanted students to understand that who we are influences our career choices. I wasn't expecting the experience to inform my understanding of who *I* am and what constitutes effective school leadership.

You see, I'd been questioning my ability to be an effective principal, based on how the role is described in school leadership literature. So many of the tasks considered most important for leading a school were things that neither interested me nor brought out my best qualities. Learning about personality type changed how I viewed my communication style, my work habits, and even the tasks themselves, empowering me to take the next steps as principal. I discovered that my personality type is significantly underrepresented in the principal population, but I could get the job done—and do it well—in my own style.

Just as important as understanding my own strengths, though, is understanding my staff. Currently, as an Extraverted principal leading an almost entirely Introverted staff, without type knowledge of our very different styles I would either be asking "What's wrong with me? Why can't I get them excited?" or "What's wrong with them?"

Jane: I've now worked with Beth and her staffs at three different schools, as well as with countless other schools. It's been exciting to translate the theories and techniques that work so well in executive coaching and training into sound practices for school leadership. However, I've found one huge difference between business leaders and education leaders. In businesses where as many people roam the halls as you find in an average school, the visionary and managerial roles reside with different individuals. In education, principals and district personnel are often expected to do it all!

So this book is in part a story about how we introduced type theory into schools, embedded it within our professional development of teachers by making it useful and practical in the classroom, and empowered students to advocate for how they learn best.

More important, we aim to broaden the perspective of what constitutes an effective leader and, in particular, an effective school leader. Although we don't argue with the literature describing the various tasks or duties of a principal, or even the need to carry out these tasks, we do believe that how the tasks are addressed can look very different, depending on one's personality preferences. No one personality type makes the best leader. Instead, leaders are most effective when they understand their own styles, work from their strengths, and compensate for their blind spots by developing skills or teaming with others.

We hope that the information in this book can help all people in school leadership positions realize their unlimited potential.

Acknowledgments

O ver the past eight years, we've had the privilege of working with the students and staff of several schools. They have embraced the concepts of personality type and strengthened our understanding of how best to put the theory to use in school leadership. Students willingly shared what they were learning about themselves, their teachers, and how they might best succeed academically. Teachers willingly tried new ideas, provided feedback, examined their classrooms in different ways, and worked with us to strengthen our overall focus on student learning. We also benefited from other school principals and leaders who shared not only their wisdom but also stories and examples of how their personality types influenced their leadership style and experiences.

We would also like to thank Jane's mentor, Sandra Krebs Hirsh, for all of the information and experience she shared regarding leadership and coaching, and Beth's mentor, Dave Peterson, who is also her personality type opposite and helped her examine leadership in many valuable ways.

The contributions of the following reviewers are gratefully acknowledged:

Jan Borelli
Principal
Westwood Elementary School
Oklahoma City, Oklahoma

Bruce Deterding
Principal
Wichita Heights High School
Wichita, Kansas

Anne Roede Giddings
Assistant Superintendent
Ansonia Public Schools
Ansonia, Connecticut

James Kelleher
Assistant Superintendent
Scituate Public Schools
Scituate, Massachusetts

Theron J. Schutte
Superintendent
Boone Community School
    District
Boone, Iowa

About the Authors

Jane A. G. Kise, EdD, is an educational consultant, specializing in team building, coaching, and school staff development. She is also the coauthor of more than 20 books, including *Differentiated Coaching: A Framework for Helping Teachers Change, Differentiation Through Personality Types, Introduction to Type and Coaching, LifeKeys,* and *Work It Out.* She holds an MBA in finance from the Carlson School of Management and a doctorate in Educational Leadership from the University of St. Thomas.

Kise has worked with diverse organizations, including Minneapolis Public Schools and various public and private schools, The Bush Foundation, Twin Cities Public Television, and numerous other institutions. She is a frequent workshop speaker and has presented at NSDC, World Futures, and APT International conferences. She has taught writing at the university level. She is a faculty member of the Center for Applications of Psychological Type and an executive board member of the Association for Psychological Type. In 2005, she won the Isabel Briggs Myers Award for Outstanding Research in the Field of Psychological Type.

Workshop descriptions, speaking schedule, and contact information are available at www.edcoaching.com.

Beth Russell, EdD, is a principal in a Minneapolis public school. She holds a BS in Child Development and Family Relations from Colorado State University, a Master's in Social Work from the University of Minnesota, and a doctorate in Educational Policy and Administration from the University of Minnesota.

Russell has worked in both urban and suburban school systems introducing type. Coauthor of a *Principal Leadership* article entitled "Are They Really Problem Students?", she views type theory as a vehicle for helping students self-advocate for how they learn best and helping teachers to identify new strategies so that all students can learn. She has presented at NSDC, World Futures, ASCD, and National Urban Alliance conferences. Russell volunteers as an assessor for the University of St. Thomas Principal Assessment Center and provides peer reviews for educational books for a local publisher.

Introduction: Leading Through Your Strengths

A deluge of recent books address the issue of *what* school leaders need to do to increase student achievement. Some even provide clear strategies. However, some very important *how* questions go unanswered. *How* do you help independent teachers form professional learning communities when their natural inclination is to work alone? *How* do you establish an atmosphere of trust when past betrayals and opinions create very real barriers? *How,* when teachers are sure they are doing all they can, do you help teachers believe that effort creates ability in students and that all can succeed? And *how* do you cover all the bases of leadership that research says are key to student achievement?

This book uses a single framework, that of personality type, to provide workable strategies to answer these questions and put into practice the research-based ideas that work.

What is personality type? While the concept is fully explained in Chapter 1, at its core, *type* describes normal, natural differences in how people

- Gain energy
- Take in information
- Make decisions
- Approach work and life in general

Look at the list again. Each item deals with processes that are essential to how we lead, collaborate, communicate, and learn, making it a valuable tool for school leadership teams.

The first step in using type, though, is acknowledging that the job of school leadership is too big for any one person.

Solo School Leadership? An Ideal Past Its Prime

Marzano, Waters, and McNulty (2005) listed 21 "responsibilities" that are key to effective school leadership. Cotton (2003) found 25 categories of principal behavior that correlate with student achievement. Reeves (2006) pointed out that effective performance on every dimension of leadership is impossible for a single individual, stating, "The task of the leader is to create an organization that is exemplary in every dimension and not engage in behaviors suggesting that a single person bears the burden of exemplary performance in every area" (p. 24).

Marzano agreed:

In short, our research and that of others validates the conclusion that leading a school requires a complex array of skills. However, the validity of this conclusion creates a logical problem because it would be rare, indeed, to find a single individual who has the capacity or will to master such a complex array of skills. . . . Taken at face value, this situation would imply that only those with superhuman abilities or the willingness to expend superhuman effort could qualify as effective school leaders.

Fortunately, a solution exists if the focus of school leadership shifts from a single individual to a team of individuals. (p. 99)

This book gives you the why, and then shows you how, using the research-based theory of type as a framework to

- Identify your natural strengths as a leader.
- Focus on where you can build on your strengths via training and practice.
- Pinpoint areas that, because of how you are wired, may take more effort than they're worth to reach adequacy, let alone leadership effectiveness.
- Build a leadership team that optimizes student achievement by carefully and effectively distributing leadership responsibilities.
- Help your leadership team—and your teachers—communicate, collaborate, and resolve conflicts in ways that improve student achievement.
- Work with parents and students.

People, not programs, make change possible. A principal who understands his or her own strengths can more readily transform individuals into a collaborative leadership team whose members grasp their own strengths and corresponding blind spots *and* can provide the support that teachers need.

1

What Type of Leader Are You?

It has been said that if you want to change the world, start by looking in the mirror. Given the strong correlation that we have found between leadership and student achievement, the same notion may apply to leaders who want to change their schools. (Waters, Marzano, & McNulty, 2004, p. 51)

What words might you use to describe your role as a school leader? Exciting? Challenging? Unpredictable? Never-ending? Paradoxical? Think for a moment about the synonyms for *paradoxical*: inconsistent, absurd, ironic, contradictory, illogical, and impossible are some of the main ones.

When one considers all that school leaders are asked to do, *paradox* takes on more meaning. Consider some of your key responsibilities:

- How easy is it to be both a reflective leader, taking time alone to rethink events and plan for the future, and a visible leader, interacting with students and teachers in the halls and classrooms? Further, most of us prefer one set of activities over the other.
- What about the conflicts between day-to-day managerial tasks and being a visionary leader? Most corporations divide those duties among different individuals because they require different skill sets and interests.
- Similarly, what about grappling with data and assessment strategies versus grappling with issues around teacher collaboration or building relationships with students? One requires attention to detail and logic, while the other requires attention to values and emotions.

- Finally, what about the charge to monitor and evaluate progress toward school reform goals, which requires creating action plans, versus the call for flexible leadership, which requires letting go of plans?

In other words, school leadership requires handling priorities, responsibilities, and goals that are in opposition to each other.

Leaders, though, don't have the luxury of worrying only about their own priorities. They need to influence the priorities of every adult in the building—especially as the evidence mounts for professional learning communities as a key to student achievement. Schmoker (2006) wrote

> If there is anything that the research community agrees on, it is this: The right kind of continuous, structured teacher collaboration improves the quality of teaching and professional morale in virtually any setting. Our experience with schools across the nation bears this out unequivocally. (p. 177)

Note the qualification, though: "The right kind of continuous, structured teacher collaboration. . . ." Leaders are charged with taking a group of independent workers, each isolated from the others, who often choose the profession because they like to work solo, and turning them into effective teams. Fullan (1993) pointed out that many teachers don't have the skills required for collaboration. Hargreaves (2002) discussed the very real barriers to the process of creating professional learning communities.

Thus, school leaders need to determine how best to carry out the huge task of organizing for student achievement—concentrating on giving teachers the training and support they need in their classrooms—*and* help teachers develop the skills they need to implement key elements such as collaboration. How?

Personality Type Theory

For decades, researchers and practitioners have used the theory of personality type in businesses to develop leaders and create high-functioning teams. The theory explores diametrically opposed yet normal *preferences* people have for

- Gaining energy
- Taking in information
- Making decisions
- Approaching work or life

These are key processes in education. What do we mean by preferences? Let's look at a physical example to be clear about the concept. In the space below, sign your name with your nonpreferred hand. What adjective might you use to describe the process?

Most people say that writing with their nonpreferred hand feels awkward, clumsy, or childish. They have to think about how to form the letters. Now sign below with your preferred hand:

_____

Most people say that writing with their preferred hand feels natural, smooth, or easy. They don't have to think. In the same way, type theory says that we have mental preferences for how we gain energy, take in information, make decisions, and approach life.

However, our preferences do not keep us from developing skills with the opposite mental processes. For example, almost all of us can write with our left hands. We can pick up a pencil and scribble something. We can *use* our left hand.

Now, can you and others read what you wrote with your left hand? If so, you have some skill with your left hand. Through practice, all of us could improve our handwriting and increase our skill at it.

But are you left-handed? If so, it's a physical preference that just *is*. You didn't decide to be left-handed. Further, it's equally good to be right-handed or left-handed, although at some points in human history, people have been biased against the latter.

Our mental preferences work the same way. All of us can *use* the eight mental preferences described below. With practice we can become more skilled with those we don't prefer. But we're hardwired to prefer four of the eight preferences; research shows differences in brain patterns (Myers, McCaulley, Quenk, & Hammer, 1998). And just like people, systems, organizations, or cultures usually favor one preference over another, even though all are equally valuable, viable processes. This chapter provides information for determining your own preferences and the ones your school or district administration might favor.

This theory of opposites puts patterns to strengths and struggles and provides developmental paths that have worked for others who share your preferences. Further, type theory *values* rather than evaluates differences. Fitzgerald (1997) pointed out several advantages of using type in leadership development:

- The focus on valuing natural differences halts the search for perfection in leaders since each personality has its own gifts and its own imperfections.
- The theory allows for enhanced self-awareness in leaders, including accurate assessment of predispositions, strengths, and blind spots.
- The emphasis changes from individual achievement to collaboration and teamwork to take advantage of differing gifts effectively.

Let's first explore your preferences. Then in Chapter 2, we'll examine different models of leadership through the lens of type—which roles are easiest for leaders with various preferences? What do you naturally do well as a leader?

Extraversion and Introversion: Gaining Energy for Leadership

The first preference pair describes how we are energized:

Extraversion (E):   Gaining energy through action and interaction, the outside world

Introversion (I):   Gaining energy through reflection and solitude, the inner world

Note that Extra*version* is spelled differently from extroversion; the words describe two different concepts. In the following scenario, which sounds more like you?

> Jane and Beth attended a conference together. Toward the end of the session, Beth invited the other school leaders at their table to join them for coffee and conversation. The group of seven then spent another two hours discussing the theories they had heard and what might or might not work in their own buildings. Beth then joined another group for dinner. Jane went back to her hotel room and ordered room service.

Note that both of us benefited from being with a group, and we would each eventually reflect on what we'd learned, but while the interaction was *energizing* for Beth, who prefers Extraversion, Jane felt *drained* by the end of the afternoon. She prefers Introversion.

Extra*version* isn't about sociability, shyness, or being the life of the party. While by definition, people who prefer Extraversion get their energy from the outside world—being with people, engaging in activities, exploring outer experiences—some prefer crowds while others prefer being with just a few close friends. Some enjoy a wide variety of activities while others have a favorite few. Either way, given a choice, they would rather pursue those activities with at least one other person than alone.

In contrast, people with a preference for Introversion gain energy from reflection and solitude. Yes, they have friends, and yes, they pursue activities, but the outer world is draining, whereas the inner world of thoughts and ideas brings renewal. Usually, they delve deeply into a few interests and activities and maintain a few close friendships. When they're with a crowd, they often converse with one or two people for long periods rather than mingle with different people.

To gain an understanding of the difference, think back on meeting dynamics. Recall a brainstorming session around student discipline, for example. Most Extraverts jump right into the conversation, adding ideas. They actually process thoughts by talking. Most Introverts hold back, perhaps not adding ideas until 10–15 minutes have passed. They process thoughts internally and are seldom comfortable sharing their ideas until they are fully formed.

One of the axioms of people who use type professionally is "If you want to know what Extraverts are thinking, listen. If you want to know what Introverts are thinking, ask!" Know, though, that if Introverts know the topic in advance and have time to reflect on it before the conversation, they can be as vocal as the Extraverts.

All of us have both an extraverted and an introverted side. The question is, how many people do you prefer to be with and for how long? For the moment, forget about what your job requires of you. Also, set aside escapist daydreams brought on by stress. Instead, think of what you really *prefer* as you place yourself on the continuums on page 8. The goal is not to be an "ambivert," showing equal skill with each preference, but to know which preference is easiest for you so you know when you have to adjust.

Below, circle the letter that describes you best:

E   **I**

(Extraversion)   (Introversion)

Ponder this: Which preference is favored in the United States? We value people who speak up quickly with ideas and participate actively in groups and events. We worry about quiet children and frequently question the mental health of people who spend time alone. The United States is biased in favor of Extraversion, even though about half of our population prefers Introversion.[1]

Which preference is favored among staff at your school? Most schools and other organizations develop an archetypal personality (Bridges, 2000). The personality may reflect that of the founding leader, the current leader, the organization's purpose, the majority preferences of the employees, or any combination of these factors. Understanding the personality of your school brings insights for change efforts as well as day-to-day management.

- Does most communication happen verbally, in face-to-face meetings or via phone (E), or through e-mail and other forms of writing (I)?
- During staff development events, are there chances for interaction (E), or is a lecture format used (I)?
- Are decisions and goals formed in conversation (E), or do conversations take place after time for reflection (I)?
- Is there a balance in classrooms between conversation and activities (E) and quiet time and reflection (I)?

One note: Perhaps due to their natural bent to spend more time in reflection, Introverted leaders are often, though not always, more aware than Extraverted leaders of how others view them (Walck, 1997).

Sensing and Intuition: Your Preference for Gathering Information

People—adults and students—take in information in two profoundly different ways:

Sensing (S):   Gathering information through the five senses, first paying attention to facts and reality

Intuition (N)[*]:   Gathering information through hunches, connections, and analogies, first paying attention to what could be

---

* Note that *N* is used for Intuition because *I* was already used for Introversion.

E | | | | | **I**

I'd rather be out and about,
visiting classrooms and
chatting with students.

I'd rather be in my office,
working on projects but
available if needed.

E | | | | | **I**

Interruptions often
energize me.

Interruptions drive me nuts.
It takes too long to get my mind
back to what I was doing.

E | | | | | **I**

I like gathering information
through site visits, conferences,
and conversations.

I like gathering information
through reading and research.

E | | | | | **I**

I usually take action
and then reflect.

I usually reflect and
then take action.

E | | | | | **I**

In groups, I offer
ideas quickly.

In groups, I form ideas
internally and offer
them somewhat later.

E | | | | | **I**

I prefer breadth—knowing
something about a lot
of topics in education.

I prefer depth—knowing
a lot about my specialty
areas in education.

E | | | | | **I**

I prefer communicating
face-to-face or via
telephone.

I prefer communicating
via e-mail or memos.

E | | | | | **I**

To work through my
problems, I like to talk
them out with someone.

To work through my
problems, I like to think
them through on my own.

One way to characterize the difference is that Sensing types first focus on the trees while Intuitive types first focus on the forest. Note that all of us use both Sensing and Intuition, but we (a) prefer to start with one or the other and (b) are usually more comfortable using one or the other. Which sounds more like you in the following story?

> Beth was in a cohort of principals studying Lauren Resnick's framework of the nine principles of learning. Her school's initiatives at the time included:
>
> • Becoming authorized as a Middle Years International Baccalaureate program
> • Implementing an antibullying curriculum
> • Using type concepts in lesson planning
> • Adopting common literacy strategies
>
> Beth, who prefers Intuition, clearly saw how the principles of learning framework could organize all of the school's initiatives. However, when she shared it with her leadership team, most of whom prefer Sensing, they were overwhelmed. They told her not to present the entire framework but to introduce it in pieces, step-by-step, and tie it clearly to their current tasks. Beth was energized by the BIG idea while her teachers felt overwhelmed by it.

In general, people with a preference for Sensing like to build on past experiences, work with verifiable facts and data, take a common-sense approach to problem solving, and deal with reality.

In general, people with a preference for Intuition like to build on new possibilities, work with ideas and theories, take an innovative approach to problem solving, and deal with future potential.

Aram (1990) pointed out the tensions between Sensing and Intuition in leadership:

> Managerial ideas and tools are often ill-suited to address the complex character of large organizations. We have theories and practices of innovation and concepts and policies of control; rarely do we seek conceptually or practically to integrate innovation and control. Many extol the virtues of change. Why isn't comparable emphasis placed on benefits of stability, and why not address ourselves more to the important challenge of balancing stability and development? (p. 35)

The Sensing gifts of leadership often involve stability and control; the Intuitive gifts often involve innovation and change. Where are your strengths? Again, as you mark yourself on the continuums on page 10, think about what comes more naturally for you.

Below, circle the letter that describes you best:

S   **N**

(Sensing)   (Intuition)

Which preference is favored in the United States? We value accuracy, common sense, and learning that has real-world applications. Further, think of how

S | | | | | N

I put together detailed procedures and policies. — I concentrate on the big picture of strategy and vision.

S | | | | | N

I tend to focus on a narrow band of initiatives. — I tend to be attracted to several new initiatives at once.

S | | | | | N

Past experiences and facts are reliable guides. — Future possibilities and ideas are reliable guides.

S | | | | | N

I prefer receiving relevant facts and examples. — I prefer receiving relevant theories and metaphors.

S | | | | | N

I excel at maintaining order in my building. — I excel at challenging the status quo in my building.

S | | | | | N

I gather facts and then determine direction. — I often "know," then look for facts to back up my hunch.

S | | | | | N

I'd rather perfect skills before learning new ones. — I love learning new skills but often start learning another set before using the first ones.

S | | | | | N

I use proven methods to solve problems. — I like solving new problems in unusual ways.

the country has framed educational reforms: the emphasis is on measurable results via standardized tests, consistent standards, and replicable methods. Approximately 65–70 percent of the population prefers Sensing.

However, when it comes to intellectual performance, what our educational institutions value is clearly biased in favor of Intuition. The following statistics show how *type bias* may be more harmful and far more difficult to detect than race or gender bias.

- 82 percent of Merit Scholarships (which are based on PSAT scores) go to Intuitive students, even though Intuitives account for only 30–35 percent of the population (Myers, 1993).
- Measures of creativity favor the Intuitive style (Hammer, 1996).
- The higher the level of education, the greater the bias toward Intuition. Consider how graduate-level education courses favor theory over application, for example. About 64 percent of university professors prefer Intuition; in some fields, such as philosophy and architecture, nearly all professors prefer Intuition.
- In a study of Teachers of the Year (Rushton, Knopp, & Smith, 2006), while 63 percent of the comparative group of elementary teachers preferred Sensing, 72 percent of the awards went to Intuitive teachers. Three of the 16 personality types accounted for nearly 60 percent of the awards. One way to interpret this data is that one has to teach like the role models in *Dead Poet's Society* or *Stand and Deliver* to receive an award, when in truth, *every* type has a distinct form of excellence in teaching.

Is Sensing or Intuition favored among staff at your school?

- Are teachers commended for following curriculum (S) or creating their own curriculum (N)?
- Is it safer to support the status quo (S) or to support change (N)?
- Are traditions and past successes honored (S), or are new practices and innovations (N) honored?
- Does the curriculum emphasize facts, procedures, algorithms, and designated texts (S) or creativity, self-study, individual expression, and constructivism (N)? Research shows, for example, that Sensing teachers favor a phonics-based approach to reading instruction while Intuitive teachers favor a whole language approach. In truth, to *know how* to read, write, and perform math for standardized tests and to *understand why* for higher-level thinking and problem solving, all students need both Sensing and Intuitive approaches to learning at every grade level and in every subject (Kise, 2007).

Note that your school's culture for students may be different from the culture for teachers. At one school for example, while teachers were encouraged to try innovative practices, students were seldom given choices in assignments, and independent study was discouraged because of the push to provide the knowledge needed for Advanced Placement tests.

Thinking and Feeling: How We Make Decisions

People approach decisions through two rational but psychologically opposite processes:

Thinking (T):   Basing decisions on principles, objectivity, and logical if-then, cause-effect reasoning

Feeling (F):   Making decisions based on values, considering the impact of each alternative on the people involved

People who prefer Thinking tend to be analytical, impartial, fair but firm, and logical. They tend to identify first what is wrong with a situation or an idea.

People who prefer Feeling tend to be empathetic, subjective, harmonious, and accepting. They tend to comment first on what is right with a situation or an idea. Which sounds more like you in the following scenario?

> Beth, who prefers Feeling, was discussing plans for school workshop week with a colleague who prefers Thinking. "As usual, we'll start with a movie written by some of our staff members—a parody of *The Wizard of Oz*—which will set our staff development theme for the year. We'll show it right after our breakfast together."
>
> "Breakfast?" her colleague replied. "Doesn't your staff just want to get through the agenda so they can work in their classrooms? I'm passing out the staff development schedule, going over open house arrangements, and releasing them."
>
> "I think we need that time to connect, to catch up on what happened over the summer, make new staff feel welcome. . . ."

Beth planned her activities based on her values for community building and her belief that activities like the movie creation helped energize staff for the new year. Her colleague planned her activities based on efficiency and maximizing time for tasks at hand. Note that considering values is every bit as rational as considering logic. If teachers at your school value group consensus, then a mandate for change, no matter how logical, may never get the careful consideration it deserves. However, traditional models of management and leadership favor the Thinking style—and no wonder. In business and in education, 75–80 percent of leaders have a preference for Thinking!

When leaders underestimate the importance of "soft" factors in decision making—things that can't be quantified but are still very real—they often find that results vary widely from what they envisioned. Consider how the theory of emotional intelligence brings the Feeling function into the theory of management. Sparks (2005) pointed out that, "Initiating and maintaining the momentum of significant change requires experiences that appeal to the heart as well as the head. Intellectual engagement alone is usually insufficient to produce such changes" (p. 1).

The heavy emphasis on Thinking in management texts can make it difficult for Feeling leaders to recognize their natural preference. Consider performance reviews where you need to give negative feedback to a teacher. Is it easy for you

T |_____|_____|_____|_____|_____| **F**

I enjoy working with data, identifying patterns and useful information.

I enjoy working with people and building relationships.

T |_____|_____|_____|_____|_____| **F**

My decisions come from logic, awareness of precedents, and cause-effect reasoning.

My decisions come from values-based analysis and the impact on people involved.

T |_____|_____|_____|_____|_____| **F**

I value being viewed as competent.

I value being viewed as caring.

T |_____|_____|_____|_____|_____| **F**

I prefer to work through conflict.

While I know how to work through conflict, I prefer to avoid it.

T |_____|_____|_____|_____|_____| **F**

I emphasize fairness through adherence to rules.

I emphasize fairness through consideration of circumstances.

T |_____|_____|_____|_____|_____| **F**

I tend first to see the flaws in ideas and practices.

I tend first to see the positives in ideas and practices.

T |_____|_____|_____|_____|_____| **F**

I tend toward skepticism.

I tend toward acceptance.

T |_____|_____|_____|_____|_____| **F**

I'm at ease when providing constructive criticism.

I dislike telling people unpleasant things.

to give a direct critique for essential improvement (Thinking), or would you rather deliver "bad news" by sandwiching it in with good news or through indirect means such as suggesting a book to read or another teacher to observe (Feeling)?

As you mark yourself on the continuums on page 13, consider your *natural* approach. For example, we're both inclined to make exceptions on assignment due dates when students have reasonable excuses—we both prefer the Feeling decision-making style. However, we know that to be fair to all students, we need to set clear rules about late work, a strength of the Thinking preference.

Below, circle the letter that describes you best:

T
(Thinking)

F
(Feeling)

While the United States population is split fairly evenly between Thinking and Feeling, our culture favors Thinking. However, this is the only preference pair with a gender bias: about 60 percent of males prefer Thinking while 40 percent prefer Feeling. The opposite is true for females; 60 percent prefer Feeling while 40 percent prefer Thinking. An accurate catchphrase would be "Thinkers are from Mars, Feelers are from Venus."

Feeling males report that they were often labeled as crybabies, wimps, or worse. Thinking females report labels such as catty, bossy, and far worse. Each gender is biased toward one of the preferences, and individuals are criticized when they don't fit the stereotype. This is another example of type bias.

Which preference is favored in your school?

- Is logic (Thinking) or values (Feeling) favored in decisions?
- Is the staff more concerned with each other's competency (Thinking) or ability to build relationships (Feeling)?
- Do teachers tend to critique (Thinking) or praise (Feeling) each other?
- When disciplining students, do staff stick to the rules (Thinking) or take into consideration individual nuances in each situation (Feeling)?
- Does staff understand the concept of "leveling the playing field" for special needs students by modifying assignments (Feeling), or do they think they are watering down expectations by changing or modifying (Thinking)?
- When conflict arises, do people address it head-on (Thinking) or prefer to ignore it (Feeling)?

Note that logic, values, competency, relationship building, critique, praise, conflict resolution, and conflict avoidance are all useful and important, but type theory is about what we *prefer.*

Traditionally, elementary schools have a Feeling personality; by high school, though, Thinking often defines the culture as teachers prepare students for the less-forgiving environments of college and work.

As a whole, teachers value meeting the needs of students as individuals, helping them build social and intellectual skills, developing their community values, and so on. However, a Feeling culture does not necessarily mean a harmonious culture, nor does a Thinking culture indicate an insensitive or contentious culture. Thinking types often address conflict head-on, make their feelings known, work through it, and move on. They may not even see such encounters as conflicts.

In contrast, if an organization continually buries conflict as Feeling types may do, eventually that conflict resurfaces, often in a violent, bitter episode. Frequently, we've conducted team interventions because Feeling types, teachers and other professionals, have engaged in vicious behavior toward each other.

Judging and Perceiving: Our Approach to Life

The final preference pair is perhaps the most visible in terms of outward behavior. What is your preferred approach to life?

Judging (J):   Preferring to plan your work and work your plan. Judging types are not more judgmental but rather prefer to come to judgments, bring closure, and wrap things up.

Perceiving (P):   Preferring to stay open to the moment. Perceiving types are not more perceptive but rather prefer to continue to perceive (gather more information), process, explore options, and allow for spontaneity.

In the following scenario, which sounds more like you?

> Beth and Jane were working together on a grant proposal. Thirty-six hours before they needed to turn in the 40-page application (it also happened to be the Saturday before Mother's Day), Beth showed up at Jane's with 13 new pieces of research that she thought would bolster their argument. Jane had already completed formatting the document but went through all of the articles with Beth and agreed on ways the information could be included. She then printed off a copy of the article for Beth and said, "Make any changes you want that improve clarity or flow, but we have to be done adding new information—or we'll either miss Mother's Day or the deadline!"

You might think of Judging types (Jane prefers Judging) as the "early starters" of the world. They like to plan ahead, set schedules (and follow them), be on top of their work, take care of responsibilities before relaxing, and come to closure rather than leave decisions hanging. For Judging types, productivity comes when they feel in control of their work—they know they'll be done with time to spare.

Perceiving types (Beth prefers Perceiving) like to stay more open to new developments or changing circumstances. Some are truly the "last-minute" people of the world who like to stay open as long as possible to new "perceptions" or information. Productivity or creativity for them flows from the adrenaline that time pressure produces. They usually work best in bursts of energy rather than via schedules. Often, they find ways to combine work and play or can move fluidly between the two. And they resist coming to closure too soon—they are keenly aware that there may be more options to explore and information to discover.

Not only are both styles valuable approaches to life, but the quality of people's work actually depends on being able to operate according to their own preference. Yet the United States is clearly a Judging culture. Planes are to leave on time, stores usually close promptly as posted, and tardiness is frowned on. About 60–65 percent of the population prefers Judging.

Schools, too, emphasize Judging, with bells and schedules and curriculum maps and pacing schedules and standardized tests for all students at the same time, no matter how different their learning needs might be.

Before you mark yourself on the continuums on page 17, be aware that 80–85 percent of school principals in the United States prefer Judging. Perceiving school leaders may either feel out of the mainstream or develop skills that make it difficult for them to recognize their natural preference. Remember, both Judging and Perceiving are valuable styles for leadership, learning, and life.

Below, circle the letter that describes you best:

J   **P**
(Judging)   **(Perceiving)**

Which preference best describes the culture of your school? Note that because our schools for the most part still follow an industrial model, where students are supposed to be moved through the system at a constant rate, any Perceiving tendencies may be viewed as irresponsible.

- Are teachers expected to follow set pacing schedules or curriculum maps (J), or are teachers allowed flexibility in how they address standards and curriculum (P)?
- Are there regular meetings with clear agendas (J), or are meetings more erratic with emergent agendas (P)?
- Are teachers commended for planning out lessons in full (J), or are teachers commended for developing and adjusting units as student needs and interests emerge (P)?
- If students fail to show proficiency with a skill or concept, do they move on with the class to the next unit (J), or does the school schedule allow more time for them to grasp the concept before they move on (P)?

Note that the educational principle that effort, not inborn intelligence, creates ability, championed by Resnick (1999) and The Efficacy Institute (2006), incorporates Perceiving through the principle that all students can learn when given enough time and support to master concepts.

One other important statistic with Judging and Perceiving: Most studies of at-risk students, whether for behavior or academics, show that a preponderance have a preference for Perceiving. At one school where we used type with students, only 8 percent of the at-risk students reported a preference for Judging. Is this a coincidence when about 70 percent of elementary teachers prefer Judging? Do we set up these students to be at risk? Perhaps using type in elementary school would help mitigate the challenges students have and provide a way to build on their recognizable strengths.

J | | | | | P

I like to work on big
projects at a steady pace.

I like to do more of
the work close to the
deadline.

J | | | | | P

I do my best work when
I'm not under pressure.

I do my best work
when an upcoming
deadline adds pressure.

J | | | | | P

I have a built-in clock;
I know how long
something will take.

It's hard for me to
estimate how long
something will take.

J | | | | | P

I feel better if my work is
done before I play.

I might work first, play first,
or combine work and play.

J | | | | | P

I know when I have
too many things to do;
then I can say no to new
commitments.

I say yes to new commitments,
then struggle to keep things
under control.

J | | | | | P

I like to implement
a plan.

I like to respond to
a situation.

J | | | | | P

I naturally come to conclusions
and definite choices.

I naturally enjoy finding
more options.

J | | | | | P

Producing a product in
line with a timetable is
appealing.

I enjoy the process of
searching and creating
more than finishing.

Below, record the preferences you chose as best describing your natural ways of being energized (**E**xtraversion or **I**ntroversion), gaining information (**S**ensing or I**n**tuition), making decisions (**T**hinking or **F**eeling), and approaching life (**J**udging or **P**erceiving).

     E or I   S or N   T or F   J or P

If you still aren't sure about some of your preferences, several options might help you clarify them.

- Resource A, Descriptions of Leadership Styles of the 16 Types, contains detailed whole-type descriptions. If, for example, you're struggling to decide whether Extraversion or Introversion describes you best but have chosen Sensing, Thinking, and Judging, try reading the ESTJ and ISTJ pages. Does one sound more like you?
- Take the Myers-Briggs Type Indicator (MBTI®) by contacting a qualified practitioner in your town. Consult the referral list at http://aptinternational.org. Or you can take the MBTI online at http://mbticomplete.com, the official site created by the MBTI's publisher. The MBTI is a well-researched instrument designed to help people determine their "best-fit" type.
- Use some of the exercises in Resource C, Making Type a Schoolwide Language, with your staff or leadership team. Sometimes as people participate in these exercises, which allow for experiencing the preferences, their "best-fit" type becomes apparent.

Personality Patterns in Leadership

When looking at type distributions, remember that the types are not evenly distributed in the general population. To summarize, numerous studies have shown the following distributions of type preferences in the general population of the United States (Myers et al., 1998):

- Extraversion and Introversion: These preferences are just about equal.
- Sensing and Intuition: About 65–70 percent prefer Sensing.
- Thinking and Feeling: These are just about equal, but about 60 percent of men prefer Thinking and 60 percent of women prefer Feeling.
- Judging and Perceiving: About 60–65 percent prefer Judging.

Table 1.1 shows the distribution of 276 elementary and secondary principals (Macdaid, McCaulley, & Kainz, 1991) in comparison to the distribution of the general population in the United States and to the distribution of teachers.

Table 1.1   Type Distribution of Principals and Teachers

ISTJ	ISFJ	INFJ	INTJ
Principals 25.4%	Principals 4.7%	Principals 2.2%	Principals 8.7%
Teachers 10.7%	Teachers 17.9%	Teachers 5.1%	Teachers 2.1%
Gen. pop. 11.6%	Gen. pop. 13.8%	Gen. pop. 1.5%	Gen. pop. 2.1%
ISTP	**ISFP**	INFP	INTP
Principals 2.5%	Principals 2.5%	Principals 1.0%	Principals 1.0%
Teachers 1.7%	Teachers 4.7%	Teachers 4.6%	Teachers 1.5%
Gen. pop. 5.4%	Gen. pop. 8.8%	Gen. pop. 4.4%	Gen. pop. 3.3%
ESTP	**ESFP**	ENFP	ENTP
Principals 2.2%	Principals 1.8%	Principals 2.2%	Principals 1.5%
Teachers 0.9%	Teachers 5.7%	Teachers 10.2%	Teachers 1.5%
Gen. pop. 4.3%	Gen. pop. 8.5%	Gen. pop. 8.1%	Gen. pop. 3.2%
ESTJ	ESFJ	ENFJ	ENTJ
Principals 26.1%	Principals 5.4%	Principals 2.5%	Principals 10.1%
Teachers 8.5%	Teachers 12.4%	Teachers 7.2%	Teachers 5.2%
Gen. pop. 8.7%	Gen. pop. 12.3%	Gen. pop. 2.5%	Gen. pop. 1.8%

Remember:

E: Extraversion	I: Introversion	*Energy*
S: Sensing	N: Intuition	*Information*
T: Thinking	F: Feeling	*Decisions*
J: Judging	P: Perceiving	*Approach to Life*

Note that 70 percent of the principals are the four Thinking and Judging types (ISTJ, INTJ, ESTJ, ENTJ), in the corners of the table, compared with only 27 percent of the teachers. This is similar to the representation of these types in business leadership. Kirby (1997) described the resultant bias in leadership literature:

> Because Thinking and Judging types are so prevalent in organizational leadership, it may be that Thinking and Judging behaviors have become the accepted definition of what it means to lead, and, therefore, people displaying these behaviors are seen as "leadership material." Other styles of leading may then not be seen as "leadership" because they do not fit the standard definition. (p. 18)

As you work through Chapter 2, you'll have a chance to ponder whether this bias is true of literature on school leadership. How are the essential roles identified and defined? In terms of type, what is missing? And how do your own strengths fit in with expectations? How can you lead from your strengths?

Note, also, in Table 1.1 that for both teachers and principals, the shaded boxes—the SP, or Sensing and Perceiving types—are significantly underrepresented. Studies of at-risk students show that as many as 90 percent prefer Sensing and Perceiving. Perhaps one reason is that few adults in schools can step into the shoes of these students and understand what motivates them.

Chapter Summary

There is a strong correlation between the "type" of leader you are and how you might best get the results you seek. To best manage the multiple demands of the school leader, understand the ways in which your strengths, if used appropriately, can help move a school to continuous improvement and increased student achievement. Leaders increase their effectiveness when they understand their own style, the general culture of their school, and the styles of the teachers in the school.

The chapter also discusses the personality type distribution of teachers and principals and their preferences for learning.

Reflection

Which of your beliefs about leadership and education come from your personality type?

- Journal: What are your strengths as a leader? After you've written them down, compare your list to your type page in Resource A. What is similar? Different? What patterns do you see? Turn to your opposite (e.g., ISTJ, look at ENFP). What do you notice?
- What are the characteristics of an excellent teacher? What do you expect to see in a classroom? Reflect on whether your expectations tend to honor your own personality preferences. Or do they acknowledge how different styles can still show best practices? You might look at the teacher type descriptions in *Differentiated Coaching* (Kise, 2006). What is your reaction to the teacher type description opposite your own?

Note

1. All type distribution information is from the database of the Center for Applications of Psychological Type, Gainesville, Florida.

2

Strengths-Based
Leadership Priorities

You Can't Do It All

> Great leaders are not mythological composites of every dimension of
> leadership. Instead they have self-confidence, and without hubris
> they acknowledge their deficiencies and fill their subordinate ranks
> not with lackeys but with exceptional leaders who bring complemen-
> tary strengths to the organization. (Reeves, 2006, p. 33)

That's right. The task of school leadership is too big for any one person.
Further, as we'll see below, the responsibilities are paradoxical; one can't be
interactive and reflective at the same time, for example. But one needs a framework to dissect and determine for which roles one is most suited, a framework
backed by research, so that it doesn't seem as though you're shirking responsibilities but instead acknowledging the wisdom of current research.

In this chapter, we will look at the research on type and leadership, examine
the various educational leadership roles that are connected with student
achievement, and then compare those roles to the natural strengths of each type
preference. The chapter will conclude with tools for examining your own strengths
as a leader and strategies for enhancing your effectiveness.

Research on Type and Leadership

Over 40 years of research on type and leadership provides several key insights.
As we saw in Chapter 1, there are clear patterns in the personality preferences

of managers; study after study—involving thousands of managers and executives—consistently show that 75 percent or more have preferences for Thinking and Judging. Further, the same pattern exists in Japanese, British, and Latin American corporations (Macdaid, McCaulley, & Kainz, 1991). A strong argument could be made for the current emphasis on emotional intelligence in leadership as an addition of the strengths of the Feeling function to the overwhelmingly Thinking literature on leadership.

Other key research findings (Walck, 1997) are the following:

- Leaders with preferences for Sensing, Judging, and/or Thinking are generally recognized for their administrative skills. This doesn't mean that leaders with Intuitive, Perceiving, and/or Feeling preferences can't handle administrative tasks but that these are seldom their *preferred* tasks. Further, such leaders can be overlooked for key administrative positions when organizations seek and value the Thinking/Judging style.

- Leaders with preferences for Intuition and/or Perceiving are more often associated with creativity, managing change, and transformational leadership roles. This doesn't mean that leaders with preferences for Sensing and Judging aren't creative or can't function as change agents, but the nature of these roles is more naturally appealing to the other preferences.

- Type preferences do not predict who will be successful as managers. First, there is a profound difference between having a preference and being skilled with that preference. This is why using type as a basis for hiring decisions is unethical. Second, although the world of management may have a bias toward Thinking and Judging, the best managers tend to lead from their strengths rather than by developing skills with their least-preferred type preferences.

- Successful managers are significantly clearer about their own preferences (Johnson, 1992; Rytting, Ware, & Prince, 1994). Learning about type concepts does not lead to success. Rather, success comes from having enough self-awareness to be able to say, "These are my four preferences," rather than, for example, "It's situational. Sometimes I'm an Extravert, sometimes an Introvert." The latter is true for everyone, but those who are clear on their preferences know which bring energy and which drain them and can, therefore, develop better strategies. Remember, type is hardwired. Brain research shows distinct EEG pattern differences in people with different preferences.

Reread the opening chapter quote from Dennis Reeves (p. 33). The job of school leadership is overwhelming. As we review the principal roles identified in research in terms of the preferences they require, keep in mind that your best chance for success is to build on your strengths. McCaulley (1990) wrote that asking which type makes the best leader is the wrong question. Instead, in this chapter, we will examine the strengths of each type in leadership. Chapter 3 provides insights into how people with different preferences best handle change. Then in Chapter 4, we'll look at how to use the framework from this chapter to build the best leadership team possible.

The Literature on Principal Responsibilities

Because research confirmed that effective school leaders have a positive impact on student achievement, several authors set out to define the key roles or responsibilities that lead to effective school leadership. We reviewed the following texts and then categorized the responsibilities identified by the type preferences most aligned with that role.

- Marzano, Waters, & McNulty (2005). *School leadership that works.* Through meta-analysis of 35 years of research on school leadership, the authors identified 21 leadership responsibilities that correlate with student achievement.
- Reeves (2006). *The learning leader.* Reeves identified seven dimensions of leadership that "describe the components of leadership that are necessary in every leadership team, but rarely present in a single leader" (p. 34).
- Whittaker (2003). *What great principals do differently.* Whittaker studied the differences between effective and ineffective school leaders, including where they focus their attention, what they emphasize in decision making, and how they view their schools.
- The Institute for Learning (Resnick, 1999) trains school leaders to become instructional leaders capable of guiding teachers in creating classrooms that act on the belief that effort, not inborn intelligence, creates the ability to learn. They emphasize nine schoolwide principles to carry out this shift in beliefs, practices, and results.
- Sparks (2005). *Leading for results: Transforming teaching, learning and relationships in schools.* Sparks identified "results skills" that are essential for school change leaders.
- Danielson (2002). *Enhancing student achievement: A framework for school improvement.* Danielson provides school leaders with a framework for coordinating key efforts in curriculum, team planning, policies, and classroom practices that impact student performance.

As we review our synthesis of the roles identified in the above research, note that they are organized by the order of preferences, with Extraverted and Introverted roles explained first, rather than in the order of importance. Chart 2.1 lists the 26 separate leadership roles we found in the research, categorized by the type preferences that are naturally best suited to the roles. The rest of the chapter describes these roles and the research that connects them to student achievement. You can approach this information in the following different ways:

- If you're interested in the research and theory, read straight through the definitions.
- If you prefer first to understand how you can put the information to use, review Activity 4.4, Team Reflection on Leadership Roles, or skim through the other activities in Chapter 4.
- If you prefer to focus on what seems most relevant, use Chart 2.1 to select the leadership roles that are least familiar to you.

Chart 2.1   Leadership Roles Categorized by Type Preferences

Interactive Leader (Extraversion)

1. Being visible
2. Being situationally aware
3. Gathering input
4. Advocating for the school

Reflective Leader (Introversion)

5. Providing time for reflection
6. Learning from positive and negative results
7. Delaying decisions to allow for reflection

Administrative Leader (Sensing)

8. Establishing standard operating procedures and routines
9. Maintaining school focus and monitoring strategy implementation
10. Managing school administrative processes
11. Setting clear expectations and providing related feedback

Visionary Leader (Intuition)

12. Setting school direction
13. Acting as a change agent and optimizer
14. Influencing beliefs

Systemic Instructional Leader (Thinking)

15. Gaining extensive knowledge of curriculum, instruction, and assessment
16. Being involved in instructional decisions
17. Aligning curriculum and standards
18. Using data, assessment, and testing effectively

Community Instructional Leader (Feeling)

19. Building relationships
20. Team building for effective collaboration
21. Incorporating qualitative data into decisions
22. Showing appreciation and recognizing accomplishments

Planful Leader (Judging)

23. Using "next action" thinking
24. Establishing goals and maintaining focus

Flexible Leader (Perceiving)

25. Being flexible
26. Being open

Extraverted Responsibilities: The Interactive Leader

Action and interaction are the hallmarks of the Extraverted preference. Successful school leaders know firsthand what is happening in their building. They're in hallways and classrooms, observing and communicating with others. They gather information from students, teachers, and office and maintenance staff so that multiple perspectives inform their view of school functions and policies.

Marzano et al. (2005) identified four responsibilities that fall under Interactive Leadership:

1. **Being visible**: Making systematic, frequent visits to classrooms; being highly visible to teachers, students, and parents; and interacting frequently with each group.

2. **Being situationally aware**: Understanding informal relationships among staff members, noticing potential issues, and using their understanding to predict potential problems. Constant interactions keep leaders aware of the detailed life of the school.

3. **Gathering input:** Seeking staff involvement in setting priorities and goals and gathering input on important decisions.

4. **Advocating for the school**: Reaching out and speaking for the school to all stakeholders, including staff, students, parents, and the community.

Reeves (2006) listed the same need for input from others and shared decision making in his description of the dimension of collaborative leadership. Fink and Resnick (2001) emphasized the role of visibility for principals who are truly instructional leaders, saying that they "are in teachers' classrooms every day, and it is difficult to draw the line between observations that have an evaluative intent and those that are part of the professional support system" (p. 606). Further, they need input from beyond the hallways of their own building; Resnick and Hall (1998) suggested that school leaders join with peers from other districts in learning communities:

Principals need to be students in their own district-wide learning communities, participating in study groups, university programs, and targeted learning activities; conferring regularly; visiting each other's schools; and routinely drawing on one another's expertise—as well as that of professional developers and senior administrators—to become more effective instructional leaders. When educators observe each other and allow themselves to be observed, they move back and forth between teacher and learner, developing their knowledge core and pedagogical intelligence in the process. (p. 113)

The responsibilities of the Interactive leader clearly call on the strengths of the Extraverted preference, including natural preferences for (Hirsh & Kise, 2000, 2001):

- Enjoying variety and action
- Understanding how others do their jobs
- Communicating in person or via telephone
- Working in an environment filled with people
- Focusing on the outside world, what is happening
- Talking through ideas and options
- Networking with others
- Moving about to reenergize

Yes, Introverted leaders can excel at the Interactive role; in fact, we'll see that effective leadership for *all* types requires both the Interactive and the Reflective role we describe next. However, Introverted leaders will lose rather than gain energy from Interactive responsibilities.

Introverted Responsibilities: The Reflective Leader

To emphasize the diametrically opposed nature of Extraverted and Introverted leadership responsibilities, let's look first at the natural strengths of the Introverted preference (Hirsh & Kise, 2000, 2001):

- Gaining energy by time alone for reflection
- Focusing on the inner world of ideas and what could be
- Communicating through the written word
- Reflecting on options and ideas before acting
- Understanding their own strengths and blind spots
- Developing expertise in a few areas of interest
- Concentrating for extended periods on one project or task
- Preparing in advance to discuss plans and give presentations

Many of the above strengths fall under educational leadership literature responsibilities we characterize as the Reflective Leader role. Reeves (2006) said, "Reflective leaders take time to think about the lessons learned, record their small wins and setbacks, document conflicts between values and practice, identify the difference between idiosyncratic behavior and long-term pathologies, and notice trends that emerge over time" (p. 49). Sparks (2005) called on leaders to gain clarity through writing and reflecting on actions. Resnick (2005) emphasizes reflective activities for both staff and students.

The most current brain research emphasizes that none of us can make meaning without reflective time (Jensen, 1998). Further, the theory of type development shows how *all* types need both action and interaction to (a) be effective and (b) reach maturity. (See the next section on "Type Development.")

The Reflective Leader puts into practice the following:

- **Providing time for reflection:** Giving time to self and staff to reflect on actions, interactions, goals, and possibilities. Further, staff development is inquiry-based, with reflection for synthesis of ideas and invitation of questions.
- **Learning from positive and negative results**: Using processes that help teachers and administrators look beyond obvious factors to others that might influence outcomes. For example, our teachers did a relationship audit, starring the names of students with whom they had relationships. When given time to analyze what students with few or no stars had in common, they realized that they'd been ignoring students with a preference for Introversion. This led to a deep discussion of their tendency to stereotype students of one type as "good" and another cultural group as "prone to behavior problems" because of the more Extraverted style of their home culture; the Introverted students were just as likely to struggle, but their behaviors were less obvious and, therefore, often ignored.
- **Delaying decisions to allow for reflection:** Building in time for stakeholders to reflect before coming to closure, whether for an hour, a day, or a week, depending on the magnitude of the decision. The importance of this becomes apparent when one considers type dynamics and development (see below).

Yes, Extraverted leaders can excel at the Reflective Leader role and need to develop some skills with it to be effective. However, the Reflective Leader role will usually take energy from Extraverted leaders, working against their natural strengths.

Type Development: Why We Need to Access Our Extraverted and Introverted Sides

The tug between the Extraverted and Introverted leadership roles can feel like a tug-of-war. Extraverted leaders sometimes describe periods of solitude for reflection as "being in jail" while Introverted leaders can view a day out in classrooms and meetings as "drowning in people." But type research and theory bear out why *both* practices are essential for *all* leaders.

Type theory is a description of *dynamic development,* not a static picture of who we are. Above all, it emphasizes developing balance as we mature, balance between our inner and outer world, and our ability to gather enough information to make good decisions.

In type theory, Sensing, Intuition, Thinking, and Feeling describe how we *function,* so they are referred to as functions as well as preferences. Chart 2.2 shows the order in which these functions develop in most people of a given type.

(Continued)

(Continued)

Chart 2.2   Order in Which the Four Functions Develop

Key: D: dominant function; A: auxiliary function; T: third or tertiary function; I: inferior function

ISTJ	**ISFJ**	**INFJ**	**INTJ**
D: Sensing A: Thinking T: Feeling I: Intuition	D: Sensing A: Feeling T: Thinking I: Intuition	D: Intuition A: Feeling T: Thinking I: Sensing	D: Intuition A: Thinking T: Feeling I: Sensing
ISTP	**ISFP**	**INFP**	**INTP**
D: Thinking A: Sensing T: Intuition I: Feeling	D: Feeling A: Sensing T: Intuition I: Thinking	D: Feeling A: Intuition T: Sensing I: Thinking	D: Thinking A: Intuition T: Sensing I: Feeling
ESTP	**ESFP**	**ENFP**	**ENTP**
D: Sensing A: Thinking T: Feeling I: Intuition	D: Sensing A: Feeling T: Thinking I: Intuition	D: Intuition A: Feeling T: Thinking I: Sensing	D: Intuition A: Thinking T: Feeling I: Sensing
ESTJ	**ESFJ**	**ENFJ**	**ENTJ**
D: Thinking A: Sensing T: Intuition I: Feeling	D: Feeling A: Sensing T: Intuition I: Thinking	D: Feeling A: Intuition T: Sensing I: Thinking	D: Thinking A: Intuition T: Sensing I: Feeling

In the chart, the preference, or function, listed first below the four-letter type code is referred to as the *dominant* function. For example, under ISTJ, "D: Sensing" is the *dominant* function. Find your own dominant function and think back to childhood.

- Dominant Sensing types often agree that they were known as sensible or matter-of-fact children.
- Dominant Intuitive types were often viewed as imaginative children (or as daydreamers).
- Dominant Thinking types were often known for asking questions, wondering "Why?" and "How?"
- Dominant Feeling types were often seen as empathetic children, aware of the feelings of others and concerned that everyone be included.

Now look at the next function in the list for your four-letter type code, the *A*, for *auxiliary,* function. If the dominant function describes how you take in information (Sensing or Intuition), then the auxiliary balances this with your preferred method for making decisions (Thinking or Feeling). If the dominant describes how you make decisions, the auxiliary describes how you take in information. As you develop your first two preferences, you gain balance between these two processes. Think about it. *Immature* people either

- **Can't make up their minds:** They keep looking for more information or vacillating among options. In this case, they haven't developed a method for making decisions (Thinking or Feeling preference).
- **Make decisions too quickly:** They don't explore enough options, or they ignore pertinent information. In this case, they haven't developed a preferred way to gather information (Sensing or Intuitive preference).

Just as significant to leadership style is the second way in which your first two preferences balance each other:

- Extraverts use their dominant function in the *external world*. They use their auxiliary function in the *internal world*.
- Introverts use their dominant function in the *internal world*. They use their auxiliary function in the *external world*.

Thus, to take in information and make decisions effectively, we need both Extraverted and Introverted time. Our own types serve as an illustration of this concept.

Beth: ENFP	Jane: INFJ
Dominant function: Intuition	Dominant function: Intuition
Auxiliary function: Feeling	Auxiliary function: Feeling
My Intuition works best in the outer world of people and activities. It's through interaction that I brainstorm, discover new possibilities, and make new connections. When I withdraw to my inner world, then my Feeling function has a chance to determine my reaction to each idea. Which are worth pursuing? Which do my values support?	*While our first and second functions are the same, I use my Intuition in the inner world. When I'm alone, I can brainstorm, synthesize various thoughts, and develop new insights. Often when I'm talking through these ideas with others, I suddenly realize which ones I like and don't like—my Feeling function works best through interaction.*

Even though we have the same dominant and auxiliary functions, we operate very differently. Why is this so significant? Because in a preponderance of executive coaching incidences, where leaders are struggling to be effective, the first suggestion we make is to "switch worlds."

- When Introverted leaders are unsure what to do, they often retreat to their preferred world of reflection. This actually cuts them off from their auxiliary function, which they need to balance information gathering and decision making. Thus, we coach them to talk with other leaders, observe classrooms, interact with students in the halls—to get out of their offices and into the external world.
- When Extraverted leaders are unsure what to do, they often continue at a high pace of activity and interaction, cutting themselves off from their auxiliary function. Thus, we coach them to reflect on specific questions, withdraw until they have a short list of priorities, read or study a text—to stop acting and start reflecting.

(Continued)

(Continued)

> Try it! If you prefer Extraversion, make room for reflection. If you prefer Introversion, make room for being out and about. Does the other "world" provide new pathways for effectiveness?
>
> Note that in Chart 2.1, your *tertiary* and *inferior* functions include preferences that aren't in your four-letter code.* Remember, we can all use all of the preferences. And to develop fully, we need some skill with each.
>
> - Everyone needs other people. Extraverts and Introverts just need differing amounts of time with others and alone.
> - For true understanding, we all need to perceive both the details (Sensing) and the big picture (Intuition).
> - For balanced decisions, both logic (Thinking) and the impact on the people involved (Feeling) are important.
> - A full life includes both planning (Judging) and making room for unexpected events (Perceiving).
>
> The theory of type, therefore, isn't a one-dimensional box of who you are but a dynamic model for lifelong growth.
>
> ---
> * What happened to Judging and Perceiving? The answer delves deep into type theory, deeper than you may want to explore! Myers expanded on Jung's theory of psychological type by including Judging and Perceiving to point to the function each type uses in the outside world. Refer back to the example of Beth's and Jane's types. Beth, with a last letter of P, uses the perceiving function of Intuition in the outside world. As an Extravert, it is also her dominant function. Jane, with a last letter of J, uses the judging function of Feeling in the outside world; however, she uses her dominant function of Intuition in the internal world. All of us use our dominant function in our preferred world.

Sensing Responsibilities: The Administrative Leader

One interesting note on the educational leadership literature synthesized in this chapter: Very little attention is paid to the administrative duties of school leaders, such as budgeting, scheduling, compliance, and other day-to-day tasks. While they may not correlate directly with student achievement, few school leaders can escape these time-consuming responsibilities without getting fired!

The role of Administrative Leader includes:

- **Establishing standard operating procedures and routines** (Marzano et al., 2005; Sparks, 2005)
- **Maintaining school focus and evaluating strategy implementation** (Marzano et al., 2005; Whittaker, 2003; Reeves, 2006).
- **Managing school administrative processes**: Managing budgets, overseeing compliance requirements, filing reports, scheduling, and other detailed administrative tasks. Beyond the need for consistency, this responsibility is seldom mentioned in leadership literature.
- **Setting clear expectations and providing related feedback:** Providing teachers with sufficient information and examples for them to understand what should happen in their classrooms and their roles in other efforts (Marzano et al., 2005; Whittaker, 2003; Resnick, 1999).

The above responsibilities draw on the strengths of the Sensing function, including (Hirsh & Kise, 2000, 2001):

- Valuing accuracy and precision
- Taking a methodical, step-by-step approach
- Trusting experience more than inspiration
- Concentrating on practical applications and results
- Gauging success in concrete terms and by reaching measurable goals (test scores, budget targets, discipline statistics, etc.)
- Avoiding generalities in favor of specifics
- Adding standardization, replication, and efficiencies
- Applying what they have already learned

Yes, Intuitives can handle the Administrative Leader responsibilities. However, consider that while all types can set goals, *limiting* them and staying focused can be difficult for Intuitive leaders because they are naturally pulled toward new possibilities, even after their school improvement plan is finalized. Intuitive leaders also often struggle with being specific.

Intuitive Responsibilities: The Visionary Leader

To contrast the Administrative and Visionary Leader roles, let's look at the strengths of the Intuitive preference (Hirsh and Kise, 2000, 2001):

- Trusting hunches, intuitions, and connections
- Concentrating on the big picture of ideas and possibilities
- Taking creative, novel approaches
- Using imagination and inspiration as reliable guides
- Focusing on how things could change rather than on what is right with the status quo
- Learning new things rather than practicing skills
- Looking to the future
- Valuing insights and innovations

Specific responsibilities listed in the literature on educational leadership that correspond with the Visionary Leader include:

- **Setting school direction:** Communicating strong ideals and beliefs that lead to student achievement (Sparks, 2005; Marzano et al., 2005; Resnick, 2005; Whittaker, 2003; Danielson, 2002)
- **Acting as change agent and optimizer**: Challenging the status quo and inspiring others, leading them in new innovations (Marzano et al., 2005)
- **Influencing beliefs**: Transforming assumptions to change habits and affect practices (Sparks, 2005; Resnick, 1999)

The Visionary Leader role is mentioned in all of the leadership texts we reviewed. As the above factors show, there is natural synergy between the Visionary and Administrative Leader roles. However, the Administrative role comes more naturally to the Sensing leader and the Visionary role to the Intuitive leader. Being aware of one's natural tendencies allows for developing ways to compensate—or to develop partnerships to cover each role in depth.

Thinking Responsibilities: The Systemic Instructional Leader

In examining Thinking and Feeling leadership roles, we're going to look at two forms of instructional leadership: Systemic and Community. The Thinking preference lends itself to some of the systematic, in-depth practices that add up to schoolwide accountability for curriculum and assessment. Resnick (2005) emphasized that principals are to function as instructional leaders; Whittaker (2003) defined instructional leadership as teaching teachers what you want them to do and know.

Specific responsibilities mentioned include:

- **Gaining extensive knowledge of curriculum, instruction, and assessment**: Studying and providing information to staff on cutting-edge theory and practice (Marzano et al., 2005)
- **Being involved in instructional decisions** (Marzano et al., 2005): Understanding and working with teachers on decisions about content and processes in the classrooms.
- **Aligning curriculum and standards**: Understanding and guiding teacher efforts to align what they teach with what students need to know. This responsibility was mentioned in all the leadership texts we reviewed. Working with standards draws on the Thinking ability to organize and systematize the outer world. Resnick (1999) described this in the "Clear Expectations" principle of learning: students need to be able to understand in their own terms the goal of each lesson.
- **Using data, assessment, and testing effectively** (Whittaker, 2003; Reeves, 2004): Thinking types are attracted to *data* while Feeling types prefer to deal with *people*. The Community Instructional Leader role (see below) incorporates qualitative data to present a comprehensive picture of what and how students are learning.

The Systemic Instructional Leader role often involves taking a tough stance against current teaching practices. For example, such leaders may require teachers to discard favorite units that don't tie to state standards. They may set strict accountability procedures for teachers and teams that relate directly to school goals, such as specifying goals and reporting requirements for team meetings. They might standardize curriculum maps or lesson-planning formats so that teachers can more easily share ideas and learn from collaboration. Actions like these may threaten harmony among teachers or between the leader and teachers, but they may also be necessary to move the staff toward a common vision. Reeves (2006) says

The best analytical leaders are not masters of answers but rather persistent questioners. Their questions require the admission of ignorance, not the assertion of knowledge. As incongruous as it may seem, analytical leaders are so aware of the multivariate nature of life, systems, and organizations that they can be the engine that drives collaboration. (pp. 57–58)

These responsibilities draw on the natural strengths of the Thinking preference (Hirsh & Kise, 2000, 2001):

- Analyzing problems and situations
- Concentrating on the underlying principles behind decisions
- Creating or working within efficient, logical structures
- Seeking improvement through questioning and objectivity
- Putting tasks and goals before relationships
- Working with data and things
- Being firm but fair
- Finding flaws and acting to correct them

Yes, Feeling leaders can be Systemic Instructional Leaders, but many of the tasks call for them to ignore their natural drive for harmony, subjectivity, and treating each person as an individual.

Feeling Responsibilities: The Community Instructional Leader

Feeling leaders use what they know about individuals to get them to utilize their strengths, focusing on what is needed so that all students can learn. While Thinking leaders focus on data, Feeling leaders focus on the bottom line of whether students are learning. More important, is Johnny learning? Is Denisha learning?

To grasp the difference between the Systemic and Community Instructional Leader roles, let's look at the strengths of the Feeling function (Hirsh & Kise, 2000, 2001):

- Understanding the impact of decisions on those involved
- Instilling trust and harmony
- Fostering acceptance
- Working with people and relationships
- Seeking what is most important to people
- Bringing about harmonious outcomes
- Appreciating the efforts of others
- Upholding personal and organizational values

Remember that a preponderance of leadership literature reflects a Thinking type bias because 75–80 percent of executives and managers, in business and in education, have a preference for Thinking. While the Community Instructional Leader role is described in the leadership literature, far less text is given to it than to the Systemic Instructional Leader responsibilities of standards and accountability, curriculum, and instructional knowledge.

We would propose that great instructional leaders use both Thinking and Feeling. While the focus is always on whether students are learning, the Thinking leader reflects on hard data whereas the Feeling leader reflects on each student's statements, explanations regarding the learning process, and engagement in the classroom.

The leadership responsibilities that fall under the Feeling function include:

- **Building relationships:** Understanding the personal needs of teachers and the significant events in their lives (Marzano et al., 2005). Such leaders also work to build personal relationships with them. This requires face-to-face interactions. Reeves (2006) listed Relational Leadership as one of his seven dimensions of leadership and cited the following specific skills:
  o Listening
  o Respecting confidences
  o Practicing empathy through deliberate inquiry
  o Exhibiting passion for both mission and people
- **Teambuilding:** Leading for effective collaboration. Reeves (2006) described Collaborative Leadership as the ability of the leader to reach out to others, but helping others learn to collaborate is a separate responsibility.
- **Incorporating qualitative data into decisions:** The current emphasis on data in the wake of the No Child Left Behind Act may reflect an unbalanced view of data. Reeves (2006) pointed out that test score gains may reflect increased dropout rates for underperforming students or retention of students in the grade level before a high-stakes test. Further, strategies that produce immediate test score gains may not create long-lasting achievement gains (Hargreaves & Fink, 2004).
- **Showing appreciation, recognizing accomplishments**: Formalizing frequent, regular acknowledgement of effort and achievement (Marzano et al., 2005; Resnick, 1999; Whittaker, 2003). Reeves (2006) claims that appreciation, recognition, and personal contact are some of the most extraordinarily strategic uses of leadership time, yet time is rarely allocated in that way because we are too busy with expenditures of time that are distinguished only by tradition and expectation, not by effectiveness. (p. 168)

Carrying out the last responsibility listed above is especially complicated because people with preferences for Thinking and Feeling have profoundly different needs for appreciation and recognition. Hirsh and Kise (2006b) described it this way:

Thinking types uniformly say that recognition should occur when job standards are achieved or, in many cases, exceeded. They may even suspect an ulterior motive if they receive appreciation before a job is done. Feeling types uniformly want praise throughout the task cycle, acknowledgement that they are performing well, encouragement to continue, and a sense that they are contributing to the overall success of the project.

Universally, both Thinking types and Feeling types become frustrated, demoralized, and possibly angry if they do not receive recognition or appreciation in a way that appeals to them. (p. 82)

In viewing the Community Instructional Leader roles, note that building community and relationships with students is about far more than ensuring pleasant working and learning conditions. Research shows that collaboration is key to student success (Kise, 2005). The Community Instructional Leader role is essential to school change, as Fullan (2001) encapsulated:

The fallacy of rationalism is the assumption that the social world can be altered by logical argument. The problem, as George Bernard Shaw observed, is that "reformers have the idea that change can be achieved by brute sanity." (p. 98)

The role of Community Instructional Leader moves all teachers toward a collective sense of shared mission, values, and collaborative effectiveness. And the keen awareness of how practices and policies affect student and staff motivation, values, and attitudes—a focus on developing students and staff who are lifelong learners—provides data that test scores can't show.

Yes, Thinking types can carry out the responsibilities of the Community Instructional Leader, but the skills required go against their natural strengths for objectivity, problem solving, and task orientation.

Judging Versus Perceiving Responsibilities: Balancing Results and Process

Schools need concrete goals if they are to implement major changes; every author we reviewed listed this as a leadership responsibility, as we discussed above under the Administrative Leader. Carrying out plans to reach those goals calls on the strengths of the Judging preference. However, other responsibilities, such as monitoring progress and evaluating data, make clear that school leaders need to stay open to new information and be willing to make midstream course corrections if necessary. Doing so calls on the gifts of the Perceiving preference. The strengths of the two preferences are compared below.

Judging	Perceiving
• Planning their work and working their plan	• Adapting to changing situations
• Making decisions, coming to closure	• Leaving options open, changing course when needed
• Focusing on products	• Focusing on processes
• Avoiding problems by anticipating	• Solving problems on the spot
• Finishing	• Starting
• Limiting information gathering	• Expanding information gathering
• Structuring projects in advance	• Letting projects unfold
• Scheduling time and events	• Keeping schedules and timetables open

The term *change management* is close to being an oxymoron. Change by nature is chaotic, yet one is assuming that it can be structured for success. Leadership responsibilities that draw on the strengths of the Judging preference include:

- **Using "next action" thinking:** Identifying concrete actions to take once each decision is made (Sparks, 2006). Sparks also noted that requests produce results when they are specific, require action, and have a clear deadline.
- **Establishing goals and maintaining focus:** Choosing and keeping attention on the same goals throughout the school year (Marzano et al., 2005; Resnick, 1999). This involves intentional planning.

Leadership responsibilities that draw on the strengths of the Perceiving preference include:

- **Being flexible:** Adapting one's leadership style to the needs of the situation (Marzano et al., 2005) and allowing creativity in school scheduling and curriculum to give students the time they need to learn (Reeves, 2006; Resnick, 1999)
- **Being open:** Allowing dissent and diverse opinions (Marzano et al., 2005; Reeves, 2006) and allowing teachers to reach school goals in multiple ways (Sparks, 2005)

Chances are, how you are evaluated as a leader depends to a large degree on how well you manage the Judging side of leadership. A survey of evaluation experiences (Reeves, 2004) revealed that less than half of school leaders said their evaluations were related to student achievement. Instead, evaluations may rest on the more quantifiable managerial skills. Are students prepared for the state testing date? Do you meet budget deadlines? Do you comply with reporting requirements for federal funding programs? Is your school improvement plan current and complete?

Still, key leadership roles involve the Perceiving function, reflecting "thoughtful consideration of the continuous updates and modifications that make planning documents correspond to reality" (Reeves, 2006, p. 63). In other words, set the plan and get on with implementing and monitoring to see whether student achievement improves; if not, modify.

The best way to incorporate the strengths of Judging and Perceiving into school leadership is to *plan for flexibility.* Chart 2.3 contains a checklist (granted, a Judging device) that allows school leaders to navigate the Judging culture of education while still remaining open to shifting circumstances, new information, and unforeseen possibilities and ideas.

Chapter Summary

The roles of school leaders truly are in opposition to each other. Leaders need to be:

- Interactive and Reflective
- Administrative and Visionary
- Systemic Instructional and Community Instructional Leaders
- Balanced between structure and flexibility

Chart 2.3 A Checklist for School Structures and Flexibility

	Yes	No
1. Does your school have clear goals? (Judging)		
2. Do you have a system in place for monitoring progress toward those goals? (Judging)		
3. Does your system allow for periodic reexamination of those goals? (Perceiving)		
4. Does your leadership team periodically examine, "What if we'd pursued a different goal? Have we missed an opportunity?" (Perceiving)		
5. Is your leadership team able to come to closure on major decisions? (Judging)		
6. Do you have mechanisms in place to avoid rushing to closure, such as regrouping after reflective time or exploring additional options before choosing the most obvious? (Perceiving)		
7. Do you provide clear expectations to teachers as to how they can reach goals? (Judging)		
8. Are teachers allowed to explore creative, individual ways to meet the same goals? (Perceiving)		
9.		
10.		

Note that the checklist allows you to add your own items, balancing control and flexibility.

While no one individual can successfully carry out all roles, we can use type as a model to pinpoint our strengths and recognize our blind spots. Again, *all* types can be great leaders. Successful leaders, however, understand their personality type and use that knowledge to continue to grow and develop, even as they seek to partner with others who have complementary strengths so that all leadership roles are adequately covered within an organization.

Reflection

- Which leadership roles make the best use of your strengths? In which roles do you feel most effective? Rank the various roles. You might jot down examples that support your rankings.

Leadership Role	Evidence of Effectiveness
___ Interactive Leader (Extraversion)	
___ Reflective Leader (Introversion)	
___ Administrative Leader (Sensing)	
___ Visionary Leader (Intuition)	
___ Systemic Instructional Leader (Thinking)	
___ Community Instructional Leader (Feeling)	
___ Planful Leader (Judging)	
___ Flexible Leader (Perceiving)	

- Resource A contains type descriptions of each of the 16 types, focusing on general strengths, leadership style, and pathways for development.
  - Examine the page for your own type. Do you agree with the primary leadership roles for your type? Do the strengths listed capture how you view yourself as a leader?
  - Review the developmental paths for your type. Have you tried some of them?
  - Consider the leadership role listed as most difficult for your type. Reread the description of the role in the chapter. How willingly do you tackle the tasks associated with that role? Who on your leadership team more naturally fills that role?
- How are you evaluated as a leader? Does your district consider each of the leadership roles? Which are valued most?

3

Succeeding at
School Change

If we want change to matter, to spread, and to last, then the systems
in which leaders do their work must make sustainability a priority.
(Hargreaves & Fink, 2004, p. 13)

This chapter will help you look at your and your staff's propensity for change and how the personality types of key players can affect change efforts. Here's a typical scenario.

An ENFP principal, whose strengths lie within the Visionary Leader role, attends a workshop and returns to his building excited by the possibilities. He tells his ISTJ assistant principal (note that they have completely opposite preferences), "I heard so many great ideas for changing grading and assessment practices. The district's doing trainings every month—let's get the whole staff through by the end of this year."

The ISTJ, who excels at the Administrative Leader responsibilities of maintaining focus, silently thinks about all of the other initiatives and trainings the staff is already committed to. She starts to ask questions:

- What's wrong with our school's grading policies? I haven't heard complaints from parents or students.
- How much will all of this training cost?
- Will teachers walk out knowing what they need to know, or will they have to do more planning and study?
- How does this fit in with their training on grading rubrics? Or student self-assessment?

- Can you give a specific example of the problem with the current system?
- Will you wait for all teachers to go through the training before implementing, or will they each implement it as they finish the training?
- How does this rank within your priorities? What *won't* happen if you ask teachers to do this on top of everything else?

Unless the principal has a grasp of how the ISTJ approaches change, chances are at this point, the ENFP will assume that the ISTJ is being resistant. However, every question being raised has merit; they just aren't the kinds of questions ENFPs usually generate on their own, at least not in their initial enthusiasm with a new possibility or idea.

What much of the literature describes as resistance to change is in fact the result of not meeting the needs of people with various type preferences. Clancy (1997) summarized as follows:

> Without conscious attention to the impact of type diversity, we all will tend to project onto others the kind of support that we ourselves need rather than focus on their special needs that differ from our own. *And when they ask for what they need, particularly if it relates to something that is difficult for us to provide, we may interpret their requests as resisting our ideas or attempting to block them* [emphasis added]. The type lens provides a means for understanding these differing needs and can help us to hear the questions and challenges as pleas for help. But this can only happen if our understanding of type constructs is coupled with an underlying assumption that all types are striving to give their very best and a belief that ideas and plans are strengthened when diverse perspectives are incorporated. (p. 437)

Most school reform efforts fall short of their goals. An administrator's task is to structure the change effort to give it the best chance of success. The rest of this chapter outlines a process for doing so: for evaluating your own propensity for change, helping teachers understand their needs during change, and using "resistance" to examine both the *what*'s and the *how*'s of the change process.

Leadership Propensity for Change

The Chinese character for change blends two others: those for opportunity and for disaster. Depending on personality type, people view changes as either a recipe for opportunity or disaster. Chart 3.1, describing what each of the preferences needs during change, is based on the coaching framework of Hirsh and Kise (2000) and on Barger and Kirby's (1995) survey regarding what people need in times of change. Like Clancy (1997), Barger and Kirby found that resistance to change increases when these needs are not met and that leaders in general failed to recognize and deal effectively with these needs.

Read through Chart 3.1 with your own preferences in mind. Note how the needs during change correspond to the Leadership Roles described in Chapter 2.

Chart 3.1   What Each Preference Needs During Change

Extraversion (Interactive Leader)	Introversion (Reflective Leader)
• Is there time for productive conversations regarding the changes? • Are there active roles for those who want them? • Is action as well as talk taking place?	• Is information available for reflection before teachers are asked to respond or act? • Are there opportunities for communicating one-on-one, both to share thoughts and to ask questions? • Is there time to internalize the meaning of the change before having to act?
Sensing (Administrative Leader)	**Intuition (Visionary Leader)**
• Is real data available to demonstrate why the change needs to be made and why the new course of action is better than the present? • Have specific details been provided regarding schedules, costs, and responsibilities? • Have you made specific connections between the proposed changes, past practices, and other change efforts?	• Have you provided the big picture—the underlying theories and the long-term vision? • Are there options for implementation? • Do teachers have opportunities to influence the change effort design?
Thinking (Systemic Instructional Leader)	**Feeling (Community Instructional Leader)**
• How clear is the logic of how the change measures were chosen? What about the internal logic of the proposed changes? • Has leadership demonstrated competency in implementing change? • Has leadership shown the fairness and equity of the proposed changes?	• Is the change consistent with the values of the organization and people involved? • Do plans take into account the needs of people? • Do those most affected have a voice in the implementation plan?
Judging (Planful Leader)	**Perceiving (Flexible Leader)**
• Are there clear goals and time frames for the change process? • Are priorities clear? What will be left undone to implement this program? • Are surprises being minimized?	• Is the plan open-ended enough that goals and time frames can be adjusted as the process unfolds? • How will the change effort stay open to new information? • Is there flexibility for how each person implements these changes?

To add relevance, you might compare the questions raised by the ISTJ assistant principal in the opening chapter example to the Introversion, Sensing, Thinking, and Judging questions given in the chart.

Can you see how the ENFP principal probably had everything he needed to make the change? And why the ISTJ had so many questions? "Opposite" types frequently miscommunicate around details. For example, when a group of teachers, most of whom preferred Sensing and Feeling, complained that their principal, who preferred Intuition and Thinking, wasn't providing sufficient guidelines for curriculum, she replied, "I've told them that innovation is fine as long as they heed the district recommendations. What other guidelines could they need?"

During individual interviews, the Sensing teachers clearly spelled out the guidance they wanted:

- We need to be told whether to follow the pacing schedule, how many parties to hold, and whether we're self-contained or cohesive grade levels.
- Tell us what's expected. How important are test scores? What academic expectations do we have? What is our philosophy beyond "what is best for children"? What about science and social studies compared to math and reading?
- We want to know if we should all be on the same page. Some of us skip handwriting, etc.

The principal commented that she herself would be stifled by such specificity, yet she finally understood what her teachers wanted.

To use type as a framework for effective change, leaders need first to understand how their own personality type affects both the changes they want to make and how they proceed in making them. Think of a recent change initiative of some significance, perhaps the adoption of a new curriculum, homework policy, technology system, or behavior policy. Consider the following questions:

- In what ways, if any, did the change initiative reflect your own educational beliefs? You might look at your type page in Resource A for ideas.
- How many alternatives did you research?
- How much input did others have in the process?
- Have you seen clear examples of end results?
- How well did the implementation plan meet the needs of the different preferences? Use Chart 3.1 as a checklist.
- Which informational needs were met as you introduced the change?
- Do these reflect your own needs during change?
- Which teacher showed resistance? Does Chart 3.1 indicate any clues as to why? What needs weren't met?
- How did the change initiative affect other school priorities?

Did you discover any patterns? The following activity can help your staff understand their reactions to change.

Activity 3.1
Helping Teachers Understand Their Needs During Change

This activity helps normalize the change process, the feelings associated with it, and the needs of teachers. Once your staff has learned about their own type preferences (see Resource C), divide them into type-alike groups or, if you have 15 or fewer people, into dominant function groups:

- Sensing: ESTP, ESFP, ISTJ, ISFJ
- Intuition: ENFP, ENTP, INFJ, INTJ
- Thinking: ESTJ, ENTJ, ISTP, INTP
- Feeling: ESFJ, ENFJ, ISFP, INFP

Hand out copies of Chart 3.1, flip chart paper, and markers. Have the groups discuss the following scenario:

- As a group, call to mind a recent change at school that you didn't like. Record your answers on flip chart paper. Use Chart 3.1 to answer these questions:
  o What bugged us most about the change?
  o What information did we need but did not get?
  o How would *we* have handled the change?

  After all of the groups have reported out, ask your staff to reflect—do a quick-write—on the various responses. How well does your school handle change, given the varying needs of the type preferences? What one suggestion would they have? After providing five minutes or so for them to write their ideas, ask for volunteers to share their thoughts.

NOTE: The *dominant* function is explained in Chart 2.2.

Balancing Planning With the Urgency of Change

At most schools, changing is mandatory, not optional. Lorraine Monroe (Checkley, 2004) pointed out the urgency:

> Frankly, it's just galling to me how so much time can go by in some schools before something really happens. We can't have that—because the clock is ticking on our children's lives. (p. 72)

Block (2002) provided a framework for helping teachers consider whether, given the needs of their students, they need to set aside some of their own change needs. In his book *The Answer to How? Is Yes*, he points out that whenever people face seemingly impossible tasks, the most frequent question is, "How? How are we going to pull this off?" All of the following "how" questions reflect valid Sensing and Thinking needs during change, whereas Intuitive and Feeling educators tend to skip the questions and say, "Yes, we will change." However, if a change *needs* to be made to bring about student achievement, then the entire staff needs to concentrate on generating the right questions to bring about the change.

Consider how the following "how" questions can help or block change:

- *How do you do it?* Too much time can be spent answering this question, delaying change indefinitely. Given the difficulty of any major change, leaders might ask teachers to table this question until the best alternative, based on other criteria, is chosen.
- *How long?* This question points to wanting speedy answers rather than making a commitment to deep change. This is one of the biggest problems in education reform. Most experts acknowledge that major change efforts take 3–5 years to enact, yet schools are measured yearly on test scores, pressuring them for short-term patches.
- *How much?* This question monetizes values, ignores other costs, and puts people at risk. Budgets have to be balanced, but if options are eliminated too early because of relative costs, the school leaders may never explore alternatives for grant funding, partnerships, or other creative ways to implement the best solution for their site.
- *How do you measure it?* In the world of education, this question currently points to test scores. Quantifiable measures are important, but when long-term results are the goal, other measures are just as important. Focusing on quantitative data can also increase pressure for a short-term response rather than evaluating long-term benefits.

In type terms, Block was suggesting that organizations use the Visionary Leadership roles first: setting school direction, acting as change agent and optimizer, and influencing beliefs. Resnick (1999), Whittaker (2003), and Reeves (2006) agree. However, we would add that to bring about change effectively, the Visionary Leaders need to pay attention to the strengths of the Sensing function—getting to "How?" right after the vision, answering:

- What are our *specific* goals?
- When will we evaluate our progress?
- How can we measure progress? Besides test scores or other statistical measures, consider staff surveys, student focus groups, and other measures that might track changes in attitudes or beliefs long before concrete results appear.
- What data will be most meaningful? What do we need to do now to have that data when we want it?
- What concrete steps do we need to take? By when?

Balancing teacher needs while driving for change is tricky but essential. Why? Because change is so hard. Further, teachers may truly believe they have no reason to change. Kise (2005) asked a team of teachers to list why students failed in their classrooms:

Only two of the teachers mentioned any factors that were within the control of the teachers. . . . Every other factor mentioned, as listed below, was outside of the teachers' control:

- Chaotic home lives
- District automatic promotion policies
- Increasing class sizes
- Perfectionism, resulting in students' giving up on projects
- Homes that don't value education or insist on homework completion
- Student apathy, having lost hope that they can succeed in school

In separate interviews, each teacher named the percentage of students they believed would fail no matter what strategies they used. Their estimates ranged from 10 to 25 percent. (p. 51)

The teachers' viewpoint could be described as learned helplessness. They believed that they had done everything they could to help their students succeed, their students were doing as well or better than others in the building, their classrooms were under control, and they were sure that the reasons for failure were outside of their control. Why would they go through the hard work of change? When they were coached in their own styles and presented with hard evidence that their students could succeed (they reduced the failure rate to less than 2 percent on major projects), the teachers actively engaged in change.

DuFour (2004a) reported a similar experience. He asked teachers to brainstorm ideas for improving student achievement in their building. Every one of their 15 items were outside of their control. He then gave them another list, which included none of the items on the teacher-generated list. These included:

1. Clear, focused academic goals for students

2. Using timely formative assessments to monitor student progress toward those goals

3. Developing a schoolwide plan to give extra time for students to meet academic goals

4. Developing strong partnerships with parents

5. Feedback for teachers on student progress toward goals

6. Collaborative teams to analyze student achievement and develop new strategies

7. High expectations for all students

8. A safe and orderly school environment.

DuFour noted that the teachers grudgingly said that they could influence the items on the second list whereas the factors on their own list were outside of their control. However, another difference was more important:

The items on the second list have a much more powerful impact on student achievement than those on the first. Research over 35 years confirms that when schools create these conditions, they have a significant, positive effect on student learning. . . .

> Schools that resort to the "if-only" strategy [of things outside their control] spend their time looking out the window for the solutions to their problems. Schools that commit to the can-do strategy spend their time looking in the mirror. (p. 64)

The danger in trying to meet all teacher needs during change is that they will never get around to changing—there are too many needs and too many questions. However, leaders can use the framework of type to pinpoint where the change process is ignoring the needs of teachers with certain preferences, work to meet those needs, and keep the initiative moving forward.

Using "Resistance" to Examine the Change Process

One method is to consider in advance the nature of a change and which personality types will find it hardest to implement (Kise, 2006). For example, Intuitives struggle to follow detailed lesson plans, especially if others created them—they thrive on having input to the process, even if they need input from others on time lines and other details. Thinking types may not feel comfortable with community-building activities in their classrooms. Sensing types may resist a new system because they already have one that is working for them.

Once you determine which types will struggle most with the changes, consider what information those types need. And how would they prefer to proceed? In the example that opens this chapter, where the ISTJ questions a change to the school's grading system, a leader might infer that ISTJs will struggle with changes to grading systems because they no doubt already have a consistent, detailed grading method. Consider the ENFP principal's proposal in view of Clancy's (1997) description of ISTJ strengths and change:

> They predict the future based on the past, so saying that things are changing and today's system won't work in tomorrow's world sounds like speculation to them. They are not about to willingly throw out a system that's working based on speculation that it *might* not work tomorrow! They often can point to many previous predictions that didn't materialize and will want to know why this prediction is more reliable. (p. 418)

To gain buy-in from the ISTJ for changing the grading system, the principal would need to start with facts. Exactly what isn't working? How does the proposal fit with these problems? Why is this system better? Why do teachers need to be consistent? Will all teachers really be using this system? How does this fit with the big picture? And so on.

Will meeting those informational needs convince the ISTJ to change grading practices? Kise (2004) found that *evidence,* couched in the information to which teachers pay attention, changed beliefs, providing motivation to change practices. Leaders *can* structure events and situations to produce the three kinds of evidence necessary to change beliefs:

1. **Evidence that their current beliefs have failed:** For example, a middle school teacher believed that diagramming sentences helped the students who were behind grade level in reading. While several research studies show that the process is ineffective, this teacher prefers Sensing and Feeling; research isn't necessarily the most important information for her. Instead, we went through her grade book to look at an assignment her classes had just completed; she discovered that the students she thought were helped by the diagramming worksheets had in fact not done them at all or had done very poorly on them.

2. **Evidence that contradicts current beliefs.** Another group of teachers had dismissed learning to differentiate, claiming that the needs of their students were too varied—there was only so much they could do. During a staff meeting, we handed out a variety of brainteasers, each of which was geared more toward Sensing, Intuition, Thinking, or Feeling preferences. (This exercise is included in Resource C.) The teachers drew these from a hat and then had to work silently. After a few minutes, we showed them a list of all the problems and asked them to talk about the experience. Depending on which ones they received, comments varied:
   - Mine was easy.
   - If I'd had a different one, I'd have been done in no time.
   - I wanted to talk with someone to see if I was on the right track.
   - I *did not* want to do mine—I hate logic problems. But finally I buckled down.
   - I wanted to know what everyone else had; I couldn't concentrate.

   We then brainstormed together a list of ways that we could have differentiated the task so that each participant would have felt more confident: chances to work with a partner or to process out loud, examples of what the question was asking for, a choice between two similar problems where one seemed more interesting to some people, being able to use manipulatives, and so on. The teachers hadn't realized how much difference these small steps in differentiation could make until they experienced it for themselves.

3. **Evidence that helps form new beliefs:** Another group of teachers were convinced that one class of students had no interest in math, weren't motivated, and were so far behind grade level that the school simply couldn't help them catch up. Jane engaged all of the students in a little exercise on brain research and then asked the students to draw a map of what it takes to be good math students. Only three students listed active strategies—ask for help, find a homework partner, do more practice problems, or call the homework help line. The rest wrote things like "Listen better," "Show up for class," "I don't learn. I watch," "Don't talk," and "The teacher should explain more."
   - The students' responses helped the teachers understand that the students did not know how to be active learners; the students equated quickness with intelligence and felt helpless in math.

- In another class, these same students were just beginning a huge research project. That teacher immediately started using different language with her students. "You have to be active learners to research. No one's going to bring the information to you. This is different; you're used to being handed what to learn." She showed a chart of Sensing and Intuitive learning activities and had the students brainstorm ways in which research was Intuitive.

Use the information in Chart 3.1 to design experiences that produce convincing evidence for all types. Text-based discussions, actual teacher stories, video clips where teachers model sound teaching strategies, and learning theories can all introduce ideas and provide common material with which teachers can interact. They increase teacher awareness of what is and isn't working and provide an essential foundation for school change. However, when staff development can also involve action—personal experience or events in their own classrooms—existing beliefs are challenged at a deeper level, one that invites change.

A Final Step: Assessing School Capacity for Change

While leaders need to push change forward when student achievement is at stake, they can't lose sight of the difficulty of change. A final step is acknowledging the school's current capacity for change. Too often, especially when the Visionary Leader role takes precedence in the push for systemic, long-term change, some basic considerations are overlooked in the initial planning stages.

Chapter Summary

Our personality types influence whether we view change as more of a threat or an opportunity. Understanding one's own propensity for change, as well as what other people may need, can aid in implementing sustainable change efforts.

When leaders understand that what they view as resistance to change might actually reflect the wisdom and common sense of others, or even be the result of a poorly planned change process, they can assist their staff in adopting the actions that need to occur. They can also use personality type to assess and then plan within their school's capacity for change.

Activity 3.2
Assessing Change Capacity

Conduct an inventory of the following assets:

- *Do teachers have the knowledge to effect change?* For example, implementing a more constructivist approach to mathematics instruction requires that teachers have a much deeper understanding of how students acquire math concepts. *Many,* but certainly not all or even most, Feeling teachers struggled with math themselves—after all, it involves numbers and not people!—and passed tests by memorizing procedures (Huelsman, 2002). If teacher understanding doesn't go beyond the algorithms they themselves were taught, they can't evaluate whether students are using good reasoning. Similarly, Intuitive teachers who just "know" how a math concept works may not have developed thorough explanations of *why* it works or alternative methods of explanation for students who struggle to understand. Developing either kind of knowledge takes extensive staff development time.

- *Is the level of effort required to make the change understood?* If so, are sufficient resources (time, coaching, and materials) allocated to support the change? In the above example, how will teachers be given the time they need to gain mathematical knowledge? Who will explore how to embed that learning in their work? The point isn't to give up on the initiative but to identify the level of resources needed and creatively find ways to deliver them before teachers view the initiative as hopeless.

- *Is the change well researched? Can it be implemented?* For example, in Chapter 2 we discussed how aligning curriculum and standards is a sound, research-based strategy for improving student achievement. However, Marzano (2003) demonstrated that the time needed to teach all standards adequately (approximately 13,000 instructional hours) exceeds instructional time (approximately 9,000 hours); insisting on meeting all standards sets up teachers for failure. Hopefully, districts see the need to coordinate efforts to determine the essential standards.

- *Is there a long-term commitment to the changes (3–5 years at a minimum)?* One note here: Sensing types consistently identify *long-term* as 3–6 months, a year at the most, while Intuitive types view *long-term* as 3–5 years. Does the fact that 65–70 percent of the U.S. population prefers Sensing influence how little time schools are given to enact changes before being judged as "failures"? Leaders need to acknowledge the long-term nature of change while at the same time identifying short-term benchmarks that show progress toward the ultimate goals.

While change is complex, messy, and filled with uncertainty, such preparations can increase the probability of progress.

Reflection

Consider your own needs during change as you work toward distributing more responsibilities to your leadership team. How will you go about it? What will be difficult?

- Review how distributing leadership fits with your own strengths and educational beliefs.
  - o Look at your type page in Resource A for insights into your leadership style.
  - o Review your ranking of the leadership roles that you did as a Reflection activity at the end of Chapter 2. How easy or hard will it be for you to share the ones you ranked lowest? Do you have concerns about how others will view your leadership competency?
- Use Chart 3.1 as a checklist for considering teacher reactions to changes in leadership.
  - o Which questions will you need to answer? How might the changes be presented so as to gain buy-in from teachers with each preference?
  - o From a type perspective, shared leadership is the best way to lead because our blind spots can be covered by someone else's strengths. Which types might most naturally resist the changes? Which people on your staff might resist? Why?
- Turn to the Table of Contents and review the subjects of Chapters 5–10. Which seems most applicable to your school's current struggles? You might wish to read that chapter next.

4

Your Leadership Team

Distributing Roles Effectively

The essential challenge of the leader is not attaining perfection but acknowledging imperfection and obtaining complementarities. Rather than developing what they lack, great leaders will magnify their own strengths and simultaneously create teams that do not mimic the leader but provide different and equally important strengths for the organization. (Reeves, 2006, p. 23)

A braham Lincoln knew he needed the best minds in the nation to help him lead our country. He'd been elected into a catastrophe as Southern states seceded rather than submit to his government. Instead of choosing friends, he sought out the people most likely to question his assumptions, put forth opposite suggestions, and challenge his decisions—and who firmly believed he was the wrong man for the presidency. He chose the men he'd defeated for the Republican nomination, thus avoiding the "groupthink" that impairs so many leadership teams (Goodwin, 2006).

Type provides a framework for ensuring that your team covers all of the roles necessary for effective leadership *and* for learning to work together effectively. However, choosing a team on the basis of type preferences is not only unwise but unethical. Type preferences are just that: preferences. Type does not measure skill. Choosing Sensing, Intuitive, Thinking, and Feeling types for your team wouldn't guarantee you had the individuals at the table best able to cover the Administrative, Visionary, Systemic Instructional, and Community Instructional Leader roles.

This means that if you've inherited a team or are working within an existing school district structure, you needn't worry whether your group has an even distribution of personality types. This chapter will provide ways for your team to evaluate its natural strengths and blind spots. How can each member best contribute and collaborate?

If you are forming a new team, though, consider potential leaders in two ways. First, begin where you normally would, looking at the staff members that others seek out for advice, department and team leaders, teachers interested in moving into leadership roles, and individuals on whom you depend to help you develop or evaluate ideas.

Then, like Lincoln, consider your "opponents." Are they truly negative people, or is it possible that their personality is different enough from yours that it's difficult for you to understand their thoughts, motivations, or beliefs? Interpersonal issues may go far beyond type differences, but sometimes the framework of type provides sufficient insight to allow for "constructive use of differences," a motto for type professionals.

If you prefer Intuition, who in the building asks for the details? If you prefer Sensing, who in the building keeps bringing you new ideas? If you prefer Thinking, who keeps reminding you of how your decisions affect others? If you prefer Feeling, who keeps reminding you of setting precedents, logic, or systematic ways to look at data? The idea isn't to build a team of enemies but to examine your choices (or your judgments, if you've inherited a team) for type biases and thus ensure that you have considered everyone with leadership potential.

From research, we can draw several conclusions about type and teams (McCaulley, 1975; Kirby, 1997):

- *Because of the preponderance of Thinking and Judging managers, a majority of leadership teams are unbalanced.* They may not place enough weight on Feeling decision criteria, such as the impact of decisions on the people involved, the values the decision supports or contradicts, whether there is buy-in, and so on. Without Perceiving, they may also come to closure on decisions too quickly, without exploring less obvious alternatives.
- *When team members have similar preferences, they learn to work together more quickly.* However, no matter which preferences they hold, they may make poorer decisions if they don't somehow incorporate the strengths of the other preferences.
- *"Type-diverse" groups reach decisions more slowly (and painfully).* However, they often make better decisions because more viewpoints are covered. The more type-diverse the team, the longer the team members will take to understand each other and work effectively together. Chapters 5 and 6 provide exercises for team building so your leadership team can more quickly become effective.
- *If a team has a "dominant type," where the majority of its members share one or more preferences, the team may exaggerate the expression of those shared preferences.* Unless team members pay conscious attention to process, they may show bias against the other preference. Further, unless the team consciously works to include the gifts of the less-represented preferences, the

minority types may mask their preferences, unconsciously adapting their style to match that of the majority.

- *Teams that are "one-sided" (i.e., have few different types) will succeed if they use different types outside the team as resources.* They can also succeed if they make the effort to use their own less-developed functions as required by the tasks. The communication and collaboration exercises in Chapters 5 and 6, and the Problem-Solving, or Z, model, included in Resource B, are designed to help teams "stretch" to the other side.

Once you've chosen your team, type can help with three key tasks: understanding each person's strengths and how to work together, using type to examine best-fit responsibilities for each team member, and providing processes to ensure that the strengths of all type preferences are included in decisions, policies, and communications. First, though, let's look at the research on type and work styles and then apply it to your own style.

Type and Work Styles

As mentioned in Chapter 2, a preponderance of the daily responsibilities of school leaders slip through the cracks of the literature on essential school leadership responsibilities, as if budgets, schedules, hiring decisions, and managing the building happen by themselves. Some of these may be hardwired into your job description; you can't delegate them. But some of the tasks that drain your energy might actually be interesting and energizing for other members of your team. Research on the four columns of the type table, or the "function pairs" as they are called, provides insights into who likes to do what, which can also make it easier to open the conversation about distributed leadership. Heifitz and Linsky (2004) pointed out that

> Most people would rather have the person in authority take the work off their shoulders, protect them from disorienting change, and meet challenges on their behalf. But the real work of leadership usually involves giving the work back to the people who must adapt, and mobilizing them to do so. (p. 35)

As shown in Chart 4.1, the columns of the type table describe four groupings of personality types: Sensing-Thinking, Sensing-Feeling, Intuition-Feeling, and Intuition-Thinking.

The types in each function pair have in common how they gather information and make decisions. The function pairs account for specific patterns in communication styles, work habits, job focus, and career choices. They are therefore useful for examining task distribution among team members and individual effectiveness. While type preferences don't predict skill, they are a useful framework for considering natural interests and affinities for tasks.

It just may be that someone else would look forward to a task that you dread. For example, a Sensing-Feeling school leader hated working out the

Chart 4.1   The Function Pairs

Sensing, Thinking Administrative, Systemic Instructional Leader	**Sensing, Feeling** Administrative, Community Instructional Leader	**Intuitive, Feeling** Visionary, Community Instructional Leader	**Intuitive, Thinking** Visionary, Systemic Instructional Leader
ıST ı	ıSF ı	ıNF ı	ıNT ı
ıST ᴘ	ıSF ᴘ	ıNF ᴘ	ıNT ᴘ
ᴇST ᴘ	ᴇSF ᴘ	ᴇNF ᴘ	ᴇNT ᴘ
ᴇST ı	ᴇSF ı	ᴇNF ı	ᴇNT ı

details of the school schedule, even though she was good at the task, because she knew that she couldn't keep everyone happy. One of her Intuitive-Thinking teacher leaders took over the responsibility, saying that to him, it was like an intricate puzzle to solve.

Similarly, an Intuitive-Feeling principal, after spending two hours in a meeting with a documentation specialist learning a system for tracking staff development and parent involvement initiatives, exclaimed, "Someone's job is worse than mine." In truth, the Sensing-Feeling documentation specialist enjoyed her work because she was using her skills to provide needed help one-on-one.

Research on the Four Work Styles

As "proof" that the function pairs are worth studying and using as a framework, Chart 4.2, Career Data and the Function Pairs, summarizes research on patterns in career choices. Recall that because the type preferences are not evenly distributed in the population, one needs to compare career data with the distribution in the general population. For example, look at the column for Intuition and Thinking, NTs. While they represent the lowest percentage of elementary teachers, the figure of 11 percent approximates the percentage of NTs in the general population, 10 percent.

What inferences can be drawn from the data in Chart 4.2? While people with all type preferences become teachers, nurses, and so on, certain professions attract people with certain preferences. Some occupations show clear patterns, confirming the validity of type theory.

Consider, for example, that 85 percent of psychologists are Intuitive types. Psychology involves theories of human behavior; psychologists discuss patterns of behavior and possible solutions with their clients, activities that appeal more to the Intuitive strengths of dealing with ideas than the Sensing strengths of dealing with reality and concrete tasks.

Chart 4.2 Career Data and the Function Pairs

	Sensing, Thinking	Sensing, Feeling	Intuition, Feeling	Intuition, Thinking
% in the general population	30	43	17	10
% of school principals	56	15	8	21
% of elementary school teachers	23	42	23	11
% of licensed practical nurses	25	49	19	7
% of architects	13	5	39	43
% of psychologists	8	7	48	37
% of high-level managers	51	6	4	38
% of bank nonexempt employees	46	46	2	6

SOURCE: Macdaid, McCaulley, & Kainz (1986)

What about the lack of Feeling types in high-level management positions? The Feeling function emphasizes subjective decision making, treating people as individuals, and working toward harmony. Most high-level managers are rewarded for objective decision making, efficiency, and the ability to make tough decisions that may not lead to popularity.

Similarly, one can reason out why few Intuitives choose to work in banks (high structure, low creativity) or why few Sensing types go into architecture (designing with the mind rather than building with the hands).

Other research shows clear patterns in job focus, communication preferences, and tasks that people seek and avoid (Hirsh & Kise, 2001; Brock, 1997). Recall that the leadership responsibilities literature reviewed in Chapter 2 had little to say about the day-to-day duties of school administrators. We have two theories as to why this is so. Perhaps the authors take budgeting, scheduling, hiring decisions, and so on as givens so there is little point in writing about them. After all, principals *must* meet expectations in these areas. Or perhaps the lack of attention to these areas reveals type bias in school leadership information. Chart 4.3 shows how many of these functions are the domain of Sensing—Sensing-Thinking and Sensing-Feeling. Most writers, on the other hand, are Intuitives—around 75 percent. The Administrative Leader responsibilities may not be on their radar screens.

Now in Chart 4.4, let's see where the leadership responsibilities laid out in Chapter 2 for Administrative (Sensing), Visionary (Intuitive), Systemic Instructional (Thinking), and Community Instructional (Feeling) Leader roles fit in.

Why switch from focusing on the leadership roles that fit the eight personality preferences to how they fit the function pairs? Combining the roles this way reflects the career data cited above—the work activities people naturally pursue.

Chart 4.3   Workplace Patterns for the Function Pairs

	Sensing, Thinking	Sensing, Feeling	Intuition, Feeling	Intuition, Thinking
Focus on	• Efficiency • Thoroughness • Consistency • Stability • Facts and details • Data or tangible items	• Being of service • Respect • Role clarity • Facts about individuals and their needs • Details • Tried-and-true methods	• Community • Possibilities for people • Communication • Motivating people • Creativity • What could be	• Competence • Big picture • Future possibilities • Systems and structure • Theories and global concepts • Evidence that supports their mental models
Preferred tasks	• Establishing procedures • Allocating resources • Budgeting • Scheduling • Technology • Objective analysis	• Providing practical help • Determining individual needs • Office and facilities management • Budgeting	• Creative problem solving • Innovations • Developing others • Communicating • Team building • Exploring new ideas	• Goal setting • Strategic planning • Critiquing • Problem solving • Research • Data analysis
Turn-offs	• Vagueness • Factual errors • "Surprises" • Untried methods • Brainstorming without practical outcomes	• Theoretical possibilities • Criticism of others • "Cookie cutter" mentality • Logic without soul • Future projections	• Playing politics • Put-downs • Pushiness • Documentation, paperwork • Working with costs, figures	• Being given the answers • Hype • Administrative details • Repetition • Short-term outlook

- As the discussion on type development in Chapter 2 makes clear, individuals and teams *must* undertake both the Extraverted Interactive Leader role and the Introverted Reflective Leader role to gain balance in seeking information and coming to closure.
- Similarly, individuals and teams need to balance the Judging Planful Leader role and the Perceiving Flexible Leader role, adapting practices and process checks that ensure both approaches to school improvement are being honored.
- As a leader, you can't quite abdicate responsibility for any of the remaining roles, either. The four-function framework acknowledges that you

Chart 4.4 The Function Pairs and the Leadership Roles They Handle Most Naturally

Sensing, Thinking	Sensing, Feeling	Intuition, Feeling	Intuition, Thinking
Establishing procedures and routines (Administrative)	Culture: establishing trust and harmony (Community Instructional)	Setting and communicating vision (Visionary)	Setting and communicating vision (Visionary)
Managing budgets, scheduling, and other detailed tasks (Administrative)	Building relationships (Community Instructional)	Acting as change agent (Visionary)	Acting as change agent (Visionary)
Setting clear expectations, focusing on manageable goals (Administrative)	Managing budgets, scheduling, and other detailed tasks (Administrative)	Building relationships (Community Instructional)	Extensive, in-depth knowledge of curriculum, instruction, and assessment (Systemic Instructional)
Monitoring strategy implementation (Administrative)	Showing appreciation and recognizing accomplishments (Community Instructional)	Culture: establishing trust and harmony (Community Instructional)	Providing staff with cutting-edge theory and practice (Systemic Instructional)
Aligning curriculum and standards (Systemic Instructional)	Setting clear expectations, focusing on manageable goals (Administrative)	Showing appreciation and recognizing accomplishments (Community Instructional)	Effective use of data, assessment, and testing (Systemic Instructional)
Effective use of data, assessment and testing (Systemic Instructional)		Team building for effective collaboration (Community Instructional)	Analytical problem solving (Systemic Instructional)
			Aligning curriculum and standards (Systemic Instructional)

already have an affinity for two of the remaining four roles; for example, Sensing Thinkers might be drawn to both the Administrative and the Systemic Instructional Leader roles, although some tasks may appeal more than others. Look at the coding on Chart 4.4. Some of the Administrative roles fit best under Sensing/Feeling, and some of the Systemic Instructional roles fit best under Intuition/Thinking. This means that a Sensing/Thinking principal might have some natural abilities with two of the four leadership roles yet ask for team help with aspects of each of those roles. The columns help us consider the roles as the complicated frameworks they are, not as simple leadership styles that provide neat boxes for tasks.

In other words, the function pairs framework allows your team to *share* the leadership *roles* while *dividing up* the leadership *responsibilities.*

Reflecting on Your Own Responsibilities

Before you bring together a team, you may wish to do some reflection on your preferred leadership roles and responsibilities.

Activity 4.1
Leadership Roles Reflection

1. Consider the roots of your leadership philosophy. How do any of the following factors, separate from your personality type, affect your views of what you *should* be doing?

   - **District expectations:** Compare Chart 4.4 with criteria used in your performance evaluations. Which roles does your district emphasize?
   - **Your principal licensure program or ongoing staff development:** Which roles received the most attention? How has that influenced what you view as essential?
   - **Your experiences:** During which activities do you find yourself saying, "This is a waste of my time"? Does past experience tell you that no one will pay attention to your results, or does the activity not seem as important as the other roles?

2. With those factors in mind, highlight the responsibilities and tasks in Charts 4.3 and 4.4 for which you are currently responsible.

3. Fit all of the responsibilities you highlighted into Chart 4.5, Task Preference Grid. You can also add other specific duties that come to mind (for example, if you're on a specific district committee or have other roles that seem outside those in Chart 4.4).

   Most people describe "Quadrant I" activities as time givers—time flies when they're engaged in them. Quadrant IV activities are time drainers—people usually drag out these tasks by returning phone calls, checking e-mails, or anything else that seems more interesting (which is almost everything else!). Usually, people have found ways to structure Quadrant II activities so that they can be done efficiently. And they often view Quadrant III activities as a bit of refreshment. Perhaps the pleasure comes from learning something new or from doing something totally different from your normal responsibilities.
   The goal is to examine how you can be most productive. Remember that you can't do it all.

(Continued)

(Continued)

Chart 4.5   Task Preference Grid

I. Responsibilities I enjoy and do well	III. Responsibilities I enjoy but struggle to do well
II. Responsibilities I don't enjoy but do well	IV. Responsibilities I don't enjoy and don't do well

Understanding the Strengths of Each Team Member

Forming an effective leadership team requires stepping into the Community Instructional Leader role. Again, communication, respect, and trust are essential for collaboration. If team building isn't one of your natural strengths, consider hiring an outside expert to help your team understand each other's personalities and work styles, as the Annenberg Institute (2005) recommended.

Whether you do it yourself or use outside help, the following exercises will help the team move toward collaboration.

Ideally, use Activity 4.2, Type Identification, and 4.3, Using Type to Team Together, during a half-day session so that your team members can identify their preferences and learn about each other. If instead of using the workshop format for Activity 4.2, they read one of the suggested chapters to identify their preferences, allocate about 90 minutes for your first meeting to (a) answer questions that arose during the reading and (b) complete Activity 4.3.

Often, school leaders balk at the amount of time suggested for completing these team-building exercises. Remember that the "archetypal" leadership style is Thinking and Judging. The process of building a team is Feeling and Perceiving. You can't rush the process, and there's no point moving on to tasks if the trusting, communicative atmosphere needed for collaboration hasn't been established.

Activity 4.2
Type Identification

Allow team members to determine their personality preferences. There are several options:

- *Have a qualified professional administer the Myers-Briggs Type Indicator (MBTI) or other well-researched instrument.* The referral network at http://aptinternational.org lists type professionals who subscribe to the ethical use of type.

- *Have team members read through Chapter 1 in this book.* Alternatively, have them read Chapter 2, "Who You Are Is How You Teach," from *Differentiation Through Personality Types* (Kise, 2007). Note that even if people take the MBTI, ethical guidelines call for them to work through a self-selection process such as these readings encourage. The MBTI doesn't tell people their preferences. Appropriate use of the instrument includes an explanation of the preferences, self-selection, interpretation of results, and the clients determining their own best-fit type after reading type descriptions such as those contained in Resource A.

- *Take a group through the type activities described in Appendix C.* Understanding comes from seeing the preferences in action. Ideally, a school's whole staff would participate, including office, paraprofessional, and maintenance staff. However, your leadership team can also serve as a pilot group that can spread the word about the insights they gained through the exercises, paving the way for a future whole-school event. As long as you have examples (such as the "Write about a snowman" samples in Resource C) of how people with various preferences respond to the exercises, even groups of two can benefit from them.

Activity 4.3
Using Type to Team Together

This exercise helps team members learn more about their own type preferences while at the same time giving them a chance to explain their key needs in working together.

- If more than one team member has the same four-letter type code, allow them to work together on this exercise.
- Provide team members with copies of their type description from Resource A of this book. You might also make available the descriptions in Resource A of *Differentiated Coaching* (Kise, 2006) or other books listed in Resource D, For Further Reading on Personality Type.
- Choose three or four of the following prompts and have each person (or type group) record their responses on a piece of flip chart paper:
  o My strengths include . . .
  o I do my best work when . . .
  o The best way to communicate with me is . . .
  o If you want me to be productive, then . . .
  o Please know that I am working on . . .
  o On the job, I get irritated by . . .
  o I know that I annoy others by . . .
  o The most important thing(s) I want you to know about my type is . . .

Distributing Leadership Roles and Responsibilities

The next step is determining how your team will function together. What is the best use of each person's time? What might the team overlook without careful attention to the frameworks of leadership roles and type?

Activity 4.4
Team Reflection on Leadership Roles

- Have all team members complete Activity 4.1, Leadership Roles Reflection, using Chart 4.5, Task Preference Grid. This could be done before the meeting.
- Have all team members complete Chart 4.6, Leadership Responsibility Matrix.
- Reproduce Chart 4.6, Leadership Responsibility Matrix, on poster paper. Provide each team member with ten stickers, five each of, for example, red and green garage sale price stickers. Have them place their green stickers by the five roles they believe are the best match for their strengths and interests and their red stickers by the five roles they believe are the poorest match.
- Allow time for the group to reflect on the patterns they see before discussing the following questions:
  o What are our strengths as a team?
  o Which responsibilities are left uncovered?
  o Of the four leadership roles the team shares, with which will we struggle most? Administrative? Visionary? Systemic Instructional? Community Instructional?
- Have each function pair group (ST, SF, NF, and NT) discuss how they can support the principal going forward (i.e., looking at the group's Leadership Responsibility Matrix, what roles could they undertake?) Have them write their conclusions about their group's ideas on flip chart paper. When each group has presented to the whole group, lead a discussion on the results.
- As an ending reflection, have the same groups respond to the following prompt:

  To move forward as a leadership group, we need to take the following actions . . .

  The differences among the groups are usually striking and provide insights into why covering all the responsibilities is a team, not an individual, effort. See page 74 for an example.

(Continued)

(Continued)

Chart 4.6   Leadership Responsibility Matrix

Rating key:

1. I don't think I am best suited to this responsibility.
2. I understand this responsibility and could cover some of it.
3. I have strategies and ideas that work for me in this area.
4. I can do this easily.
5. I already do this and can share with others what I've learned.

Leadership Responsibilities (defined in Chapter 2)	1	2	3	4	5
Interactive Leader					
1. Being visible					
2. Being situationally aware					
3. Gathering input					
4. Advocating for the school					
Reflective Leader					
5. Providing time for reflection					
6. Learning from positive and negative results					
7. Delaying decisions to allow for reflection					
Administrative Leader					
8. Establishing standard operating procedures and routines					
9. Maintaining school focus and monitoring strategy implementation					
10. Managing school administrative processes					
11. Setting clear expectations and providing related feedback					
Visionary Leader					
12. Setting school direction					
13. Acting as change agent and optimizer					
14. Influencing beliefs					
Systemic Instructional Leader					
15. Gaining extensive knowledge of curriculum, instruction, and assessment					
16. Being involved in instructional decisions					
17. Aligning curriculum and standards					
18. Using data, assessment, and testing effectively					
Community Instructional Leader					
19. Building relationships					
20. Team building for effective collaboration					
21. Incorporating qualitative data into decisions					
22. Showing appreciation, recognizing accomplishments					
Planful Leader					
23. Using "next action" thinking					
24. Establishing goals and maintaining focus					
Flexible Leader					
25. Being flexible					
26. Being open					

Activity 4.5
Team Plan

After the large group has discussed the priorities each function pair group suggested, do the following:

- Provide each group with three strips of adding machine tape and a marker. Instruct them to choose their top three priorities for the team and write each one on a separate strip of paper. The team may benefit from starting with the School Improvement Plan.
- Have the teams tape their priorities to a wall or whiteboard. As they do so, ask them to read those already posted and place similar ones next to each other.
- When all the groups have posted their strips, look for similarities. Can any be combined?
- Consider if there are other significant ways to sort the strips:
  - Can they be split into short-term and long-term goals?
  - Do they fall under the same leadership roles?
  - Do they involve the process-oriented roles (the Interactive, Reflective, Planful, and Flexible Leaders) or those more directly related to student achievement (Administrative, Visionary, Systemic, and Community Instructional Leaders)
  - Do any of the priorities require that another priority be completed first?
- Work toward group consensus in prioritizing the priorities. The following techniques may help:
  - Ask the groups whether they would now rank any other priorities above their own.
  - Number the strips. Have team members cast ballots for the one they think should have the highest priority.
  - Have each person, without speaking, write down the priorities and how they would rank them. Read your own rank-ordered list to the group. Then have them reflect in writing on where they agree/disagree with your list. Collect their lists and reflections.
  - Estimate how long it will take to implement each priority and then how many priorities the team can work toward during the year. Then, for example, if the team believes they can work toward 8 of the 12, ask for suggestions on which 4 might be eliminated.
  - Leadership team members may wish to take the list back to their departments or grade-level teams to receive input—the Interactive Leader role.

Activity 4.6
Action Plans

Assign at least one team member to each priority. Have them develop an action plan for that item. The action plan should include:

- Their description of the priority
- The goal: What will success look like?
- The measure: How will the team know if they are making progress toward the goal?
- Specific steps to reach the goal with deadlines, resources needed, and people assigned to the responsibilities

Including the Strengths of All Preferences

The final step in establishing your leadership team is ensuring that the strengths of all preferences are included in decision making and communication processes. The time taken to develop understanding of team differences, strengths, and communication styles all goes toward reaching this goal.

Activity 4.7
Drawing on All Eight Preferences

To ensure that your leadership team considers the roles linked to each of the eight preferences, work through the following exercises together.

- *To balance Extraversion and Introversion:* Use the suggestions on pages 69–70 to balance the Interactive and Reflective Leader roles of the team.
- *To balance Judging and Perceiving:* Complete the Planful Leader/ Flexible Leader checklist on page 37 and incorporate your findings into how your team operates.
- *To balance the insights of Sensing, Intuition, Thinking, and Feeling:* Tackle solving a problem together using Resource B, Problem-Solving Model, a method that combines the work of Dewey (1910) and Myers (1998), breaking the process into four steps that correspond with Sensing, Intuition, Thinking, and Feeling and requiring all participants to spend time on each step.
  - o Resource B contains several sample questions for each step of the process as well as a sample exercise, "S'mores Dilemma," to help your team understand how the process helps cover all aspects of problem solving and compensates for team blind spots. You can start with a real problem your team faces. However, we recommend starting with the sample exercise so everyone understands the benefits of using the process before tackling a serious issue; otherwise, they may still tend to rush through steps in the process.

Chapter Summary

With personality type as a framework, school leaders can understand the roles necessary for effective leadership and effectively distribute them among members of their leadership team. Having a diverse team is certainly desirable and can provide new perspectives to a leader, thus ensuring better decision making. Each team member can draw on his or her own strengths while, at the same time, learning to appreciate how others both contribute to the group and compensate for each others' blind spots. Being aware of your team's type biases, its preferred ways of gathering information and making decisions, can help you be a better leader.

Reflection

- What evidence might teachers need to convince them that forming this style of leadership team will be worth the effort? How might you create an experience that provides that evidence?
- Assess your school's capacity for change to a team approach to leadership. The approach *is* well researched, supported by most of the experts cited in Chapter 2. Research on type, teams, and leadership shows that the type framework can help build successful teams. Therefore the biggest capacity questions are:
  - o **Time:** Have you allocated sufficient time for the team to learn to work together? Will there be sufficient meeting time to carry out identified roles and goals?

○ **Expertise:** Given the documented difficulties of learning to collaborate, does the team have sufficient expertise, or is outside help needed?

• Below are descriptions of the four main leadership styles. Read your own first, highlighting the parts that best describe your contribution. Then read the other styles. What are your blind spots—either areas where you might benefit from those with different strengths or areas of leadership that you tend to downplay in importance?

1. **Sensing and Thinking (ST):** Strengths include administrative tasks, setting up systems, providing clear expectations for various roles, using data, scheduling and implementing plans, balancing budgets, using technology to show data or to get a task accomplished. Can hold to the bottom line. Can easily establish clear positions on many issues. Dominant type for school principals.

2. **Sensing and Feeling (SF):** Strengths include handling details, scheduling (but may dislike the task because of the impossibility of pleasing everyone), assisting others in documentation. They enjoy being thorough and helpful. Can implement new programs well but are aware of the impact on staff and may slow implementation by adding steps. Good at maintaining what has been started and managing it. Often good at managing day-to-day operations.

3. **Intuition and Feeling (NF):** Strengths include starting new programs, inspiring staff to work toward challenging goals (and providing emotional support along the way), going with hunches about solutions to a problem or hiring new staff, solving problems by thinking outside the box, motivating staff, building team cohesion. Love the challenge of making things work.

4. **Intuition and Thinking (NT):** Strengths include theorizing about ways to improve student achievement and then logically testing out theories, looking at patterns in behavior or outcomes and coming up with reasons for it, setting strategic goals and organizing to meet them, and problem solving. They often enjoy analyzing data and looking at research to support their views.

5

Communicating So That What You Say Is What They Hear

Noticing what surprises and disturbs me has been a very useful way to see invisible beliefs. If what you say surprises me, I must have been assuming something else was true. If what you say disturbs me, I must believe something contrary to you. My shock at your position exposes my own position. When I hear myself saying, "How could anyone believe something like that?" a light comes on for me to see my own beliefs. These moments are great gifts. If I can see my beliefs and assumptions, I can decide whether I still value them. (Wheatley, 2002, p. 36)

Communication skills are essential for leaders. Costa & Kallick (2000) included thinking and communicating with clarity and listening with understanding and empathy as two key habits of mind. However, it's a rare leader who hasn't experienced the frustration of having a carefully crafted message be misinterpreted, even used as fuel for fostering opposition. Consider, through the framework of type, how simple interactions might be misinterpreted:

- Our preference for Sensing or Intuition influences the kinds of information we pay attention to in communications. One person's attempt at clarity can be way too much information for someone else.

- Our preference for Thinking or Feeling influences our reactions to some-one else's conclusions. Did they follow a path of reasoning with which we can agree? Did they overlook criteria that are important to us?

Add differences in processing time (Extraversion and Introversion) and our affinity for coming to closure (Judging and Perceiving) and you can see how different personality types can inadvertently miscommunicate.

For example, in one of her first administrative positions, Beth announced to her staff that a new online grading system was ready and explained how it would work. The teachers could start entering grades whenever they wanted. Several teachers were upset, telling her later in the day, "We don't have time to do grades now. Why can't we wait until our flex day as we always have?"

Baffled by their anger, Beth talked it over with the school principal. They concluded that she'd given too much information at once, which can be a blind spot for people who prefer Intuition and Perceiving. Because the message came from an assistant principal, the teachers who preferred Sensing and Judging had only heard, "Enter your grades," not that they had the option of doing it when they wanted to.

These very different communication needs, though, also mean that type provides a framework for developing *effective* communication. School administrators can use type to

- Create healthy communication patterns for the school leadership team, which will lead to more effective collaboration
- Communicate well with teachers, parents, students, and other stakeholders, all of whom have differing needs as well as a mixture of communication styles
- Provide staff development so that teachers can communicate. For effective professional learning communities to take root, teachers need to be able to communicate how and why a practice or lesson plan boosts student learning in a way their colleagues can understand—and be open to listening to other teachers.

This chapter contains exercises that help teams understand and adjust to meet the needs of each other's communication styles.

Common Communication Problems Between People With Different Preferences

One of the most common reactions to type exercises that focus on communication is, "You mean they weren't doing that just to frustrate us?"

Let's set aside for a moment the content of what we're trying to communicate and look just at common roadblocks between people who prefer Extraversion and Introversion—whether we find forms of communication energizing or draining—and who prefer Judging or Perceiving—how quickly we want to come to closure in any communication. As you read about Extraversion and Introversion, think about a colleague or staff member who often seems to misread your intentions. Do these type differences explain any of their reactions?

Common Complaints

What Introverts say about Extraverts	*What Extraverts say about Introverts*
• "They talk before they listen and want us to talk before we think." *Introverts often need time to compose their thoughts before speaking while Extraverts often clarify their thoughts through conversation.*	• "Things are set in stone before we even know they're under consideration." *Introverts, because they want to be clear, may not share that they're working on an idea or project until it's done. The Extraverts may feel cut off from the process.*
• "They didn't gather our input." *Sometimes Extraverts take silence as agreement and bring matters to a close before Introverts have formed an opinion.*	• "They're apathetic even when I share a great idea." *Introverts are often more contained. For some, a smile and a nod indicate great excitement.*

Fortunately, putting into place a few meeting protocols often increases understanding among Extraverts and Introverts. Consider the following:

Agendas. If Introverts know what will be discussed, they can start thinking before the meeting and be ready to participate. Give them an opportunity to review any data or other information in advance. This allows them to check their own understanding, look up other information they wish to review before offering their viewpoint, or to reflect silently—which meetings often don't allow for. Even a few hours' notice allows many Introverts to contribute more in meetings.

The agenda can be as informal as bullets in an e-mail, but Introverts need the content so they can come prepared.

Visual summaries. If ideas are flying thick and fast, many Introverts may lose track of what is being said. This is especially true of visual learners. Both Extraverts and Introverts benefit from a record of the ideas being discussed, especially if it's being recorded visually for the whole group. Besides keeping a list on a whiteboard or overhead, the following two techniques often improve discussions:

1. *Webbing summary.* Have the group define the main question being discussed. Write that down in the middle of a whiteboard and draw a circle around it. Then as the group brainstorms, work to create a web of what is being said. What themes are emerging? Circle those and then move comments or ideas so they surround related themes. One middle school team used this technique to narrow down all of the problems their students faced into one cohesive strategy for the start of the next school year: planning the first four weeks of school to establish a caring, academic community.

2. *Reflective brainstorming.* Provide participants with two or three strips of adding machine tape or other sizeable strips of paper. Pose a question and have everyone write down their responses. Have participants join in organizing their comments into themes. Because this process allows Introverts time to gather their thoughts, everyone is ready to participate in the ensuing discussions.

Check-ins. Include a formal time in meetings for Introverted participants to share what they're working on even if they haven't fully formed their ideas, including plans they're considering for helping a certain student, interdisciplinary units, common assessments, teacher or student recognition programs, or even summer reading lists. Normalize using phrases such as, "I'm only just starting on this, but . . ." or, "I haven't worked the bugs out, but . . ." The Introverts quickly learn that they may get valuable input from a colleague who has tried a similar idea.

Similarly, communication conflicts often arise between people who prefer Judging and Perceiving, as shown below.

What Judging types say about Perceiving types	What Perceiving types say about Judging types
• "They talk in ever-widening circles." *The strength of Perceiving is **process**—recognizing that prematurely cutting off the search for multiple perspectives or changing information can weaken the problem solving or other process.*	• "They plunge ahead too quickly" *The strength of the Judging function is **product**—recognizing that delaying decisions delays progress.*
• "They keep changing directions." *Perceiving types understand that changing directions is preferable to sticking with an unproductive plan.*	• "They're close-minded." *Judging types understand that changing directions wastes time and resources.*

To balance the Planful and Flexible leadership roles, which use the strengths of the two approaches to life, use the following strategies:

Key decision reflection. One school board spent a single day interviewing several superintendent candidates and then made the final decision over dinner that night. *Any* decision that big deserves overnight reflection, even if the group seems to be in agreement. Before your team begins discussing a major issue or idea, agree whether postponing the final decision would be beneficial, even in the event that the outcome seems clear. Schedule in advance for when that decision will actually be made, perhaps the next morning in a brief meeting. The purpose is to allow time for any subtle warning signs to emerge—or for people to remember any key information not considered.

Problem-Solving, or Z, Model. Resource B contains the full problem-solving model that helps groups use Sensing, Intuition, Thinking, and Feeling to reach decisions. Use the model as a protocol for decisions, *especially* if the course of action seems obvious, to ensure that the team's blind spots aren't hiding other perhaps better alternatives.

What-if exercise. When a decision seems obvious, consider some outlying what-if scenarios. What if a key teacher leaves? What if class size increases? What if school district priorities change? The point isn't to stymie the process but to ensure that the decision holds well under very different circumstances.

Backward planning. Because Perceiving types often prefer delaying decisions until the last minute, backward planning can help a team decide when the "last minute" for making a decision really is. For example, think how often the new curriculum arrives too close to the start of the school year for teachers to plan adequately. Backward planning might look like this:

- Sept. 5:   School starts, so materials and lesson plans need to be ready.
- Aug. 5:   Teachers need materials in hand so they have time to plan.
- June 5:   Materials order placed; publishers quote eight-week delay.
- June 1:   Final decision on curriculum made so administrator has time to place order.
- May 15:   Final teacher input to curriculum decision needed.
- May 1:   Curriculum display and information go to teachers on various curriculum.
- April 1:   Final curriculum alternatives selected so sales reps can deliver samples for teachers.
- March 1:   Curriculum alternatives researched and ranked by committee; report given to task force team.

Note that Judging types usually plan forward—wanting to reach closure as soon as possible. Backward planning helps everyone understand that each deadline is real and important to the overall process. A similar process for helping students finish major projects is described in *Differentiation Through Personality Types* (Kise, 2007).

The above protocols aid the *processes* of communication. Let's look now at the *content*. What is most important to those receiving your communication? How can you adjust your style so that what you say is what they hear?

Creating Healthy Communication

If you want someone to listen and understand your message, adapt your communication style to match theirs. You *know* what you want to say; they don't.

At the heart of good communication is giving people the information they need, whether they prefer Sensing or Intuition, in ways that honor how they make decisions, whether they prefer Thinking or Feeling. The four-function framework that we used for examining team tasks also works, then, for communication.

Sensing and Thinking (ST). Be brief; focus on reality.

As much as they want details, STs also want efficiency in communication. They concentrate on reality and measurability. Form your communication around

- Proof that the idea, tool, or program works
- Efficiency—time, effort, or cost savings
- Cost/benefit analysis to show worth
- How results were/could be measured
- Specific applications—how they can use something immediately
- Opportunities for answering all of their questions

Sensing and Feeling (SF). Be friendly; focus on people-centered information.

SFs want to know how ideas or strategies might affect people they know. Frame your communication with examples about specific students, people in positions similar to theirs, problems they faced recently, and their own experiences in helping individuals. Focus on

- Practical results for people
- Individual needs
- Benefits for individuals they care about
- Immediate results, not future goals
- Personal testimonies from people in very similar situations
- Showing respect for their concerns, questions, values, and viewpoints

Intuition and Feeling (NF). Be idealistic; focus on potential.

While NFs enjoy exploring ideas, they're usually more interested in envisioning how those ideas might foster human growth and potential than in the details of the theory. Focus communication on

- Impact on relationships
- The strengths of those involved
- New insights and perspectives
- Elements of fun or enjoyment
- Avenues for meaning and purpose
- Evidence that others will be drawn to the idea and to those who support it

Intuition and Thinking (NT). Be theoretical; focus each person's expertise.

Any idea has to fit into the NT's own schema of the world. Their questioning may be taken as skepticism, resistance, or even arrogance if their drive for understanding is misinterpreted. Focus communication on

- Research
- Theoretical underpinnings
- Relationship to strategies and goals
- Building competency
- Future possibilities
- Concepts and the fascinating possibilities they present

Again, to be heard truly, change your style. Doing so takes practice, especially in group situations where people with all of the preferences are present.

One way to frame such communications is to provide at least some information for everyone:

- Facts for the STs
- Stories for the SFs
- Potential for the NFs
- Theory for the NTs

Let's work through a couple of examples. As you read them, jot down what you would naturally do. Then read the suggestions. Would you need to make further adjustments to your style to communicate effectively with this teacher?

A very angry Sensing/Thinking teacher comes into the administrator's office, announcing total frustration with what she perceives as a lack of detailed planning. She gives her opinion and stalks out, leaving the Intuitive/Feeling administrator with her mouth hanging open. What might the administrator do?

The first step in solving the above communication dilemma is for the Intuitive/Feeling administrator to acknowledge that she doesn't communicate or process details in the same way as the Sensing/ Thinking teacher. (Remember the opening example in Chapter 3, where the ISTJ assistant principal has dozens of questions about the new grading system?) After this acknowledgment, she might quickly summarize how the plan fits with the overall school strategy and point out that this is her strength. Then, if she has a more detailed plan, she can show it to the teacher and ask her to voice her concerns. If not, the administrator might suggest that because understanding the detailed process is one of the teacher's strengths, the administrator would very much appreciate receiving a list of questions from her. What hasn't she covered?

An Intuitive/Thinking administrator is observing the classroom of a Sensing/Feeling teacher. Chaos is reigning. Only two of 24 students are participating in a warm-up exercise. Several girls have their backs to the teacher and are sitting on desks, styling each other's hair and creating a student survey on who likes whom. Another group of boys are discussing their fantasy football teams. After 10 minutes of hoping things will get better, the administrator intervenes, helping the teacher insist that students do the work and suggesting a reflection/answer process so that all students generate answers. Afterward, the teacher is furious, complaining that she's lost her credibility with the students.

Remember that Sensing/Feeling teachers value harmony, in this case so much so that the teacher was afraid to confront students on their behavior. Becoming authoritative probably won't help your message be heard. You might be able to diffuse her anger with an appeal to other values. The students were showing total disrespect for her and for each other; no learning was taking place. Students who really wanted to learn (be specific, with examples of the effort individual students show in other classes) are being prevented from doing so. Acknowledge her frustrations—the difficult dynamics of this particular group of students (even if you've seen them behave perfectly well in other classrooms).

Then provide specific offers of help. Explain how the reflection/answer process required each student to engage and was relatively easy for her to manage. Offer to discuss other warm-up activities that work with diverse learning styles. Ask her if she would like to visit the classroom of a teacher who excels at getting all students to put forth effort—be specific that the teacher has strategies to pass on what she's learned. Sensing/Feeling teachers don't want generalities but rather specifics that they are confident can be replicated in their own classrooms.

Concrete Steps to Improving Communication

While a school's leadership team can facilitate the processes described below, you might want to consider hiring an outside facilitator if communication has already broken down. How can you tell if you need one? If staff members have stopped communicating with each other, if team or staff meetings have resulted in explosive interactions, or if your staff has already taken sides on issues, then you may need help from a third party.

If your team feels capable, you can improve communication in your building through exercises that lend themselves to embedded staff development, working on topics that you can leverage for other purposes. Chart 5.1 summarizes the information on the ways each function pair prefers to communicate.

For example at one elementary school, communication had all but ground to a halt among the different grade levels. After the teachers identified their own type preferences, Jane asked them to meet in function pair groups and answer the question, "What do we need to go forward as a team?"

> The *Sensing/Thinking* teachers asked questions to clarify the task and pointed out that they didn't think they had much authority to determine what would happen next.
>
> The *Sensing/Feeling* teachers wrote a list of values the team needed to honor going forward: honesty, caring, respect, patience, tact, and so forth.
>
> The *Intuitive/Feeling* teachers filled three flip chart pages with community-building activities they thought would help pull the staff together.
>
> The *Intuitive/Thinking* teachers displayed a seven-point plan for improving staff meetings.

After all of the groups had reported, the room went silent, pondering the differences. One of the teachers then asked, "Can we sit in these groups at all meetings so we remember that we speak 'foreign languages'?"

To use type concepts to improve communication, team members need first to believe that the differences are real—actually see the differences as the teachers just described did —and then practice adjusting to meet the communication needs of others.

Chart 5.1   Function Pair Communication Styles

	Sensing, Thinking	*Sensing, Feeling*	*Intuition, Feeling*	*Intuition, Thinking*
Communication keys	• Be brief • Be sequential • Be responsible	• Be friendly • Be practical • Be respectful	• Be idealistic • Be growth oriented • Be fun	• Be prepared • Be credible • Be open to their conclusions
Tips for persuasion	• Provide the facts • Get straight to the point • Answer all questions • Demonstrate how/why it will work • Refer to time or cost savings • Emphasize measurable results	• Set ideas or facts in a personal context • Concentrate on immediate results • Understand individual needs • Show loyalty • Be specific, with no surprises • Use personal testimonies	• Don't use pressure tactics • Be honest and personal • Provide individual treatment • Avoid details • Focus on people's strengths • Relate to meaning and purpose	• Convey in-depth knowledge • Provide information requested • Be business-like • Show knowledge of needs • Discuss research and theory • Point out intriguing possibilities
Planning horizon	• Establishing short-term goals (3–6 months)	• Establishing short-term goals (3–6 months)	• Establishing long-term vision (3–5 years)	• Establishing long-term vision (3–5 years)
Decision-making style (Haley & Pimi, 1994)	• Fact-based, focusing on past effectiveness, structure, and "fit" with standard practice • May ignore patterns	• Based on opinions of trusted people, paying attention to what people involved need or want • May ignore data	• Grounded in symbols, metaphors, and novel ideas, focusing on their vision of the future • May ignore practical considerations	• Based on systematic patterns, focusing on logic and their conceptual pattern • May ignore data that doesn't fit their mental mode

Step 1: Demonstrate the Differences

Choose any of the following exercises. Tailor the questions or prompts to matters your leadership team or staff needs to address.

Activity 5.1
Understanding Differences in Priorities

Break participants into the four groups: Sensing and Thinking (ST), Sensing and Feeling (SF), Intuition and Feeling (NF), and Intuition and Thinking (NT). Provide each group with flip chart paper and markers. Have them work together to answer *one* of the following prompts:

- What are our top priorities for this year?
- If we could wave a magic wand, what two things would we change about this school?
- What do we need to move forward in our teams?
- What do students need during the first week of school?

For any of these prompts, the Sensing and Thinking teachers will tend to focus on concrete details: schedules, physical facilities, class size, specific policies that need clarification, or staff consistency on certain school, classroom, or team rules.

The Sensing and Feeling teachers will tend to focus on concrete needs: whether students can get enough individual help, whether their practical needs are being met for supplies or food, and suggestions for student and teacher overall well-being, such as maintaining a respectful climate or finding ways to reward small acts of kindness or helpfulness.

The Intuitive and Feeling teachers will advocate for ideas to promote student growth, intellectually and socially. Their suggestions may include ideas for adding fun to the year for teachers and students, ways to help students be more self-motivated or have higher expectations for themselves, and suggestions for fostering creativity and enthusiasm from students and staff.

The Intuitive and Thinking teachers often put forward systems or strategies: better use of data, improved meetings, more efficient planning formats, incorporating goal setting for students, or competitions to motivate students to try harder.

Activity 5.2
Focus on Communication Styles

Divide participants into the four function groups (Sensing/Thinking, Sensing/Feeling, Intuition/Feeling, Intuition/Thinking). Have them answer the following prompts:

- If you want me to understand your message, please . . .
- If you want me to understand your message, please *don't* . . .

Study Chart 5.1 to understand the common ways the groups respond.

Activity 5.3
Learn From the Past

In the same groups, have teachers think about a past policy, rule, or other change that they felt would have benefited from better communication. They need not all consider the same past event. Have them work together to answer the following questions on flip chart paper:

- In communication about change, we need . . .
- When we *don't* get what we need, we . . .
- We felt misunderstood because . . .
- Next time we hope . . .

For any of the above exercises, a logical next step would be for teachers to gather as teams, by either grade level or subject area, to discuss the results.

- How are our communication styles the same?
- How are our communication styles different?
- What should we keep in mind going forward to communicate most effectively?

To help them consider the impact of their communication styles at a deep level, have them develop a "Team Operating Manual" that captures their discussion.

Step 2: Practice Communicating

Just as writing and speaking skills improve with practice, so do everyday communication interactions. The following exercises can be adapted to link with current discussion topics your staff needs to consider, providing practice in communication while concentrating on school goals and strategies. Note that you can use them with your leadership team first and then, as you gain experience in using type to "translate," with teaching teams to help them prepare for more effective collaboration.

Activity 5.4
Basic Communication Exercise

Provide participants with copies of Chart 5.1, the communication styles and concerns for each of the function pairs.

- Form groups by function pairs: Sensing/Thinking (ST), Sensing/Feeling (SF), Intuition/Feeling (NF), and Intuition/Thinking (NT).
- Instruct the groups to design a communication, using real-life examples or the following scenarios, to a teacher of the opposite function (STs to NFs, SFs to NTs, etc.).
  - o STs: How would you inform an NF of rules that teachers must enforce uniformly in their classroom?
  - o SFs: How would you communicate to an NT a good method for breaking down a big school project into chunks a student can manage?
  - o NFs: How would you convince an ST to try a new teaching method?
  - o NTs: How would you help an SF teacher give and grade an open-ended assignment?

Let the opposite groups give feedback on the others' communication. Do they think they understood it clearly? How could it be adjusted to be more effective?

Activity 5.5
Communication Habits

Have teams consider the specific ways they communicate with each other—meetings, e-mails, voice messages, written documents, in-the-hall conversations, etc. How effective is current communication? How might meetings and written documents be improved to meet the needs of the different communication styles?

Your leadership team might examine overall school communication. Consider the information shared in writing and in meetings. Use Chart 5.1 to evaluate which communication style is most often left out. What would best be conveyed in writing? In meetings? In other ways?

Activity 5.6
School-Based Case Study

Bring to mind a past conflict over curriculum, discipline, or a teaching practice not everyone implemented. Have teachers gather in the four function pairs to discuss

- What we agreed with
- What we didn't agree with

Note differences in the concerns of each group. Then ask the entire group to reflect on whether the change, and how it was communicated, met the needs of some groups more than others.

Chapter Summary

People screen or filter what they read and hear through their personality preferences. Thus, staff members with different preferences can easily misconstrue or even be offended by an administrator's message because of the choice of words, precision of communication, or timing. Type provides a framework for leaders to plan *how* a message needs to be communicated, *what* information needs to be communicated, *how much* information needs to be communicated, and *why* the communication is necessary.

Taking into account a person's preference for gathering information (Sensing or Intuition) increases the likelihood that the person receives the intended message and understands it. Taking decision-making styles into account (Thinking or Feeling) allows the receiver to feel valued or respected. The framework can thus minimize *mis*communication and increase the chance that all staff feel valued and heard.

Reflection

- Review Chart 5.1. Which elements of communication are hardest for you to address? You might also look at the page for your type in Resource A. Which "Practical Next Steps" might improve your communication skills?
- Think of a time when you were misunderstood or had to mediate in a misunderstanding. Could the type concepts in this chapter have improved communication? How?
- How might you use this information with your school board? Think through interactions. Could any communication problems be solved by using type concepts?

6

Making Professional Learning Communities Worth the Effort

The broad literature on school renewal describes many failed attempts to build learning communities, attempts mounted by sophisticated people, armed with considerable energy and carefully constructed strategies. There are successful cases, of course, but generalizable strategies have been elusive. I do not want to see a positive movement turn out just as the systemic, strategic, comprehensive, whole-school varieties did. Our collective past experience can help us know what to avoid and may help us devise ways of succeeding. (Joyce, 2004, p. 77)

Educational literature is filled with the call to develop professional learning communities. DuFour (2004b) distinguished these from other team efforts as follows:

As the school moves forward, every professional in the building must engage with colleagues in the ongoing exploration of three crucial questions that drive the work of those within a professional learning community:

- What do we want each student to learn?
- How will we know when each student has learned it?
- How will we respond when a student experiences difficulty in learning?

The answer to the third question separates learning communities from traditional schools. (p. 8)

The goals for professional learning communities, with the shift in focus from how we teach to how students learn, is touted over and over as *the* solution—overlooking one very real fact. Few people naturally excel at collaboration. Instead, working effectively with others takes time and skill development. Saying "must" or "should" doesn't by itself create communities. Indeed, Hargreaves (1994) pointed out that setting aside time for team meetings and mandating goals usually only results in what he calls "contrived" collaboration, not the deep conversations required to change classrooms.

Kise (2006) delineated three levels of collaboration; traditionally, teachers have struggled to work effectively at all three levels (Lortie, 1975; Little, 1990):

Level I: Superficial collaboration. This includes teaming for administrative tasks such as fundraising, field trips, procuring resources, or discussing interventions for specific students. Ensuring that staff is building relationships with all students, while important, still falls within this level of teaming.

Level II: Segmented collaboration. Teaching teams might engage in cross-disciplinary efforts such as conducting an experiment in science and composing a related essay in language arts. Or, elementary teachers may divide up subjects, one teaching math in both rooms while the other teaches social studies. Team expectations for behavior or uniform rules and consequences might also fall here . . .

Level III: Instructional collaboration. Teaching teams engage in deep discussions about teaching and learning, serving as resources to each other in developing curriculum and lessons that meet the needs of all learners. Together, they unearth assumptions about teaching and learning, gain from each others' natural strengths, share strategies and ideas, and learn more regarding what is possible in the classroom. (pp. 54–55)

We've seen teachers spend hours debating snack policies, bus duties, field trip details, or how to improve one student's behavior—all Level I topics—and thus seldom have time to examine whether their students are truly learning. Part of the problem is that these kinds of urgent agenda items will always take precedence over deeper but less urgent issues, unless collaborative teams carefully consider their goals and how to best use their time together.

However, while lack of collaboration skills plagues teams in all kinds of organizations, schools contain even more barriers to collaboration, such as professional norms that guard against teachers' criticizing each other, teacher isolation in single classrooms, the fact that many teachers go into the profession because of the autonomy it provides, the lack of team time in the school day, and teachers' fears about disclosing problems in their classrooms (Kise, 2006).

Joyce (2004) asked, "How, aside from talking about it, does one change the way school staffs are organized and how they interact?" He pointed out that no one has done the research to identify *how* to create professional learning communities effectively—the nuts-and-bolts process that consistently transforms independent teachers into Level III collaborators. However, type provides three ways to help teachers overcome these barriers and form true learning communities. First, type provides a common language for focusing on how students learn rather than on who is right or wrong. Second, teachers can use the lens of type to examine their own strengths and difficulties with collaboration. Third, type has been a standard tool for team building and collaboration within businesses and other organizations for more than three decades, providing research and strategies for helping teaching teams to learn to collaborate.

In this chapter, we'll examine the climate needed to establish a learning community, explore how teams and individuals can assess their collaboration skills, and introduce exercises and initiatives designed to increase the kind of collaboration that will improve student achievement.

A Climate for Collaboration

Trust, respect, honesty, a willingness to probe and question personal beliefs about teaching and learning—collaboration thrives when all of these are in place. Building this climate takes time; most businesses devote at least two full days to the process of improving a team's ability to work together. Yet school staff development time is so limited that we often rush past this essential step, instead thrusting teachers into community without giving them the skills to succeed. This is true in classrooms as well—in building a learning community of students, we rush to content, glossing over relationship building, developing trust, and teaching collaboration skills.

Hargreaves (2002) explored how teachers describe betrayal—the opposite of trust—as one of the strongest emotions connected with colleagues. In his study, teachers described three kinds of betrayal by their colleagues: not meeting professional expectations or engaging in self-serving practices; accusations of incompetence resulting in shame; and gossip or verbal negativity about colleagues or school goals, including being shamed in front of students or colleagues. Without trust, teachers will struggle to share ideas, take suggestions for improvement, or deal with conflict productively. He concludes

> If betrayal bedevils improvement, it is important to understand more about the organizational conditions and policy strategies that give rise to feelings of inequity in workload and professional dedication, that spread misunderstanding, gossip and self-servingness, and that give rise to insensitive attributions of incompetence. As we deepen such understanding, we might learn not only how to create more active professional trust in schools, but also how to avoid the recurring and corrosive effects of betrayal. (p. 405)

Trust comes about through effective communication (see Chapter 5). In addition, sometimes the staff needs to deal with past events that led to mistrust. Leonard and Leonard (2001) linked past problems to the climate needed for change:

> Without freedom from fear of failure and retribution, without assurance that support and encouragement are implicit and explicit, without

confidence that what teachers are doing through collaborative practice is both admired and beneficial, sustained teacher collaboration as a norm of behaviour (not just normative behaviour) is doubtful. The emergent effect may be the sustenance of schools that are characterized less by true elements of the moral community than they are by those that reflect a desire to create the image of being so. (p. 396)

As a school begins the hard work of establishing professional learning communities then, the leadership team can increase the chance of success by helping teachers process barriers, past conflicts, the skills their team needs, and the school goals that may be unattainable without Level III collaboration.

Step 1: Assess the Administrative Leadership Team's Ability to Help Teachers Collaborate

The exercises in this chapter are designed to allow a school leadership team to establish collaborative professional learning communities. However, ponder the worst-case scenario: a leadership team jumps on the "learning community bandwagon," forming its staff development calendar around the suggestions given below.

Teachers on more than one team do not trust each other, even though they show professional courtesy. Perhaps leadership is aware of this, but we see two general ways of dealing with the problem: plunging ahead with the hope that the plan will produce dialogues that will help teachers understand each other, or pushing forward with exercises that focus on student learning while assuming that the common mission will unite the teachers. During staff development, teachers on these teams refrain from critiquing each other or sharing ideas because of past episodes of betrayal.

The teachers, after a few months, determine that learning communities are yet another time-consuming, ineffective school reform.

In other words, before you form professional learning communities, or any other new team structure, work through the following activities.

Activity 6.1
Collaboration Climate Assessment

As a leadership team, consider the following questions:

- Are there existing issues among staff members that need resolving?
- Are we devoting enough time to helping teachers build collaborative skills?
- Do we as a leadership team have the skills necessary to establish a school climate where collaborative teams can thrive?
- Do we need help in considering ways to remove obstacles to collaboration, such as schedule and workload issues?
- Do we have the right people on this team, with the right skills, to move staff toward Level III collaboration?

Depending on the school climate, a leadership team might take the step of hiring an outside consultant to train them to work with the teacher teams or to work directly with the teachers until they see the benefits of collaboration. Outside facilitators can be essential when schools lack an atmosphere of trust. One school described the contributions of an outside facilitator:

> They recognized his ability to "build a nonthreatening environment" where people felt able to express their thoughts; his skill in "keeping the group together" despite the range of personalities and "making people's contributions feel valued and worthwhile"; his high level of credibility with the staff which enabled them to cope with the "fuzziness" of parts of the process and his role as a critical friend offering a different (and inherently neutral) perspective. (Andrews & Lewis, 2002, p. 248)

New school leaders might have the fresh slate needed to establish a community of trust—or they might underestimate existing issues. Established leaders may have the requisite relationships with staff and the training skills, or they may need the help of an outsider to put misunderstandings to rest. The point is for the leadership team to dialogue and reflect on whether they would benefit from a facilitator.

Step 2: Assessment of Current Collaboration Level

The next step is assessing the current level of collaboration. Often this varies widely from team to team. A note of caution on surveying staff on collaboration: People tend to overestimate their effectiveness. K. Zais (personal communication, August 9, 2006) found that as she trained teachers in collaboration, their definition of *effective* changed as their skills improved. Their postintervention ratings of how they had improved matched the administrative team's assessment of their progress. They had learned what it means to collaborate and developed skills to succeed.

When looking at initial survey results, then, often the relative rather than absolute ratings have the most meaning. For example, a team might rate themselves as "effective" to "very effective" on every item. Concentrating on skill development for the "effective" ones may bring significant improvement in collaboration if they believe themselves more effective than they really are.

Activity 6.2
Assessing Current Teacher Collaboration

Chart 6.1 provides a way to help teachers understand their current level of collaboration.

- Have individuals rate their teams/departments on how often/well they engage in collaborative activities.
- Display aggregate data. If teams vary greatly, you might share data just with the teams.
- Because teachers tend to overrate their collaboration abilities, school leadership might complete Chart 6.1 using their perceptions of each team. In most cases, this would not be shared with the team. The purpose is to record where you hope to see each team improve in collaboration skills.

Chart 6.1 Collaboration Activity Survey

Rate your team on how often and effectively they collaborate on the following:	Never	Seldom	Frequently	Nearly always	Not very effectively	Somewhat effectively	Effectively	Very effectively
Planning field trips and other events								
Action plans for struggling students								
Rules for homework, grading								
Rules for behavior, consequences								
Lesson planning								
Common assessments								
Coteaching								
Examining frequency with which students encounter similar learning activities (worksheets, freewriting, objective tests, etc.)								
Developing and teaching a common lesson plan								
Examining student work to set common expectations								
Agreeing on and implementing teaching strategies								

Step 3: Assessment of Individual Collaboration Strengths and Styles

Leonard and Leonard (2001) listed several skills needed for effective collaboration:

> Effective collaboration requires sophisticated skills that do not simply materialize when teachers come together, either voluntarily or otherwise. Collaborative skills need development. If collaborative endeavors are to meet with any degree of success, then teachers need to develop proficiency in consensus building, decision making, and the process of conflict resolution, whereby the means become as important as the ends. (p. 394)

Let's look at how type can help teachers assess and develop skills in each area.

Consensus building. Chapter 4 discussed how leadership teams can examine the overall "group type" and use the information to avoid pitfalls while making use of each team member's strengths. The information can also be used to help teachers understand the biases the team may have—an option may seem like the "best" decision when in actuality, most group members are considering the decision from the same viewpoint, biased by their common preferences. Further, teams can choose among the strategies given in Chart 6.2 to ensure that each person's viewpoint is heard before decisions are made.

Decision making. The Problem-Solving Model, Resource B, is designed to slow down decision making, ensuring that each step is given careful consideration. It suggests a way to use the process to set a team goal for collaboration, helping them build decision-making skills *and* move forward on developing their learning community.

Conflict resolution. Conflict resolution is often especially hard for teachers. They tend to avoid conflict through norms of politeness and noninterference (Little, 1990) or by only communicating with colleagues who share their educational beliefs (Fullan, 2001).

Considering the lens of type, school cultures have a *Feeling* archetype, with an emphasis on community values, harmony, and meeting the needs of each student. Often, people who prefer Feeling would rather avoid or bury conflict than deal with it. Killen and Murphy (2003) described the different approaches to conflict of people with preferences for Thinking and Feeling:

> Our preferred decision-making process determines where we focus our attention in conflict. In a conflict situation, those with a preference for Thinking (T) tend to pay most attention to or focus most strongly on
> - What the conflict is about
> - Opinions and principles
> - Analyzing and tolerating differences
> - Succinct delivery
> - Maintaining a firm stance

Those with a preference for Feeling (F) tend to pay most attention to or focus most strongly on

- Who is involved
- Needs and values
- Accepting and appreciating differences
- Tactful delivery
- Ensuring give and take (p. 11)

In addition, people who prefer Judging often seek rapid closure in conflict situations while those who prefer Perceiving often seek to process what happened thoroughly to avoid recurrences.

Activity 6.3
Conflict Styles

- Divide your staff into small groups (five or six per group) of those who prefer Thinking and those who prefer Feeling. Provide each group with flip chart paper and markers. Ask them to record their answers to the following questions:
  o Define conflict.
  o How do you handle conflict situations?
  o What do you need when conflicts arise?
- After each group has reported, ask everyone to reflect on the differences they see between the Thinking and Feeling perceptions of conflict by freewriting. Then ask for volunteers to share their thoughts.
- In teams, have teachers discuss this information and how it relates to past conflicts they've had. If past team dynamics have been heated, they may need a facilitator. Consider using the Problem-Solving, or Z, Model, fully explained in Resource B, to guide a discussion, using the following prompts:
  o Sensing:
    – How many team members prefer Thinking? Feeling?
    – What specific examples show how our personality types have affected past conflicts?
    – What positive and negative results have come from how we handled conflict?
  o Intuition:
    – What analogy describes how we handle conflict?
    – How can we use type to better handle conflict? What processes might help?
    – What benefits might result from a better conflict process?
  o Thinking:
    – What are the pros and cons of each suggestion for handling conflict?
    – Are the proposed solutions fair to all?
    – What are the consequences of not deciding or acting?
  o Feeling:
    – Who is committed to carrying out the solution? Has everyone been heard?
    – How will each possible solution contribute to harmony and group values?
    – What are each person's own reactions to the proposed processes?

Note that in conflict situations, the above process cannot be rushed—in fact, because the process sometimes brings about the first deep, civil discussions a group has had, they may volunteer to meet again to continue rather than cut the process short. The investment of several hours in discussion (no more than two hours at a time!) can bring substantial improvements in the team's ability to engage in Level III collaboration.

Activity 6.4
Collaboration Styles Exercise

Chart 6.2 provides a way for school staff to understand and evaluate their collaboration styles, skills, and difficulties. Teams can use the chart by first having individuals reflect on how the information applies to them. Second, the team can use individual responses to develop norms and choose strategies.

Chart 6.2   Type Preferences and Collaboration Styles

Extraversion	**May benefit from . . .**
• Natural desire to process through interaction with others • Usually can engage with little prior reflection • Quick with feedback and ideas • Input from outer world—class visits, conversations • Focus on a wide range of topics	• Listening protocols • Coming with specific task completed • Recording and then choosing best ideas to share • Reflection activities on their impressions before discussion • Clear expectations on mandatory shared tasks
Introversion	**May be more effective with . . .**
• Natural desire to process alone • Share when ready • Put forth full ideas, not ideas in process • Overwhelmed by fast brainstorming • Focus on one topic at a time	• Clear meeting purposes so they can be ready to interact • Visual brainstorming aids, wait time • Jotting down initial thoughts and sharing them immediately • Talking tokens • Group thinking maps to depict topics and their interrelationships
Sensing	**May be more effective with . . .**
• Communicate in facts, details, practical reality • Standards and curriculum guide lessons • Hesitate to go beyond personal experience • Want concrete goals, realistic time frames, clear next steps	• Using tools to brainstorm, such as considering metaphors or analogies, thinking maps to draw conclusions, concrete list of what isn't working • Looking for patterns in which students aren't helped by curriculum • Analogies: Why/how is this like ___? • School protocol for practical meeting practices
Intuition	**May be more effective with . . .**
• Communicate in new ideas and possibilities • Talk in general terms; grow excited about new directions • Push for changes • View standards and curriculum as a launching pad for ideas	• Time built into meeting for reality check on ideas • School protocol on "next steps" • Clear identification by team of what is working well • Focus on what students need for learning, not on right and wrong
Thinking	**May be more effective with . . .**
• Communicate through questioning, finding flaws • Add logic, weigh pros and cons, consider precedents • Bring models, theories, and research to the table • Underestimate the importance of relationships, buy-in, and values in their drive for logic • Look externally for problem sources	• Team exercise concerning how individuals like to give and receive feedback • Protocols about brainstorming • Requiring close-to-home application or concrete way to use it • Team operating manuals: "What you need to know about me to function as a team. . . ." • Using the Problem-Solving Model, using prompts to consider external and internal causes
Feeling	**May be more effective with . . .**
• Look internally for problem sources • Communicate about values, common ground; place emphasis on all students	• Using the Problem-Solving Model, using prompts to consider external and internal causes • Team goals and tasks concerning instructional and curricular strategies

(Continued)

(Continued)

• Hesitant to critique and may not want to be critiqued • May not voice dissent—don't speak up but then don't comply with group decision • Relish social, relationship-building side of collaboration	• Team exercise on how individuals like to give and receive feedback • Team protocol to check buy-in • Clear goals and purposes for meetings, even clocking and limiting social time
Judging • Focus on conclusions, goals • Expect schedules and agendas • Understand how long projects will take, reasonableness of action plans, fit with other priorities • Dislike surprises	**May be more effective with . . .** • Protocols that ensure processing of ideas before coming to closure • Being put in charge; asking at start for Perceiving consent to agenda (or additions) • Balancing with "The answer to how is yes" ideas in Chapter 3 • Building buffers into meeting and plan schedules
Perceiving • Bring possibilities, options • Struggle with set times for collaboration; may rush in or multitask • May continue to process even after team has reached conclusion • Work best under pressure	**May be more effective with . . .** • Time lines for decisions • Purposeful meetings, clear ground rules with buy-in from all • Protocol for moving on • Fake deadlines: *their* class observed first, plan with a J before the meeting, etc.

To help individuals apply the information in Chart 6.2 to themselves, ask them to

- Think about their own personality preferences and whether the collaboration style described for each of their preferences applies to them.
- Highlight in one color the items in the left column that describe their strengths or natural approach to collaboration
- Use a different color to highlight areas that are difficult for them.
- Based on their responses, freewrite for the following prompts: "I bring the following strengths to collaboration. . . ." and "I hope to find strategies to help me with. . . ." Inform them that they will be sharing this information with their teammates.

Individuals might complete this task before teams gather. Then during the team session, two different approaches can be used.
- Teams might use a round-robin written dialogue next. Each person starts to write about strengths in collaboration and what they need help with to collaborate. Then all pass their sheet to the next person, who writes how they can help support them to be more collaborative. Send all sheets all the way around the group. Each person ends up with written support, commitment, and acknowledgment of how they will work together toward deep collaborative efforts.
- Use the Problem-Solving Model, Resource B, to process the results. Ask teams to
  o Share from their freewriting, taking notes on common concerns (Sensing facts about their collaboration skills).
  o Look at the strategies in the right-hand column of Chart 6.2 (Intuitive possibilities). Which might help them succeed as a team?
  o Use Thinking to consider which strategies might be most effective and efficient. While some norms and strategies bolster collaboration, the Annenberg Institute (2005) warned

    The use of structural processes and protocols helped facilitate group efforts and develop norms and habits necessary to engage in collaborative conversations. However, in many instances, this led to a strong focus on process with lesser emphasis on and attention given to engaging in content-based, instructionally focused discourse. (pp. 5–6)

Clear product goals for collaboration, tied to student achievement, can help avoid this trap.
- Finally, the group can assess whether everyone actually buys into the chosen strategies (the Feeling function).

Step 4: Collaborate to Create a Vision

As teachers work to improve their effectiveness in collaboration, they need a common vision of *why* they are collaborating and the overall goal—that their efforts will make a difference. Saphier (2005) commented

> Belief in effort-based ability makes a huge difference in how well staff members use the collaborative structures we create on behalf of student learning. It provides the energy and motivation needed to persevere when the work of schools is tough. (p. 86)

He continued that such schools constantly give students three crucial messages:

> ... and they receive them at every turn from every adult and from the policies, practices, and procedures of the institution. These crucial messages say
> 1. What we're doing here is important.
> 2. You can do it!
> 3. I'm not going to give up on you—even if you give up on yourself. (pp. 89–90)

While the overall goal of professional learning communities is to focus on and improve student learning, schools have different ways of articulating and focusing this goal.

For example, one school developed a vision of the values and character they expected their students to uphold and then planned ways to impart those values to students. In a study of an elementary school in North Carolina, Strahan (2003) noted the importance of this common vision:

> One teacher reported, "We do things according to Archer pride. That is something we emphasize to the student. To be polite, have integrity, respect, discipline, and excellence here at Archer School. It is not an option. You have to do your best. It is something we chant in our classroom. 'Do your best. Have you done your best? Is this your best work?'"
>   This stance has emphasized a shared sense of responsibility. Students have learned that they are responsible for their own learning, for pushing themselves, and for helping their classmates. (p. 134)

Based on this stance, teachers developed shared norms around active student engagement in learning that helped teachers assess students' understanding of concepts. They use data on student results to evaluate strategies for whether they help students achieve excellence.

Another school developed a shared definition of teacher excellence and a set of eight questions to guide their practice, focusing on how students develop skills (Andrews & Lewis, 2002). One teacher described the change in her practice:

> When I plan now, I think of the eight concepts and ask myself the questions. . . . I mentally tick off all that, and I think "OK, I'm not going to teach this unless I'm really sure it's what I want to teach or it's the right way. . . ." It makes me justify my position before I go into the room. (p. 250)

Other teachers said that the eight questions led them to treat their high school students more like adults, preparing them to move on to college and community roles.

"Together We Can" expresses the values of a third school faculty, emphasizing the values of "relationship, responsibility and results-oriented efficiency" (Strahan, 2003, p. 137). Teaching criteria include high expectations for every student, clear objectives communicated to students for each lesson, and getting help whenever needed. Again, data drives discussion of student problems. A teacher described her understanding of the school's stance on collaboration:

> I'm expected to know what is in their folder and if they have any difficulties or learning differences in their folder. If I continue to see a problem, I would talk to another teacher, "What can I do about this?" Then if it still continued, I would go to my buddy teacher and ask for the Student Support Team (a team of teachers who assist their colleagues with students who are not making progress) and talk about different strategies to use. (p. 138)

In other words, both processes and expectations are in place for Level III collaboration. Further, staff development time often gives teachers practice with strategies that can be implemented across grade levels and subject areas. Teachers also identify ways they can use the strategies immediately.

Successful learning communities define not just the vision, then, but set clear expectations as to what that vision means for classrooms, student achievement, and collaboration.

Activity 6.5
School Vision

A school can use the Problem-Solving Model, Resource B, to put the vision of student achievement into its own words. Questions to guide the process might include:

- **Sensing**
  - What phrases, values, or policies exist that reflect our stance toward student achievement?
  - What parts of the school district vision might we echo?
  - What do we know that is working at other schools?
- **Intuition**
  - What new phrases or values might we consider?
  - What words might students suggest?
  - What metaphor or analogy might guide our vision?
- **Thinking**
  - Which might provide the most leverage for helping students believe in their abilities and take responsibility for learning?
  - What objective criteria need to be satisfied?
  - Which lend themselves to efficiency—easy to teach and to remember?
- **Feeling**
  - How does each of us react to the choices?
  - Are the underlying values consistent with our vision?
  - Who is committed to this as a guide for practice?

Step 5: Practice in Collaboration

Using the Problem-Solving Model to articulate a staff vision is a good example of how leadership teams can provide teachers with practice at collaboration while moving forward on the actual collaboration goals: practice-embedded staff development. Below are four other collaboration exercises that also serve these dual purposes.

Activity 6.6
Looking at Student Work

When teachers are first learning to collaborate, we recommend that they examine a lesson planned by an outside party or samples of student work from an outside party's classroom. If using a lesson plan, the team uniformly teaches the lesson and then critiques and shares experiences with, and student work from, that lesson. Usually, teachers feel more free to discuss what did and didn't work when the lesson wasn't planned by a team member.

Resource C contains exercises to use with staff to help them understand student learning styles and how to use the exercises with students; these are ideal for gaining experience in collaborative examination of student work. Teachers can plan together how to introduce a type concept to students, each try teaching the lesson, and then meet again to discuss student reactions, results, and work.

Differentiation Through Personality Types (Kise, 2007) contains several lessons that could be used for this purpose.

Activity 6.7
SMART Goals

Have teams articulate a SMART goal for collaboration. SMART stands for:

Specific

Measurable

Achievable

Results oriented

Time bound

Have team members use the Problem-Solving Model to design their action plan and ensure buy-in. Make sure they're clear on what success will look like. Leadership team members who have used the model can act as coaches to the group, using cognitive coaching techniques (Costa & Garmston, 1994), where respectful questioning, rather than providing interpretations and input, helps the person think more deeply about their ideas, beliefs, and strategies. Schedule specific staff meetings for action plan progress and results.

Activity 6.8
Lesson or Unit Plan Differentiation

Teachers can work together to evaluate an assignment in terms of type. Again, the discussions may be more fruitful if they begin with lessons developed by people not on the team so the teachers don't need to critique each other. Guiding questions might be:

- In terms of type preferences, which learning style might find the assignment easiest? Extraversion? Introversion? Sensing? Intuition?
- Were any aspects of the assignment unclear or uninteresting for students with different preferences?
- In examining student work for the assignment, are there patterns in student comprehension and work quality? If the teachers know the students' personality types, they might examine the work of four students who prefer Sensing and four who prefer Intuition, for example. If they don't have information on student types, they might hypothesize about the reasons for common errors or common exemplary work in terms of type preferences.
- How might you improve the assignment to better meet the needs of all learners?

Have teachers conclude the session by freewriting about three things they learned from looking at student work together and three things they hope to keep in mind when designing lessons and activities.

Chapter Summary

Collaboration thrives in professional learning communities where there is trust, respect, honesty, and a willingness to probe and question personal beliefs about teaching and learning. Type can serve as the common language for establishing this environment, helping staff understand that people need different things to feel safe, to talk, and to share and that they communicate in different ways and their filters for hearing information differ. Staff learn to challenge thinking in ways that others don't take personally. They are better able to talk about their beliefs and behaviors as teachers or leaders without feeling judged as ineffective or inefficient or "poor" or "good."

Further, they understand that the best schools and teams need diverse views to be as comprehensive as possible in their approach, propelling them to work well together. Yet these understandings develop through time and effort; practical steps and exercises are provided to assist professional learning communities become truly collaborative and effective.

Reflection

- Freewrite on your own collaboration abilities: skills at communication, consensus building, decision making, and conflict resolution. Revisit your type page in Resource A, "Practical Next Steps," or Chart 6.2 for action steps you might take.

- What is your assessment of your staff's ability to collaborate? Identify what they might need before establishing professional learning communities. Examples of needs might include:
  - Resolution of past conflicts to establish trust
  - Skill in decision making
  - Clear goals for collaboration
  - Protocols so that teams meet expectations
  - Practice in listening to one another
  - ???
- What is your vision for collaboration? Freewrite on what will happen in team meetings and, as a result, in classrooms.

7

Observing All Types of Teachers

The implicit contract in many schools leaves matters of instruction to teachers, with principals carrying out largely ritualized evaluation functions and seldom visiting classrooms except on special occasions. Thus for most principals in districts moving toward the new core of knowledge-based constructivism and effort-based learning, there is a complex new role to be learned. (Resnick & Hall, 1998, p. 113)

After spending two days in a workshop on using personality type concepts to coach teachers, a teacher leader wrote that the experience

... helped to put in perspective how administrators and colleagues could very easily give-up on teachers who they have difficulty understanding and communicating with. My own experience with practice coaching at the workshop brought to light my own tendency to become frustrated with a teacher who is dedicated and passionate but whom I did not understand. Having personality type knowledge and tools helped me to realize that the issue was mine and not that of the struggling teacher. Very eye-opening! (J. Woodling, personal communication, September 8, 2006)

All of us walk into classrooms with preconceived notions of what teachers and students should be doing—and those notions come from how we teach and learn. A school leader's approach to classroom observation often comes from training and personal style—and may not meet the coaching needs of teachers with very different styles.

Preaching Styles, Teaching Styles

Delpit (1995) examined the question of how culture affects teaching practices. She reviewed attempts by educators to develop fair and culturally sensitive training and assessment models for teachers based on the law, business, and medical professions. She wrote

> After trying to identify points of intersection between these professions, I've realized that teaching does not closely resemble any of them. The more I pondered their lack of similarity, the more I have been drawn to the resemblance of teaching to another profession—preaching. This may seem an unlikely comparison at first blush, but consider this: ministers are the only professionals who, like teachers, see their clients in a group. Further, they must not only present subject matter, but must also convince clients to incorporate that subject matter into their lives. In teaching as well as preaching, there are components of both content and motivation, of values and technique. (p. 137)

She points out the futility of using standard criteria for evaluating the abilities of a black Southern Baptist style, where the emphasis is on emotion, gestures, and audience participation, and a white Boston Episcopalian style, where the emphasis is on word choice, logic, and knowledge. The same standards don't work because the audiences are different, as are the training and skills of the preacher. What is more important is the impact on the audience. Are they learning? Are they motivated or inspired?

Returning to education reform, standardizing criteria for teaching poses the same hazards. McNeil (2000) recorded the impact of this emphasis in Houston:

> They tried to teacher-proof the curriculum with a checklist for teaching behaviors and the student minimum competence skills tests. By doing so, they have made schools exceedingly comfortable for mediocre teachers who like doing routine lessons according to a standard sequence and format, who like working as de-skilled laborers not having to think about their work. (p. 187)

If this seems like an exaggeration, consider just one difference in how educational beliefs can impact classroom observations: is it more important for teachers to have sound content knowledge and research-based teaching methods or sound skills at building relationships with students? In truth, both are extremely important. Obviously, teachers need content knowledge if they are to help students master materials, but brain research (Jensen, 1998) showed that negative emotions and stress actually block learning. Many educational leaders, however, are biased toward seeing one or the other as more important, as Delpit (1995) illustrated in the story of one teacher candidate:

The assessment candidates were asked to teach a familiar lesson to a group of students brought together solely for that purpose. The candidates, for the most part from other parts of the country, had never met the students. An African American teacher received poor marks for his lesson, which appeared scattered and illogical to the assessors. To one sensitive to alternative concepts of good teaching, however, it was clear that he was a teacher who believed it was necessary to establish a relationship with the students before then moving on to teach content. He appeared incompetent because he vacillated between trying to establish a rapport—to know and be known by the students—and attempting to teach the subject at hand. (pp. 140–141)

Think of the above dilemma in terms of personality type concepts. The evaluators were using a Thinking model, looking for content and logic. The teacher operated from a Feeling model, emphasizing relationships. *Both* are valid ways of teaching—an increasing number of studies show that the relationship between teacher and student may affect achievement more than teaching skills. Teachers need both Thinking and Feeling skills for their students to achieve at high levels.

Delpit (1995) gave further examples of how cultural differences can affect teacher evaluation. Kise (2007) described how type concepts can be used to identify cultural *archetypes*—which type preferences are emphasized within a culture—and can thus serve as a bridge among cultures for productive conversations around similarities and differences. While specific cultural information remains important, as we move toward more culturally diverse teachers and students working together—students in Minneapolis and St. Paul have over 90 different first languages, for example—administrators may struggle to know enough about each culture to understand differences in teacher values and practices. Thus type helps bring understanding to a complex arena for misunderstanding.

In this chapter we will look at

- Type biases in traditional models for classroom observation
- How teachers with different type preferences might carry out the framework for student achievement outlined by the Institute for Learning (IFL) in Pittsburg (Resnick, 1999).

Why use the IFL framework? Because the principles of learning it espouses, based on over 30 years of educational research, emphasize what brings about student achievement rather than specific teaching behaviors. Further, the principles help school administrators balance the Interactive and Reflective leadership roles, emphasizing that instructional leaders spend time in classrooms. Type adds a framework for avoiding bias in those observations.

Think back to the difference between Baptist and Episcopalian ministers; the key to effectiveness was audience engagement, not specific preaching skills, and the two preaching styles accomplish the same goals through very different channels. The same is true in classrooms: the correct key is student engagement in worthwhile efforts that lead to achievement. We know that the more effort students put forth, the more ability they will develop to achieve at high levels. While the IFL guiding concept, that effort creates ability, guides classroom practices, type provides a differentiation framework. How will teachers with different preferences carry out the principles of learning? How will students with different preferences be motivated? Classrooms with very different atmospheres can still be carrying out the principles of learning. Observers can use type to set aside biases based on how they teach and learn and instead focus on whether students in a particular classroom are learning from a particular teacher.

The Function Pairs and Classroom Observation

If the function pairs determine our general focus, communication style, and coaching preferences, as shown in Chapters 4 and 5, then they influence what we look for when we enter a classroom. Pajak (2003) identified four distinct models of clinical supervision, each of which fits one of the function pairs. Chart 7.1, Models of Teacher Observation, describes the models, given in the order in which they emerged in education literature.

Chart 7.1   Models of Teacher Observation

Intuition and Thinking Original clinical models (Goldhammer, 1969; Cogan, 1973)	These models concentrate on competence, theoretical concepts, and developing personal teaching styles.
Sensing and Feeling Artistic/humanistic clinical models (Eisner, 1979; Blumburg, 1974)	Rather than step-by-step procedures, these models emphasize interpersonal relationships, harmony, providing support, and meeting the needs of each teacher.
Sensing and Thinking Technical/didactic clinical models (Acheson & Gall, 1980; Hunter, 1984)	These models measure performance against set processes and procedures for teaching that are based in research, striving for efficiencies.
Intuition and Feeling Developmental/reflective clinical models (Costa & Garmston, 1994)	These models encourage reflection and emphasize fostering personal growth, guided by ideals and values.

Consider for a moment which of the above models most closely resembles your own practice and emphases in classroom observation. Which models did your formal training emphasize? You might also look at Chart 7.2, The Function Pairs and Teaching Styles. Does the information for your own style reflect your teaching beliefs and strengths?

Then, consider how each group of teachers would fare under the opposite model, using Chart 7.2 to review their natural styles. For example, how will Sensing and Thinking (ST) teachers be viewed by observers who operate from the Intuitive and Feeling (NF) model?

Chart 7.2   The Function Pairs and Teaching Styles

	Sensing, Thinking	Sensing, Feeling	Intuition, Feeling	Intuition, Thinking
Common educational beliefs	• Tried-and-true methods are best • Structure leads to learning • Basic skills come first • Objective assessments are best	• Tried-and-true methods are best • Relationships and self-esteem lead to learning • Basic skills come first • Practice leads to mastery	• Choice and creativity help students succeed • Interest and engagement lead to learning • Variety provides motivation • Goal is to develop potential of every student	• Students need to be responsible for work and grades • Curriculum should be both engaging and challenging • Students need to think for themselves • Goal is for students to apply theories and concepts
Teacher strengths	• Clear expectations • Classroom procedures • Breaking concepts into steps • Managing details such as grading, attendance, etc.	• Building one-on-one relationships • Providing individual help • Finding reliable methods • Creating classroom community	• Flexibility • Creativity, engaging and inviting lessons • Constructivist, inquiry, process-oriented learning • Patience as students work toward mastery	• Rigorous lessons that encourage thinking and creating • Teaching concepts and models • Constructivist inquiry, project-based learning • Helping students think logically and justify
Evidence of success	• Test scores, grades	• Classroom harmony, cooperation	• Student engagement	• Student curiosity, command of theories
Instructional stretch	• Constructivist teaching, letting go of procedures	• Constructivist teaching, losing control of outcomes	• Following set lesson plans	• Providing ample time for students to make meaning and understand concepts
Blind spots	• May overstructure open-ended problems and tasks • May adhere to timetables even if students need more time	• May overstructure tasks that allow for creativity • May struggle to move from teaching facts to helping students make connections	• May not evaluate whether an engaging activity results in student achievement • May fail to set clear expectations and learning goals	• May ignore role of emotions and relationships in learning • May fail to explain concepts in terms students can understand
Administrator's natural emphasis when observing teachers	• Adherence to lesson plan, curriculum, standards	• Impact on individual students	• Motivational impact on students	• Rigor of thinking and academic goals

The following examples come from classroom observations of a sixth-grade teaching team. Each teacher happened to prefer a different function pair. Read the examples and see if you can determine who prefers Sensing and Thinking (ST), Sensing and Feeling, (SF), Intuition and Feeling (NF), and Intuition and Thinking (NT).

Here is an excerpt from the first teacher observation:

> [The teacher] asked if there were questions about the homework. Some wanted to turn it in. He said, "It isn't done because you haven't finished watching *October Sky*. Did the sub explain what you were supposed to do?" Some said yes, some said no.
>
> He walked over to the side whiteboard where the assignment was written out. He said, "Here's the first question. 'Explain'—I've got a box around the word *explain* because that's the important part of this. 'Explain all the problems the Rocket Boys had to solve and how they solved them.' Does someone have an example?"
>
> The hands of a couple of the girls went up. They had their homework papers in hand. One said that the fuel had burned too rapidly. The teacher asked, "And how did they solve that problem?" Another student mentioned they'd put in an additive. Another mentioned the special nozzle they'd designed.
>
> He then read the next question: "Describe how the Rocket Boys are like scientists. Let's have an example."
>
> A different student answered, "They set goals." The teacher said, "That's right." The second panel of the whiteboard showed how they could set up their homework as a table. He pointed this out to them, emphasizing that they didn't have to write in paragraphs. He suggested that they copy down the example so they could see later how to do it. (Kise, 2002, pp. 7–8)

This teacher has preferences for Intuition (N) and Thinking (T); he enjoys letting students think for themselves, setting up projects where students discover concepts, and being a facilitator rather than a director of learning. Note the open-ended nature of the assignment questions. Students were to make connections, not just report on what happened. When Sensing/Feeling types observe his classroom, they might be disturbed by the lack of clear answers for assignments, wondering whether students might feel unsure of what to do. While the teacher provided a table for data, nothing in the assignment helped them organize the facts of the movie; the teacher leaped directly to concepts.

Let's look at another teacher:

> [The teacher] gave them a handout on how to fill out book orders. When she said, "Okay, everyone turn to this side," she added, "Thank you for following directions."
>
> She walked around to see if students were in the right spot and several times said, "Help your neighbor. Feel free to help your neighbor if you know what's going on." When students answered her questions, she often said, "Thank you."

Using a sample form on an overhead, she took them through step-by-step. "What book is the first book this child is ordering?" The class answered and she said, "Thank you." Things got just a little bit loud with the interaction and she said "Listen closely. Wait." Then she waited, and finally said in a very quiet voice, "Let's listen." Then she went on.

At one point she put her finger to her mouth until all were silent and they quieted down. Also, she smiled at some students who were talking and waited until they were respectful again. She passed papers from the front and thanked the group for helping to get them to the back of the room. . . . Then she put a bin on the floor for them to put any forms they didn't want. (Kise, 2002, p. 13)

This teacher prefers Sensing (S) and Feeling (F). She naturally breaks assignments into steps, works to create harmony in the classroom, and organizes details to minimize confusion and time-wasting. An Intuitive/Thinking observer might be frustrated by the slow pace of instruction, all of the "warm fuzzies," and attention to instruction that seemingly has little connection to academics—can't students just fill out book orders? But this teacher has learned from past problems that instruction on following directions is worthwhile.

Here is a third example:

As [the teacher] collected the quizzes, she was silent until she got to one where the student had gotten almost all of them right. Then she said, in a very surprised tone, "Good job!" Then as she collected the rest, she said, "Good, good job," a few more times.

Then as she looked through the scores, she said, "Now, are you ready for a speech? When did you start learning your multiplication tables?"

A few said, "Third grade." "Fourth." "I don't know . . ."

She went on, "How many of you know your phone number? How many of you know your address? Those are numbers. You just memorize them. That's all multiplication facts are, are numbers. So you can memorize these too. What helps? You can practice. You can help with flash cards. Have you heard of flash cards? If there's one thing that bugs me about sixth graders, it's those who don't know their multiplication tables. I had a hard time learning them. My mom drilled with me with flash cards. A lot of times after school, I couldn't watch TV or read a book until I'd gone through my flash cards. We won't have to take these tests anymore if you start getting them right. Are you sick of these? Then practice until you get them right." (Kise, 2002, p. 3)

This teacher prefers Sensing (S) and Thinking (T). Facts and basic skills come first, and she expects the students to put in the effort to get them down. She has a grounded-in-reality, bottom-line approach. She gives them practical strategies—in addition to flash cards, they can take home one-minute practice tests—and relates how she herself used them. Intuitive/Feeling observers might react negatively to her emphasis on rote drill as well as her matter-of-fact tone.

Here is one last example:

> Students were working in groups of four or five. Each group was examining a reproduction of an artifact from ancient Rome. The teacher asked them to first work silently, filling out a "thinking sheet" on the artifact. Questions on the sheet included "Does it remind you of anything you use today?" "How might a child use it? An adult?" "How might you use it in the kitchen? Bathroom? Outside? Other places?"
>
> As students worked, she whispered to me, "After the first round I made up this worksheet so that all students, high and low, could contribute to the discussion. They all have time to think. I've seen the groups really listening to each other."
>
> After students had worked silently for a few minutes, she informed them that the group's assignment was to agree on one hypothesis as to how the artifact was originally used. "That means you have to listen to each other's reasons. Who can best support his or her idea? You have to work together to come up with the best guess." (Kise, 2003, p. 66)

This teacher prefers Intuition (N) and Feeling (F). She enjoyed creating the lesson from scratch, making the artifacts, and working on the group process until all students could contribute and feel valued. Her goals for the lesson were clear to her: productive group decision making and helping students learn to conjecture and make inferences based on prior knowledge. A Sensing/Thinking observer, though, might question whether the lesson goals are clear to students, whether it ties closely enough to standards, or whether the teacher can measure individual performance and growth.

Envision for a moment how you might teach any of the concepts embedded in the above examples: What do scientists do? How do you fill out forms correctly? How can you master basic math skills? How do you make inferences? Chances are, you'd feel comfortable recreating one of the four examples and feel compelled to approach some of the others quite differently.

Given, then, our deep type-based biases about appropriate teaching methods and Delpit's research (1995) on how we can misconstrue cultural differences in approaches to instruction as deficits in a teacher, it makes more sense for observers to concentrate on students rather than how the teacher is teaching. Are the students motivated and engaged? Are they working on high-level tasks that tie to standards?

Let's turn to examining the Institute for Learning's (IFL) nine principles of learning, one framework for improving classroom instruction so that all students succeed.

The Institute for Learning's Principles of Learning

Resnick (1999) stated that our school systems and efforts at reforms are trapped by incorrect beliefs about the nature of intelligence and ability:

> What we learn is a function of both our aptitudes for particular kinds of learning and the effort we put forth. Americans mostly assume that

aptitude largely determines what people can learn in school, although they allow that hard work can compensate for lower doses of innate intelligence. Our schools are largely organized around this belief.... Assumptions about aptitude are continually reinforced by the results of practices based on those assumptions. Students who are held to low expectations do not try to break through that barrier, because they accept the judgment that inborn aptitude matters most and that they have not inherited enough of that capacity. Not surprisingly, their performance remains low. Children who have not been taught a demanding, challenging, thinking curriculum do poorly on tests of reasoning or problem solving, confirming many people's original suspicions that they lack the talent for high-level thinking. (p. 1)

Recall from page 11 that type research shows that our educational systems favors the Intuitive preference as a sign of aptitude and creativity; the higher educational level Sensing students attain, the less likely that schools will honor their ways of being creative or provide them with tools to synthesize what they know. Instead, it is assumed that you either can or can't embrace higher-level thinking.

To ensure that all students have access to a demanding curriculum, Resnick (2005) proposed nine principles to guide schools in moving classrooms to support the belief that *effort*, not *aptitude,* creates ability. The nine principles, and how type research supports their effectiveness in raising student achievement, are given in Chart 7.3, Type and the IFL Principles for Learning.

These principles, then, are universal, regardless of the personality preferences of the teacher, student, or classroom observer. However, how teachers put the principles into practice may vary greatly. Let's examine the four principles that perhaps have the most to do with day-to-day classrooms that carry out the belief that effort creates ability: organizing for effort, clear expectations, academic rigor, and accountable talk. What might they look like in a Sensing/Thinking, Sensing/Feeling, Intuitive/Feeling, and Intuitive/Thinking classroom? How might each teacher struggle?

The Sensing and Thinking Teacher (ST)

Chart 7.2 lists the basic strengths of ST teachers as

- Clear expectations
- Classroom procedures
- Breaking concepts into steps
- Managing details such as grading, attendance, etc.

Organizing for effort. Walk into a ST teacher's classroom, and you'll likely see evidence of organization. These teachers often have systems to help students remember to complete assignments, including reminders on classroom calendars, systems for students to record assignments in their planners, or set routines, such as using the first five minutes of class to correct work or the last five minute for students to start homework and ask questions.

Chart 7.3   Type and the IFL Principles for Learning

Principle of Learning	Evidence of Principle in Action	Connections With Type: Differentiation Concepts and Research
Clear expectations. Students need to understand what it means to achieve at high levels, what they are to learn, and how they will be evaluated. They must understand the minimum high standards their work is targeting.	• Learning goals, in understandable language, communicated to teachers, parents, the community, and students • Clear focus for each lesson—how the student recognizes accomplishing the goal • Examples of rigorous work • Criteria charts of what constitutes quality work	Books on using type to differentiate instruction (Kise, 2007; Murphy, 1992; Lawrence, 1993) emphasize how teachers with both Sensing and Intuitive preferences need to give directions in ways that set clear expectations for students with either preferences; meet the needs of Sensing students for detailed examples and the needs of Intuitive students for personal expression; and provide tools students can use to evaluate their own progress toward proficiency.
Organize for effort. Schools assume that all students can learn with enough time, expert instruction, and effort.	• School schedule provides extra time for students who need it • Teachers provide multiple paths to understanding if students fail to grasp a concept	Judging and Perceiving students organize differently for work completion. Teaching all students to use Perceiving strategies can significantly increase their completion rate on rigorous projects (Kise, 2005).
Recognition of accomplishment. Schools need to recognize when students meet standards and intermediate goals frequently.	• Frequent acknowledgement of small accomplishments through stickers, notes to parents, etc. • Classroom celebrations • Access to motivating events or activities for students and families • Setting goals, meeting goals, celebrating success, and then setting more goals	Type helps teachers adjust their views of rewards and recognition; recall in Chapter 1 the role that Thinking and Feeling play in how we view recognition. Introverted and Extraverted students also differ in how public they prefer such recognition to be.
Fair and credible evaluations. Tests need to be fair *and* tied to the expectations set for students.	• Student progress assessed in terms of progress toward standard, not on a curve • Regular assessments help students see intermediate progress • Assessments guide changes in instruction to ensure all students learn rather than evaluating whether students learned • Assessments modified to allow more time • Choices in assessment offered so students can use their strengths to show what they know	Type research shows clear biases in teacher test question design (Murphy, 1992). Teachers can use type to provide students with choices of ways to show what they've learned, design fair objective tests, construct rubrics for fair grading of subjective assessments, and guide students in evaluating their own progress (Kise, 2007).

Principle of Learning	Evidence of Principle in Action	Connections With Type: Differentiation Concepts and Research
Academic rigor in a thinking curriculum. Students need foundational knowledge *and* the ability to apply that knowledge to problem solving, thinking about what they know.	• Inquiry-based learning, with students learning habits of persistence, commitment to understanding, and getting it right • Students initiate new avenues of thought or exploration • Students access prior knowledge for new situations	Type strategies help Sensing students, traditionally underrepresented in honors classes and gifted programs, to trust and develop their ability to think in complex ways (Felder, 2002). Scaffolding assignments to allow Sensing students access to rigor builds self-confidence in their ability to tackle complex issues.
Accountable talk. Classroom discussions focus on responding to the ideas of others and developing them further. Push for clarification, using evidence.	• Student discussions are accurate and relevant • Students respect each other's ideas • Students use evidence to support their ideas	Teachers can use the concepts of Extraversion and Introversion to invite all students to participate in discussion; the Z Model to separate facts, opinions, and possibilities; and Thinking and Feeling to examine alternatives, similar to the information for leaders in Chapters 5 and 6.
Socializing intelligence. Teachers "teach" intelligence through daily expectations that students can think, use accountable talk, and meet standards.	• Learning tasks require thinking • Teachers ask for evidence and justification • Students are encouraged to think beyond the questions being asked for further insights • Service learning with a focus on reflection is key to understanding applied concepts	Type is a strengths-based model that provides strategies for all students to attain mastery, rather than describing who can learn or what each student learns best. This helps students increase self-expectations.
Learning as apprenticeship. Using extended projects, presentations, and assignments that require complex thinking so students are engaged in authentic work.	• Extended projects that require sustained, complex thinking • Interdisciplinary efforts that simulate real-world complexities • Tying what is being learned to practical abilities students may use outside of school	Type provides strategies for scaffolding major efforts, assisting students in planning for success, and ensuring that students engage at a rigorous level (Kise, 2005; Murphy, 1992).
Self-management of learning. Students take responsibility for their own learning, understanding when they need help, monitoring the rigor of their thinking, and striving for success as independent learners.	• Students engaged in monitoring their own progress • Students seeking opportunities to practice skills until mastered • Students engaging in homework as path to learning, not for grades	Type provides a framework for students to understand which tasks come easily, based on their learning styles, as well as strategies for learning when content or tasks require them to learn in another style (Kise, 2007).

ST teachers, though, often feel the pull of curriculum expectations. The concept that students need different amounts of time to reach mastery is difficult for them to deal with. They often feel singularly responsible for student learning, perhaps to the extreme of wanting to act as tutor or homework helper rather than have anyone else provide explanations that might confuse a student. They can thus set unrealistic standards for themselves rather than searching for other ways to provide students with extra time to master concepts.

Further, Sensing teachers in general have difficulty setting aside any part of a curriculum; they tend to move through it sequentially. They may be helped by the concept of "power standards," described by Reeves (2005) as having three key criteria:

1. **Endurance:** "A characteristic of those standards whose importance lasts longer than a few nanoseconds after the termination of a state test" (p. 50)

2. **Leverage:** "Success in one standard is very likely to be associated with success in other standards" (p. 51).

3. **Essential for the next level of instruction:** Reeves pointed out that teachers usually insist that each part of their curriculum is vital,

   but when I ask the same group to give advice to teachers in the next lower grade about what students must know and be able to do in order to advance to the next class with success and confidence, I have never—not a single time in thousands of cases—heard the words, "The teacher in the grade lower than me should cover every single standard." Rather, when giving advice to colleagues in a lower grade, educators are remarkably brief and balanced. (pp. 51–52)

In other words, ST teachers often do best when given systematic ways to provide time for all students to learn. Once they have those systems, though, their classrooms can serve as models. The ST teacher, for example, may find resources that can serve as curriculum extensions for students who have mastered standards so that extra time can be given to those who need it. Or they'll work out the details of how to trade students with other teachers to provide the lessons the different student groups need.

Clear expectations. ST teachers may be the first in a building to post standards and expectations. However, their first inclination may be to post state standards as written—or to post *all* of them in one big list. While they excel at breaking concepts into steps, they may unconsciously take written standards and benchmarks as "gospel" and hesitate to involve students in writing their interpretations of the standards in understandable language. To the ST teacher, involving the students may also seem inefficient when standards are already spelled out. An observer, then, needs to look not just for the standards but for whether students understand how the tasks they are doing connect to standards.

ST teachers can also be quite task oriented and matter-of-fact, focusing on progress yet to be made. They may appreciate modeling of how to motivate their students and suggestions for recognition of accomplishments that seem worthwhile.

However, when they design reward or recognition systems, they excel at carrying them out fairly and consistently. We've seen ST teachers accurately track whether each middle school class comes with appropriate supplies, keeping track of points on the front board. In another room, an ST teacher had a consistent "ticket system." Students earned tickets for engaging without being asked in warm-up problems, completing work on time, solving problems collaboratively, and helping each other. In another room, pizza parties happened whenever all students reached a certain high expectation.

The clear expectations of an ST teacher, once mastered, can be so organized that they can appear rigid or impossible to maintain to Intuitive/Feeling (NF) observers (who would probably forget to hand out tickets if trying to implement a similar system!). The ST teacher may so consistently post lesson goals in the same way that the NF fears students will stop noticing them. However, the processes work for STs—and they generally also have systems in place for ensuring that students pay attention.

Academic rigor in a thinking curriculum. ST teachers usually excel at transmitting knowledge to students. They develop tried-and-true methods, tweaking them until all students perform well on assessments.

They may, however, struggle to devise assignments that go beyond knowledge. They are far more comfortable grading assignments that have one right answer; otherwise they worry about fair evaluation. To be comfortable with subjective assignments—which can include everything but objective tests—they learn to use rubrics, checklists, or examples from other teachers of acceptable work. To move toward rigor, the ST teacher needs to develop skills in this area.

ST teachers may also repeatedly use the same teaching methods to engage students in problem solving or other ways of applying knowledge. For example, they may favor a certain graphic organizer, group process, or assignment. NF observers might worry that students will be bored. However, many students thus master multiple uses of the same tool and then have it available to them in new situations. What is important is whether the students understand why they use a graphic organizer or tool—what cognitive thinking skill does it support?

Accountable talk. ST teachers often excel at guiding group discussions. They understand their lesson goals and can ask questions that test whether students grasp core concepts. They are also generally good at asking students to justify their answers. They may have systems for ensuring that all students participate. Often, they prefer whole-class discussions so that they can monitor the quality of student responses. It may be difficult for them to allow students to drive the discussion or leave open what may transpire in a discussion. NF observers might misinterpret the ST drive to ensure that the discussion covers the appropriate content, viewing it as overstructuring or disregarding student ideas.

ST teachers are often early embracers of accountable talk, seeing the guidelines as an excellent structure for ensuring quality small-group discussions. Observers might see posters listing question stems that students develop and then use when needed. Discussion sessions might start with the teacher modeling how to refer to text to support ideas, even if students have been using accountable talk for several discussions.

The Intuitive and Feeling Teacher (NF)

For contrast to the ST teacher, let's turn next to the NF teacher, whose strengths are

- Flexibility
- Creativity and engaging and inviting lessons
- Constructivist, inquiry, process-oriented learning
- Patience as students work toward mastery

Effort-based ability is inherently appealing to NF teachers, for most of them want to see each student reach his or her highest potential. Many are frustrated by grading systems and promotion policies that discourage rather than encourage student success. When asked what she'd do if she could wave a magic wand at her school, one NF teacher put it this way:

> Eliminate grades . . . and that's both first, second, and A, B, C. I mean, you have to have it because the parents would freak out if you didn't. I think that then a B would mean, "This is . . . the student is learning an appropriate amount of material for where they are in this subject." An A means they've really excelled beyond that and done new, creative things. And then you need to have a thing that says, "Not yet," because . . . giving them Ds and Fs never seems to cause any new growth. It causes fears to an extent and parents get upset about it, but it doesn't seem to stimulate much in terms of growth to the kids. (Kise, 2002, p. 7)

Organizing for effort. NF teachers often enjoy organizing curriculum around themes—literature might focus on kindness, history on conflict and conquerors, science on energy, and so on. Their classrooms might be filled with artifacts relating to the theme. Organizing around themes means that plentiful enrichment opportunities exist for students who master standards quickly, allowing extra time for others.

NF teachers often gravitate toward large-scale projects for students, definitely emphasizing academic rigor. However, an ST observer may question whether the structure exists for guiding students in sustained efforts. The ST teacher plans for completion; the NF teacher tends to want to see student effort unfold and often ends up extending deadlines.

Clear expectations. NF teachers may struggle the most with tying expectations back to stated standards. Further, they may view attempts at helping them structure their curriculum around standards as stifling. Set curriculum maps or planning forms don't fit their distinctive views of how they teach. However, once they grasp that they can set clear expectations, tie to standards, *and* be creative, they embrace setting clear expectations as a way for all students to succeed.

The NF teacher may offer students the widest variety of choices in how students show what they've learned. As a culminating project on ancient Rome, for example, students had to create a product (a game, a report, a costume, a map, a scale model, and so on) and give a speech. An ST observer might question how all of the products could be graded fairly or how they helped students meet the same standard. However, the teacher had clearly targeted two learning objectives that met standards: communicate effectively through speaking and have knowledge of how people lived in ancient civilizations. The actual assignment rubric required all students to turn in a written summary of what they had learned about people in ancient Rome through their project. The details were there, and the teacher concentrated on creating an assignment that engaged students with different learning styles in the processes of speaking and writing.

Academic rigor in a thinking curriculum. NF teachers often give project-based assignments. They may hesitate to structure them for fear of stifling student creativity. An ST observer might look at the broad requirements for a student report and wonder how students know what they are supposed to do—and sometimes their question may be justified! With experience, NF teachers who embrace the principles of learning become better at setting the clear expectations that bring success to all in project-based learning. The ST observer can learn from the NF teacher how to organize for multiple opportunities to demonstrate mastery of a concept. In working together, using their strengths, they can design assignments that better exemplify academic rigor.

The NF teacher, though, counts on choice to motivate students to push their own thinking. Often, this tactic is very successful. We've seen students whose work has been mediocre turn out high-quality products on subjects that interest them. To an ST observer, the choices may sometimes seem too diverse to connect to the same standards. NFs, though, enjoy making those kinds of connections and will push student thinking to ensure that the student's work ties back to the spirit of the assignment.

Accountable talk. NF teachers hope to create communities where the opinions of each person are heard and honored. The artifact-based discussion is an example of the NF ability to structure for accountable talk. They are focused on teaching accountable talk as a way to ensure that everyone's voice is heard and respected.

To an ST observer, though, an NF teacher may not be tough enough about requiring students to use text to support their reasoning. Part of the NF's struggle with this is that personally, text is usually just a jumping-off place. What they read reminds them of at least a dozen other things they have read; they may not realize when students are diverging from the point of the discussion, because the NF teacher naturally does the same thing.

However, with practice, the NF teacher often finds ways for students to carry out accountable talk—such as the use of reflection time during the artifact discussion—so that all students have time to generate ideas and justifications to add to the discussion.

The Sensing and Feeling Teacher (SF)

The strengths of the SF teacher include

- Building one-on-one relationships
- Providing individual help

- Finding reliable methods
- Creating classroom community

Like the NF teachers, the SF teachers are attracted to an effort-based system that gives each child the time and attention they need to learn. However, like the ST teachers, the SF teachers may have difficulty seeing how structures other than their providing one-on-one help will result in all students' meeting high expectations.

Organizing for effort. SF teachers love to organize in helpful ways. Observers will find colorful classrooms with clever storage of student work, reminder systems, and displays that mark student achievement. An NT observer might see the SF efforts as robbing children of developing their own methods for staying organized. As one NT put it, "If I store their notebooks, how will they learn to keep track of them?" Most SF teachers, though, provide help that is appropriate to student development.

Like STs, SFs can struggle with accommodating differences in how long it takes students to reach mastery. Their natural tendency is to keep the entire class on a concept until everyone is ready to move on, believing that helping each child is their responsibility. The clearer they are, though, as to how other resources can be used, the more likely they are to find ways for their students to use them.

Clear expectations. SF teachers usually provide detailed assignments with step-by-step instructions. Their natural style often includes several check-in points. For example, students might need to be checked off on the three main points they will make in an essay before they begin writing. Or they may need to show how they've set up a math problem before solving it. An NT observer might feel that these structures slow down the learning process, but many students thrive on knowing they are headed in the right direction.

SF teachers appreciate setting clear lesson goals but, like STs, often appreciate help or systems for translating state standards into student-friendly language and focusing on which standards are most important to cover. Involving the students in writing standards in kid-friendly language appeals greatly to SFs.

As SF teachers explain assignments, they often show examples of past student work or create lengthy examples so that students see exactly what is expected of them. Or they may give lengthy oral directions. An NT observer might judge the examples as too explicit, stripping the tasks of rigor since students might copy from what they've seen. However, the majority of students prefer Sensing (about 65–70 percent of the population[1]) and often feel more confident about meeting expectations after seeing the clear examples.

Academic rigor in a thinking curriculum. SF teachers seldom even like the word *rigor*. To them, it seems cold and intellectual. Usually, rigorous thinking and problem solving in their classrooms includes a great deal of fun or teamwork. Problem-solving work in an SF classroom may be tied to the life of the student—multiplying a recipe to feed a crowd, determining a fair way to share the television with siblings, or writing letters to someone out-of-state so they can learn about a new place. The need to make schoolwork relevant to students is much clearer to the SF teacher than to others. Some NT observers may prefer more academically focused tasks or not catch the lesson's focus because a task seems trivial to them. An example might be the SF teacher who had even made overheads to teach students how to fill out book orders, using a simple task to set class expectations for helping each other and following directions. Without understanding the deeper purposes, an NT observer might dismiss the activity as a waste of time.

Like ST teachers, though, SF teachers may feel satisfied with a lesson plan when it allows students to master knowledge. They may struggle to find ways for students to problem-solve or think. SF teachers also appreciate tried-and-true strategies that can be used in multiple contexts.

Accountable talk. The SF teacher enjoys the way that accountable talk helps students respect each other. The SF teacher will most likely teach the process step-by-step. Students might, for example, work together to find textual evidence to support a statement the teacher makes. Next, the teacher might ask them to give an example of how to build on that idea. Or the teacher might introduce two or three discussion stems at a time, waiting until students seem to use those naturally before adding more. The SF teacher will often post the question stems, devise worksheets to help the students use them, and perhaps even give a short quiz to motivate students to study and internalize the prompts. An NT observer might view these activities as "procedures without understanding," a waste of time when the students should be learning by using accountable talk. However, the SF teacher often refers back to these activities when students are engaging in discussions and need reminders of how to use accountable talk.

The Intuitive and Thinking Teacher (NT)

The common strengths of the NT teacher are

- Rigorous lessons that encourage thinking and creating
- Teaching concepts and models
- Constructivist, project-based learning
- Helping students think logically and justify

Note that three of the principles of learning—rigor, accountable talk (logic and justification), and apprenticeship—are natural strengths for the NT teacher. The trick for them, though, is to structure their efforts in ways that reach all students.

Organizing for effort. NT teachers have no trouble setting high expectations for their students; observers in their classrooms often see them insisting that their students accomplish tasks that other teachers would be afraid to assign. One NT administrator insists that all students achieve overall grades of 80 percent or better to pass classes; he personally tutors students in math to help them reach that goal. In another school, an NF teacher was convinced that eighth graders weren't ready to write compare/contrast essays. The NT teacher across the hall had students writing multiple drafts until they mastered the format.

Usually NT teachers are at ease with students working at different paces, providing extra help to those who need it; they are comfortable with students working independently. One teacher described his method for giving directions:

> Typically I don't spend so much time in a whole group setting such that I, I mean I do kind of the introductory whatever and set them off in motion and then I sort of target the ones that have question marks on their face and I try to do one-on-one stuff with them and then . . . and then my patience is infinite. I'll stay with them as long as I need to. Or I'll invite them to come for a little extra help or, if it's a particularly tough thing I'll say, "Okay, anybody that isn't quite sure what I was talking about, why don't you all come up to this table and I'll go through it again and . . ." You know, usually I'll get 8 or 10 takers in situations like that. (Kise, 2002, pp. 25–26)

To an SF observer who prefers whole-class instruction (remember the book order forms), this approach may seem fraught with risks. One SF teacher commented, "But it's the students who *don't* ask the questions who should. They go off and do things the way they want to, and often it isn't at all what I had in mind." The NT teacher, though, is often able to multitask, observing quickly how the other students are progressing while helping those who need it.

The NT teachers may be good strategic resources for determining how to create extra time for students to reach mastery. They may think outside the box of ways to alter school schedules to add extra time for math or reading help. They might think of interdisciplinary efforts that would reinforce some skill a good number of students are struggling with.

Clear expectations. NT teachers often provide clear expectations for how assignments will be graded and what constitutes quality work. Further, they often enjoy the systematic nature of standards and the road map they provide. To the SF observer, their approaches might almost seem mechanical or cold, couched in rubrics or other structures. However, as shown in the *October Sky* example, NTs often model exactly what the final product should look like.

Where NTs often struggle is with intermediate expectations. Students might spend an entire quarter on one project, turning in the entire thing at once. The NT teacher might not naturally look for intermediate steps or benchmarks for students to track their progress. They often appreciate help from other teachers in breaking concepts into knowledge "bites" so that students can mark progress along the way.

Academic rigor in a thinking curriculum. This is the NT forte—problem solving and using models and theories to explain the world. One teacher said

> I've been known to get into long conceptual descriptions of things with kids and some will love it because they're just like, "Oh really? And so how does this happen and how do these happen and what happens then?" and others just aren't following and they go and, when I get excited about something and they're not quite staying with me, I'm like, "Come on, this

is [laugh]" . . . There'll be a formula: force equals mass times acceleration and I'll say, "You know you don't have to memorize formulas, just think. If you put a force on something, what's it going to do? You know, it's going to accelerate. But the kids want to say, "But how do you do it?" [laugh] Man, I just want you to *think* about it. (Kise, 2002, p. 25)

An SF observer might view the constructivist projects and theory-based discussions and wonder where the basic skills practice takes place. How do students pick up foundational knowledge? The practice may be there, but an observer may need to inquire. Chances are, because those aren't favorite activities for NT teachers, they don't take up significant class time. NTs believe the foundational skills will be developed as students think about concepts and applications.

Accountable talk. NT teachers encourage justification and reasoning. Of all the types, they may be best at insisting that students explain how they know what they know. SF observers might feel that they've walked into a scene from *The Paper Chase* if an NT teacher is engaging with NT students who enjoy debate. They may wonder if the teacher is pushing too hard.

How teachers approach the principles of learning, teach them to students, and use them in their classrooms can vary widely. No matter what the framework for observation, the main point is that by focusing on student achievement, instead of teacher activity, we can see whether their methods are working for their students, not whether they would work for us.

Activity 7.1
Classroom Observations

Choose one of the above principles of learning and spend time in classrooms, looking for evidence of whether the classroom and student activity reflect that principle. If you know the types of your teachers, consider in advance, using the above information, how that teacher might carry out the principles of effort-based ability. Consider visiting two "opposite" teachers, Sensing/Feeling (SF) and Intuition/ Thinking (NT) *or* Sensing/ Thinking (ST) and Intuition/Feeling (NF), focusing on the same principle. What is the same? What is different?

Chapter Summary

Many teacher observational protocols have built-in type biases. Teachers with different personality preferences, which drive their own learning styles and beliefs, will carry out the teaching and learning framework for student achievement from the Institute for Learning in different ways. Administrators observing classrooms need to understand how their own personality preferences filter what they're seeing to assess fairly what is happening in a classroom. Knowing their staff members' teaching styles helps administrators effectively coach for improved student success in every classroom.

Activity 7.2
Point-in-Time Check on Your School

How well are the needs of students with different learning styles being met? This is another classroom observation technique that avoids type bias.

- Choose several people to observe classrooms. Make sure teachers know the purpose of the visits—exactly what observers are looking for and that the data will be shown to the staff on an aggregate basis, not for individual teachers.
- Choose criteria to watch for. Samples include:
  o Extraverted and Introverted time
  o Acquiring knowledge versus applying knowledge or creative activities
  o Direct instruction versus constructivism
  o Small group work versus individual work
  Some schools devise concise checklists or observation guides so that several criteria can be tracked at once.
- At a secondary school, each observer can follow a student through several classes to record a typical day. In an elementary school, observers might spend a set amount of time in each classroom at a specific grade level.
- Alternatively, have several observers all at once observe several classes in the same department and aggregate what was found.
- Aggregate the data: total amount of observed time, percentage spent in each activity. What patterns do you see? How might students with different personality types be affected?

Reflection

- Reflect on a teacher whose instructional style you have questioned. Does type bias play any part in your opinions?
- Look at the column in Chart 7.2 that is opposite your own (e.g., Sensing/Thinking [ST] would look at Intuitive/Feeling [NF]). Highlight the strengths of teachers with your opposite preferences that you may not have valued highly in the past. How can you incorporate recognition of those strengths into your observation and coaching of these teachers?

Note

1. As noted in Chapter 1, all type distribution information is from the database of the Center for Applications of Psychological Type, Gainesville, Florida.

8

Tools for
Schoolwide Discipline

"Do you think you can maintain discipline?" asked the superintendent.
"Of course I can," replied Stuart. "I'll make the work interesting
and the discipline will take care of itself. Don't worry about me."

—*Stuart Little*, E. B. White (1945)

There's a lot of truth in Stuart Little's insights. Estimates still are that about 85 percent of classroom time is devoted to didactic instruction: the teacher passes on knowledge while students listen. Or are supposed to listen. There are two problems with this practice. First, once the test is over, without meaningful ways to apply the information, adults and students alike only retain about 5 percent of what they hear. Second, teachers dislike being lectured, especially if staff development drones on through dozens of PowerPoint slides. Why would they think their lectures will hold their students' interest?

Barth (2005) described the problem from the perspective of students considered high achievers whom he found burning their notes and notebooks on the last day of school. They saw no use for what they'd been taught as they headed off to college.

The effects, though, are even more insidious when classrooms aren't engaging for students who already question whether they can succeed. Commenting on the high incidence of disciplinary problems with African American youth, Jones (2006) wrote

> You've got to hand it to [them]. Instead of cooperating with a system
> that degrades them because of what they don't know, they're using

their meager talents to force that system to its knees. It takes genuine street skills to get kicked out of class so you don't embarrass yourself with what you don't know in front of your peers. It's an art to disrupt the formal lesson plan and force the teacher to make you the center of attention. (p. A15)

We firmly believe, then, that the first principle of effective discipline policies is to create a school atmosphere where all classrooms exhibit the principles of effort-based ability.

For us, the second principle is helping teachers understand how their own personalities affect their views of student behavior. Teachers tend to discipline students more who do not share their type preferences (O'Neill, 1986). Further, multiple studies, confirmed in our own work at many schools, show that students with certain personality types are vastly overrepresented in alternative schools and other programs for at-risk students. These same types are vastly *underrepresented* among teachers.

Even when school staffs collaborate effectively to increase student engagement and meet the needs of students with all personality preferences, there will still be disciplinary issues. After all, children and adults sometimes make poor choices.

Most disciplinary structures take into account the developmental level of the student. In elementary years, the processes are often Sensing in nature: delineating the facts of what happened with set structures for what happens next. Using type concepts helps students develop the abstract reasoning needed for them to engage actively in problem solving, a more Intuitive process, at earlier stages of development. While many programs and frameworks for school discipline problems help students reflect on those choices and plan for better ones in the future, in this chapter we'll look at some ways that the language of type might help students revisit their actions in a new light. Particularly, we'll look at how type might help the school, and eventually the student, push back at peer pressure.

Student Culture

In *all* schools, students establish a pecking order: the queen bees and wannabes of girls' cliques; the greasers and socs of S. E. Hinton's *The Outsiders*; the jocks, sporties, brains, and burnouts of the high school of one of the authors; or the preps, hicks, freaks, and Gs described by Dutton, Quantz, and Dutton (2000). The latter wrote about "the game" when they were still in high school:

The way to get more and more status within your group is to be the most popular prep among the preps, the most powerful hick among the hicks, the freak the other freaks admire, and so on. This game is getting much tougher year by year. . . . You can start to feel that if you slip up once, you will lose your standing forever. There's also a weird sense . . . that you can't really get ahead unless you destroy someone else in the process. Those who are ahead in the game harass people who get better grades or more recognition in class. They don't like sharing power. (p. 375)

These teens continue with an analysis of how adults actually reinforce the students' social structures, although they don't realize it, by the sports and clubs to which school resources are dedicated, by how National Honor Society members are selected, and by the kinds of assignments given that are more or less meaningful to certain groups.

While the open violence of street gangs may be more visible when it spills over into school hallways and classrooms, less visible social structures can be just as harmful, as so aptly described in *Queen Bees and Wannabes* (Wiseman, 2002). At far too many schools, leadership is still saying, "Kids will be kids," implying that nothing can be done. Do nothing, Dutton et al. (2000) pointed out, and things may definitely happen, "The shootings at Columbine (a school with a student population much like ours) could be mapped as two kids from the freak/G[angsta] quadrant trying to attack their enemies across the circle, who had taunted them as 'fags.' (p. 375)"

At other schools, though, administrators and teachers are working with students to help them make better choices. In this chapter, we'll suggest a way that schools can incorporate the Problem-Solving Model (Resource B) in how they teach students about respect, in helping students understand the consequences of the choices they are making, and in how they help build a better student community.

While the characteristics of a Thinking culture—analysis, reasoning, principles, competency—are extremely useful for building a culture of academic achievement, students tend to thrive academically, socially, and emotionally when schools take on a Feeling culture where

- Individual differences are honored and celebrated.
- Community values are upheld.
- People respect each other and are kind.
- Students and teachers are committed to working together so that all may achieve.
- Recognition is given for individual progress and absolute achievement levels with the belief that all students can reach the goal.
- Students and adults make decisions by stepping into the shoes of others and determining how their actions will affect everyone involved.

Compare the list above to the "game" of social hierarchy that students are enmeshed in:

- Individual differences are squelched; you win by becoming the most like the others in your group.
- Cliques have different values that often conflict with each other.
- People are not only cruel to people outside their clique but show cruelty to friends if they can win favor or recognition in the eyes of their peers.
- School policies work to support students at the top of the pecking order (Eckert, 2000).
- Recognition is given for select accomplishments, defined by faculty, the cliques, and the parental community.
- Students and adults make decisions based on rules, precedents, and cause-effect reasoning.

Another way to describe this is to say that the way gangs/cliques/school social hierarchies operate is as a permanent, unbalanced eruption of the Thinking function. It's Thinking gone awry, where faulty logic leads to lose-lose situations and rules set a high percentage of "players" up for failure.

Influencing the "Rules of the Game"

School leaders *can* influence the culture. Research upholds that the Olweus Bullying Prevention Program cuts bullying incidents at schools by 50 percent or more (Olweus, 2003). Olweus wrote

> The accumulated research evidence indicates that personality characteristics or typical reaction patterns, in combination with physical strength or weakness in the case of boys, are important in the development of bullying problems in individual students. At the same time, environmental factors, such as the attitudes, behavior, and routines of relevant adults—in particular, teachers and principals—play a crucial role in determining the extent to which bullying problems will manifest themselves in a larger unit, such as a classroom or school. Thus, we must pursue analyses of the main causes of bully/victim problems on at least two different levels: individual and environmental. (p. 14)

His program trains school personnel to be involved in warm, positive ways as positive role models, finding nonpunitive interventions for unacceptable behavior and imposing firm limits on what is acceptable behavior. Schools can influence the culture in several ways.

Recognize that "the game" is played from the first day of school. Students rightfully dread the first day of school. In most schools, students know that the wrong choice of attire, or showing that they know too little or too much, can doom them from the start. Planning activities that help a child get off on the right foot is essential. Simply appointing another student as guide may not be enough—how often in children's literature does the new child at school later have to choose between being popular and remaining loyal to that initial guide? *We* remember being the friendly guide, only to find out that the new student was destined to be best friends with the homecoming queen.

This is also why it is important to establish a learning culture in the school so that a person's experience isn't dependent on individual students but rather an overall approach to learning and being valued as a member of the learning community. Effort-based schools may find it easier to help new students buy into the culture. Some suggestions are

- Provide homeroom, advisory, or classroom activities that allow students to talk about how they've learned to persevere, seek help, and believe that they can succeed. Examples might be tangrams or logic puzzles where teachers scaffold by first providing silent work time, then letting students work with a partner, then giving hints on how to proceed. Or teachers might use books for small group discussion, such as *We Beat the Street: How a Friendship Led to Success* (Davis, Jenkins, Hunt, & Draper, 2005) or *A Hope in the Unseen* (Suskind, 1998).

- Make sure the student and parents or guardians hear together that at this school, all students do the work. Their classmates won't accuse them of selling out if they get good grades—they're all doing C or better work, or doing it over again. List the "opportunities" they will have for catching up if they fail to follow through during class. Make sure their efforts are monitored for their first week at school so that if they start to slide, adults are ready to reinforce that they can and will do the work.

- Kleiner (2000) suggested revisiting extracurricular activities. Are there some that appeal to students in all groups? If your staff tends to believe that "kids will be kids," consider using "The Great Game of High School" (Dutton et al., 2000) for a text-based discussion. This essay, by high school students, maps out the cliques in their school, the effect of the groupings on all students, and how adults reinforce what amounts to the school's class system.

Teach the values you want to see. Gather interested faculty to generate ideas of how they can encourage students to uphold the school's values. Generate ideas for discussions that reinforce the school's values. Students might discuss a movie clip, a short text, or quote and how they see it in action at the school or what it means to them as students.

Euvrard (2006) described having students define what values are and then work together to define the values they want to guide their classrooms, using a democratic process. The top values chosen, in 50 different classrooms of Euvrard's postgraduate teachers who engaged in the experiment, were respect, punctuality, responsibility, hard work, democracy/equality, and cooperation. While teachers weren't sure what to expect after the exercise was complete, they noted significant changes in their classrooms, including long-term improvement in "student hard work, cooperation, respect, creativity, honesty and responsibility" (p. 46). Further, the teachers found that they themselves changed, becoming more committed as they saw the students change:

> One wrote, "The values that we started in our class have become the culture of our class." Students showed more respect for individual differences and were more cooperative, confident, and open with their classmates. They also took more responsibility for the management of the class and reminded one another of the rules when appropriate. Most teachers confirmed that the "teacher-learner relations became healthier, with more mutual understanding." (p. 45)

Make students conscious of what they allow to trigger potentially harmful responses. Street culture, and most cliques, set clear rules of retaliation. "If you do this to me, then I do that." While we want students to take responsibility for their own actions, we also want them to see that once they buy into these action/reaction rules, others can control them and the consequences they'll receive.

For example, one sixth grader lashed out physically when another girl taunted her—a common "set point" at which students in certain groups believe they have to defend their honor. This is often a must on the street. Later in the principal's office, realizing that she faced a two-day suspension, she burst into tears at the reality of calling her grandparents with the news. She knew she could have walked away. She knew she *would* walk away the next time.

This student needed to understand the rules of school and how they differed from the street. They understand when you explain, "If you're playing football, you can't play by basketball rules. School rules are not street rules." The key is to not assume at any level that students know the school's rules. They need to become conscious of the differences; we teach the rules and the skills to provide access to learning for all. Often, Sensing or Thinking teachers become frustrated because they think students should already understand school rules, but each year, as more is at stake for the students on the streets, they need a new understanding at school of appropriate responses.

Stories can help students see how what triggers their anger or other responses can leave them vulnerable. Have teachers search texts and stories, fiction and nonfiction, for examples such as these:

- In *The Empire Strikes Back*, Darth Vader keeps Luke Skywalker from finishing his Jedi training by kidnapping Han and Leia. Vader knows Luke will think that saving his friends is more important than working with Yoda—even though the fate of the Rebellion may rest on Luke's abilities. Whether Luke's set point was right or wrong can make for a lively discussion, but the point is that Vader knew what to do to get Luke to abandon Yoda.
- In *The Lion, the Witch, and The Wardrobe* (Lewis), Edmund betrays his siblings to the White Witch because he wants more candy—and resents not being the oldest boy. He doesn't think through consequences.
- During the invasion of Baghdad, American troops broadcast insults through loudspeakers atop their tanks. The Iraqi soldiers, trained to uphold their personal honor, came out of their foxholes, essentially rendering themselves defenseless and opening the roads to the invaders (*Newsweek*, 2003).

Through accountable talk, journaling, and other activities, teachers can help students discover the set points that govern their own peer groups. Which are healthy? Which will leave them vulnerable to others, getting them into trouble? Which aren't worth it?

Using Type Concepts in Interventions

School discipline policies *have* to be more Thinking than Feeling in nature. Students talk; they know who does and doesn't get suspended, who got away with what, which teachers bend the rules and which ones write up the slightest infraction. Further, fairness rules their opinions when it comes to discipline.

One teacher put it this way, "If I stop a student in the hall for an obvious rule violation—maybe he's wearing a hood or she just threw orange peels down the hallway—and take appropriate action, that student will write me off for weeks as an idiot if he or she knows of other students who did the same thing that I *didn't* catch. That's half the dilemma; there's so much we don't see and the students shout 'not fair' when they happen to get caught."

However, the Feeling function becomes an important part of conversation with students because there are various nuances in each situation. In fact, the Problem-Solving Model in Resource B is again a useful framework.

Many schools use reflection sheets that contain aspects of the Problem-Solving Model. "How would the teacher describe what happened?" attempts to identify facts; "Besides yourself, whom did your behavior affect?" gets at Feeling; "What other courses of action could you have taken?" taps into Intuition; and "How will you solve this?" uses Thinking. The Problem-Solving Model, though, once a student calms down, can help them process the points the adults are trying to make.

Consider using Chart 8.1 as a guide to working through behavior incidents with adolescents.

Few students would sit still for all of the questions in Chart 8.1. Choose those that are appropriate developmentally and appropriate for the situation. Keys to making the process effective include:

- **Making sure the student knows the entire process:** They need to know that they'll be heard, but in turn they'll be asked to think through alternatives even if they don't think any exist, reflect on their reactions; and ponder the bigger issues of who else was affected and the overall impact on the school.

- **Acknowledging the very real dilemmas students face:** Some come from homes where retaliation is encouraged. Others have experienced that if they don't fight back at school, things may get even worse for them on the way home. In fact, they may see ignoring school rules as a pathway to safety, getting the conflict over quickly and perhaps less severely than if they get jumped on the street later.

- **Embedding the process schoolwide:** The "I-win-you-lose" mentality of the "game" affects how students interact with teachers as well as with each other. The more we can help students and staff see that "win-win" is possible or that not all encounters have winners and losers—sometimes teachers and students just exchange information or clarify expectations—the more positive the atmosphere can be.

Be aware that Thinking and Feeling students often react differently to these discussions, although students of *all* types will land in your office for disciplinary reasons. Feeling students usually become aware more quickly of how their actions affected others, even if those others are their parents or a teacher whom they admire. Feeling students who believe the teacher wrongly accused them of something may shut down and say they don't care anymore about that class or teacher. This is one reason why reflection with the teacher and students

Chart 8.1   The Z Model and Discipline

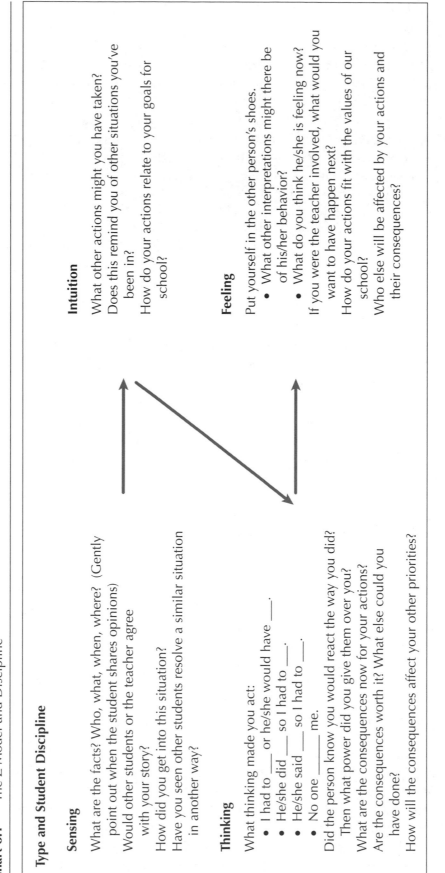

Type and Student Discipline

Sensing

What are the facts? Who, what, when, where? (Gently point out when the student shares opinions)
Would other students or the teacher agree with your story?
How did you get into this situation?
Have you seen other students resolve a similar situation in another way?

Thinking

What thinking made you act:
- I had to _____ or he/she would have _____.
- He/she did _____ so I had to _____.
- He/she said _____ so I had to _____.
- No one _____ me.

Did the person know you would react the way you did?
Then what power did you give them over you?
What are the consequences now for your actions?
Are the consequences worth it? What else could you have done?
How will the consequences affect your other priorities?

Intuition

What other actions might you have taken?
Does this remind you of other situations you've been in?
How do your actions relate to your goals for school?

Feeling

Put yourself in the other person's shoes.
- What other interpretations might there be of his/her behavior?
- What do you think he/she is feeling now?

If you were the teacher involved, what would you want to have happen next?
How do your actions fit with the values of our school?
Who else will be affected by your actions and their consequences?

about the incident helps restore the relationship again and gets the Feeling type engaged again. We remember, for example, a young boy sobbing that he wanted to apologize to the teacher for fighting before going home.

Thinking students may be far more concerned with saving face. They may respond to being involved in solutions. Prompts that might work include:

- What's your plan for keeping this from happening again?
- What do you think will happen to you if this behavior continues?
- What goal will you set for yourself? How can you attain it?

With the right spin, these students might feel that they're retaining some control in the situation.

We informally polled a group of African American students who were doing well in school about what they felt helped them succeed. All of them reported that an adult at home expected them to do well. And all reported that they'd had to fight at least once because other students had teased them about doing well. One student secretly turned in homework before school so his peers wouldn't see him handing it in during class. As school leaders, we need to do everything we can to ensure that doing well becomes the norm so that students don't have to sneak or fight to succeed.

Chapter Summary

Creating a school atmosphere where all classrooms exhibit the principles of effort-based ability and helping teachers understand how their personalities affect how they view student behavior is critical to maintaining student discipline. Teachers tend to discipline students who don't share their personality type preferences. School leaders can influence the school culture by honoring both the Thinking and Feeling styles of decision making—setting firm rules that still allow for individual needs.

Using the common language of type helps students reflect on the choices they make and eventually make better choices. Using the Problem-Solving, or Z, Model (Resource B) helps all students make good decisions—and administrators and teachers as well—as they work to accommodate the Thinking, Feeling, Sensing, and Intuitive functions.

Reflection

- How is the "game" played at your school? Do the adults do anything to reinforce the rewards of being in the most popular group? Think through awards programs, afterschool activities, and other policies.
- How often do you run into the "I-win-you-lose" attitude when dealing with students, where every confrontation has to have a clear winner? How have you diffused that when students see admitting any wrongdoing, or even misunderstanding, as losing face?
- Examine your school discipline policy in terms of the Z Model. What amount of time is spent at each step? What changes might help students better understand the choices they're making and the consequences?

9

Working With All Types of Parents

Students who succeed in school are almost always supported by their families, while other students struggle without support from home. For a school to develop a partnership program involving all parents in ways that increase student success requires new ways of thinking about family and community involvement. . . .

New approaches are needed because research shows that most parents not presently involved would like to be, if their children's teachers, administrators, and counselors showed them how to help their children increase reading and math scores, improve attendance, and meet other important goals. (Epstein & Jansorn, 2004, p. 19)

Parent involvement results in increased student achievement. Research in this area is so conclusive that The No Child Left Behind Act requires schools to develop ways for parents to get involved in their children's schools. Further, parents know that they should be involved—and they want to be involved. Drummond and Stipek (2004), in a study of low-income parents, rural and urban, from different cultural backgrounds, found

Because other studies have suggested that some parents' involvement falls short of school expectations, there are likely either additional barriers for parents in helping their children learn or there is miscommunication about participation between educators and parents. . . . Our results show that low-income parents strongly believe they should facilitate their children's success in school. (p. 207)

However, it isn't always simple for parents to be involved. Key barriers include:

- **Language:** Even when schools provide translations of communications and translators at conferences, parents report difficulties with day-to-day interactions or attendance at functions such as parent-teacher organization (PTO) meetings. Further, they may not understand directions at general meetings. For example, at a back-to-school night, many non-English-speaking parents missed the invitation to visit classrooms and instead left the building after the general session (Pena, 2000).

- **Education level:** Parental reading skills and comfort with the school environment also influence involvement. Pena (2000) found incidences where parents couldn't participate in parent night activities, such as making vocabulary booklets, because they didn't understand the words themselves. Lapp and Flood (2004) reported that many parents thought their involvement might actually harm their children, either through their insufficient knowledge or the teachers' perceptions. When asked why she didn't attend parent-teacher conferences, one parent said, "I don't like to talk to the teacher because she might think Precious ain't no smarter than me" (p. 67).

- **Culture:** Parents from some cultural backgrounds believe that schools are solely responsible for their children's education and that parents are not to meddle (Chavkin & Gonzalez, 1995; Trueba, Jacobs, & Kirton, 1990).

- **Parent social groups:** In some schools, parental cliques run PTO and other important avenues for parental involvement (Pena, 2000). They may make other parents feel unwelcome or exclude them from key roles. In schools with students from a mix of social classes, parents may hold stereotypes of lower-income parents, unintentionally structure or schedule meetings in ways that discourage their involvement, or assume they do not want to be involved (Giles, 2005). If school staff is relatively hands-off in these matters, they may not be aware of attitudes or tensions.

- **Family issues:** Time, schedules, transportation, difficulties for single parents in covering child care, and other issues can block parental involvement.

- **Lack of clarity on how they can participate:** Several studies show that parents are more likely to become involved when schools offer specific invitations or clear instructions on ways to be involved (Fields-Smith, 2005; Tam & Heng, 2005).

- **Parents' own experiences in school:** Those who had negative experiences feel less inclined to be involved.

A School's Parental Narrative

Some of these barriers are easier for schools to lower than others. However, another barrier greatly influences whether teachers and administrators think the effort will be worth it: the view the school's staff holds of parents. Giles

(2005) found that schools define distinct "narratives" (a constructed, stereo-typed view), of parents. Negative ones include:

- **The deficit narrative:** Some schools expect low involvement from parents. "Educators view the perceived pathologies and problems of families as undermining their ability as educators to successfully teach the children" (Giles, 2005, p. 3). Teachers might assume that the parents lack the education or emotional stability to help their children. Often, they claim that parents only enter the building when "bribed" with food or other tactics. "It's the only way that we can get them in here to show them what's good for them" was a representative quote (Giles, 2005, p. 4) from schools that shared the deficit narrative. Parents often report condescending attitudes from school staff. They knew principals often granted same-day meetings to white parents regarding their children, while neglecting to return phone calls from parents of color (Pena, 2000). Another parent reported scheduling a meeting with the school principal to discuss ways to improve the school. The principal handed him application letters for welfare and dismissed him (Giles, 2005).

- **The in loco parentis narrative:** Schools with this view "assume that it is their responsibility to provide an academic, and often social and emotional, education in the place of students' parents, that is, with very limited or no participation by parents" (Giles, 2005, p. 5). In contrast to the deficit narrative, these teachers believe that the students can achieve with their help. In these schools, parents are considered recipients of resources, such as workshops on parenting skills, or are given noneducational roles, such as fundraising. The educators often assume that students need skills that differ from those their background cultures value, implicitly suggesting that students distance themselves from their families and community.

- **The helicopter parent narrative:** This term was defined over 15 years ago by *Newsweek* as "A nosy grown-up who's always hovering around. Quick to offer a teacher unwanted help" (Zeman, 1991, p. 9). School staff might view parents as overprotective or overly critical, inferring that they could do a better job than the teachers. These schools may shuttle parents into time-consuming but nonacademic support roles, structure mechanisms such as signed course contracts to protect teachers from parents who want grading exceptions made, or overreact to any parent request, assuming that they'll insist on "designer," one-of-a-kind interventions for their child. Or teachers may do their best to respond quickly to all parent communications in an attempt to keep any concern from growing.

All of these narratives reflect some truth. We *do* know of teachers in a well-to-do suburban district, for example, who receive four full-page e-mails a day from one parent. We also know of schools that have tried elaborate efforts to involve parents, to no avail. However, the deficit, in loco parentis, and helicopter parent views can actually create barriers to the kind of parent involvement that research shows increases student achievement. If we misunderstand parent motivations, communication styles, or concerns, we aren't likely to extend a welcome that will reach parents.

Most schools hold a blend of the above views, but the end result is the same: these schools see as futile any attempts at getting families involved in activities directly connected to student achievement. Olivos (2004) concluded that in such schools that serve the Latino population, the lack of parent involvement is more accurately viewed as resistance, not apathy:

> Specifically, Latino parents simply refuse to attend or participate in school-related activities which they believe are useless, particularly in light of other obligations they may have in regard to home or work. Feeding this disengagement is the lack of political consciousness among many Latino parents in regard to how and why the school system frequently functions to their children's disadvantage. . . .
>
> These parents do not lack the desire or ability to participate; rather they lack the necessary appropriate avenues with which to access information concerning the education of their children and their rights as parents. Additionally, the parents also often lack opportunities in which they can begin to develop a more sophisticated political and critical consciousness that will help them increase their level of awareness of the socioeconomic and historic context under which educational injustice occurs. This "knowledge void" leads to an inability to demand what is rightfully theirs. And, more importantly, this also often misleads Latino parents to believe that they are powerless, something the school system has socialized them to believe. (pp. 7 & 10)

Because a school's parental narrative shapes the policies, opportunities, and communications regarding family involvement, it may be the most significant factor shaping how it partners (or fails to partner) with parents for student academic achievement. Parents may not be able to penetrate the barriers a negative narrative creates by themselves. Fields-Smith (2005) found that African American parents who were significantly involved in their children's schools believed they needed "a savvy network within and outside of the school . . . that may not be available to many low-income or single parents" (p. 134). Further, they concluded that these needs are greater now than before *Brown v. the Board of Education.* Thurston and Navarrette (2003) reported that low-income mothers in their study, 40 percent of whom had at least one special-needs child, wanted to be involved but found teachers intimidating.

To believe that their efforts to partner with families in more meaningful ways would be worthwhile, schools need a *fourth* narrative:

- **The relational narrative** (Giles, 2005): Schools with this view consider parents as partners with them in educating students. They take action together to address typical school issues. Parents are trustworthy and have resources to help improve the school, especially by building community partnerships.

When schools hold this narrative, they expect that parents have knowledge that can help both the school and their students. They work together to tackle community issues that influence students. They create frequent opportunities for parents to provide input and for staff and parents to interact. In such a school, Lewis and Forman (2002) reported

> Parents were rarely called upon to be fundraisers, bakers, or room moms. Instead, they were involved as members of a community, as educational collaborators with important information about their children, and as comrades in struggles related to keeping the school functioning. (p. 78)

Chart 9.1 shows six different categories of parent involvement in schools (Epstein, 2002) and the unintentional ways that a school's parental narrative might cause it to structure the opportunities represented by each category so as to deter parents or fall short of true parental involvement in student academic achievement.

So how do we interact with parents so that the relational narrative not only becomes the common belief of teachers but so that parental involvement actually reflects all the potential that the relational view has to offer? In this chapter, we'll look at type-related strategies for

- Developing a schoolwide relational narrative of parents
- Inviting parental involvement
- Partnering with parents to help their children succeed
- Mediating between parents and school staff when conflict arises.

Moving to a Relational Narrative

A school's narrative view of parents is usually the kind of mental model that Senge, Kleiner, Roberts, Ross, and Smith (1994) described as the often-unconscious assumptions or images that guide our viewpoints and courses of action—panes of glass through which we see the world. They described the task of working with mental models as bringing them to the surface, "to explore and talk about them with minimal defensiveness—to help us see the pane of glass, see its impact on our lives, and find ways to re-form the glass by creating new mental models that serve us better in the world" (p. 236).

You may have unearthed your school's view of parents by reading the above descriptions, or your school may have a more mixed viewpoint. To evaluate which is the dominant narrative, and also so that school leadership concludes for themselves the impact that narrative has on school-parent interactions, consider using Activity 9.1, an application of the Problem-Solving Model (Resource B), with your leadership team.

Chart 9.1 School Parental Narratives and Their Effect on Family Involvement Strategies

(Left-hand column from Epstein, 2002)

	Deficit narrative	*In loco parentis narrative*	*Helicopter parent narrative*	*Relational parent narrative*
Parenting • School assists families with parenting skills. • Parents assist schools in understanding culture, goals for their children.	School may only offer "remedial" parenting classes on discipline or setting limits, ignoring deeper topics such as brain research or adolescent development. Seldom seek parent input, then point to low attendance as further evidence of parents' faults.	School may assume that parental beliefs and practices are set. They work with students on developing perseverance, setting and reaching goals, and becoming self-disciplined.	Schools may defer to outside experts, channeling parents' energy into organizing one-time, big-name events, instead of developing ongoing programs with partnerships between parents and school staff.	Schools welcome parents' input in the planning process, inviting them into meetings and classrooms. Parents involved in presenting to staff on culturally relevant teaching, life experiences.
Communicating • Schools communicate about programs, student achievement. • Parents engage in two-way communication.	Schools may assume parents have little interest in hearing from the school and, therefore, spend little effort in overcoming barriers, such as language or culture.	Schools may assume that more parent involvement would harm student achievement and, therefore, only initiate one-way communication. They then state that they did their part by giving out the information. Assigning staff to work with parents is seen as the answer.	Schools may use communication to protect themselves, detailing policies and consequences, rather than seeking parental input. May structure parent input to protect themselves rather than welcome input at any time.	Schools have several channels for communication, including two-way communication.
Volunteering • Schools recruit, train, provide activities, and communicate them. • Parents serve as volunteers and as audiences at events.	Schools may assume that parents have little interest and, therefore, spend little effort on welcoming invitations, scheduling flexibility, or gathering parental input on desired roles.	Schools shape volunteer priorities and channel parents into nonacademic support roles, such as fundraising or chaperoning.	Schools may channel parental energy into significant but nonacademic events, such as school spirit events, class parties, sports team booster clubs, elaborate costuming or set building for theater, fundraising, etc.	Schools not only design volunteer opportunities but ask parents in what ways they would like to be involved, welcoming parent expertise in academic and nonacademic areas.

	Deficit narrative	In loco parentis narrative	Helicopter parent narrative	Relational parent narrative
Learning at home • Schools provide guidance for families to work academically with their students on homework, goal setting, and interesting tasks. • Parents make time for these activities.	Schools may assume that parents lack the desire to help and, therefore, do little to provide tips, suggestions, or training for parents—or to help them overcome language difficulties. They may not be clear enough about what the students are expected to know and understand, or on how they will be evaluated, based on the assumption that parents don't care.	Schools may work harder on internal assistance—afterschool help, peer tutoring, etc.—than on providing ways for families to become involved with their child's academic work. They may not take advantage of interactive assignments where parents assist their children or provide input.	Schools may be most worried about parental overinvolvement. They may offer less help to students, assuming that parents will help or hire tutors, or they may avoid some projects (science fairs, research papers) instead of working with parents to ensure that students do the work. They may avoid assigning homework for fear that the parents will do it instead of the child.	Schools ensure that parents understand standards and curriculum, providing multiple ways for parents to learn that they need to support students' achievement. Parents are involved in meaningful home activities that support learning.
Decision making • Schools include families as participants through councils, organizations, or opinion gathering. • Parents make their views known.	Schools may assume that parents lack the knowledge base to participate. Nichols-Solomon (2001) reported that parents expecting to discuss curriculum instead were asked how to communicate to other parents the importance of their students' being well-rested and fed on state test days.	Schools may assume that parental wishes would be contrary to what is best for their child academically.	Schools may resent any parental input. They may use performance data to motivate parents to fundraise, or overstructure feedback to avoid criticisms to which they aren't willing to respond.	Schools regularly seek input from all constituencies. They provide sufficient information for parents to be informed of issues, in multiple ways, and provide various forums for parents to share their views and expertise.
Collaboration with community • Schools coordinate with community resources. • Parents contribute service to the community.	Schools may assume parents have no leadership, advocacy, or planning skills to form partnerships. They may also assume parents lack skills or interest in volunteer work.	Schools may seek out and form partnerships without parental input, involving students more than families and then notifying families.	Schools may channel parental energy into fundraising or solving out-of-school behavior problems, such as substance abuse or unsupervised parties.	Schools, families, and community organizations work together to identify needs and ways that families can be involved in solutions.

Activity 9.1
Identifying Your School's Parent Narrative

1. Sensing function:

- Examine the artifacts. Gather representative communications with parents—volunteer forms, PTO responsibilities and actions, information-night topics, descriptions of school-community partnerships, activities of school committees that include parents. Under which narratives do they best fit: deficit, in loco parentis, helicopter, or relational?
- The leadership team might also record specific ways that they have heard school staff speak about parents. What do they say about parent attendance at school events? What reasons do they give for their frustrations with parents?
- Finally, look at what parents are actually *doing*. What narrative best describes their actual involvement?

Be forewarned that focusing on facts is *very* difficult as is keeping opinions and supporting examples out of this part of the conversation. For example, we know of several schools where it's hard not to use "helicopter parent" to describe what we've seen: science fair projects obviously created by a parent who works as a physicist, classes where nearly half the students have private tutors, and so on. Similarly, staffs of "deficit" schools can point to low conference attendance, lack of parent oversight of homework, and so on. The point at this stage, though, is to concentrate on evidence of school attitude or the mental model of parents: To move staff to believing that parents want to be involved and want to support their students, the school needs first to uncover the ruling negative assumptions.

Consider using the principles of accountable talk to stay on task. These include:

- Citing specific examples from texts and artifacts
- Building on each other's ideas
- Asking questions such as
  - I wonder . . .
  - Can you help me understand that?
  - I agree and . . .
  - I disagree and . . .
  - Can you say more about that?
  - Who else has an opinion on this?
  - Does anyone have an alternative explanation?

The accuracy of your assessment may depend on whose input you include. Your school might risk asking parents how they believe the school welcomes them or meets their students' needs. Chevalier (2000) reported that such a survey revealed significant differences between teachers and parents:

Parents, for example, had much higher expectations for their children than their teachers did. Many teachers believed that parents didn't care much about schools or didn't want to get involved. But 98 to 99 percent of the parents wanted to be involved. They felt shut out.

One question asked: "Do you believe all children can learn?" Most of the parents said yes. Sixty-two of the teachers said no. That was eye-opening for me; I wouldn't want my own child in the class of a teacher who doesn't believe all kids can learn. That raised some issues in terms of staff development needs for our faculty. The most chilling part was that parents correctly understood the teachers' attitudes; they knew that many teachers did not expect their children to graduate. In all of our planning sessions, we had never considered this. (p. 492)

- Once you have sorted the information, generate as a group three or four statements that summarize how your school views parents, according to the evidence you just examined. Statements might include, "Parents' reading skills are too low for them to read aloud to their children," "Parents are too overwhelmed with making ends meet to come to school functions," "Parents don't trust us to educate their children," and so on.

2. Intuitive function:

- Work as a group to develop alternative explanations for parental actions than those given during the Sensing discussion described above. For example, Nuñez (1994) found that "poor [Latino] parent participation is often interpreted as lack of concern for the education of their children; however, those that do participate often perceive their activity as demeaning and insignificant" (p. 34).

3. Thinking function:

- Analyze the logical flow of interactions and results from the alternative explanations. Consider depicting the results in a decision-making tree chart, including what possible courses of action a school might take to determine which explanation is accurate. These courses of action might also be avenues for presenting evidence to staff that their assumptions, or mental models, are inaccurate. An example is given in Figure 9.1.

Figure 9.1   Parent Involvement Beliefs, Alternative Explanations, and Avenues to Changing School Beliefs

Current belief	Alternative Explanation	Possible New Avenue
Parents don't care enough to attend school events	Parents feel patronized	Review correspondence, meeting design, content and delivery for evidence
	Topic didn't meet needs	Solicit parent ideas for future sessions
	Language barriers aren't addressed	Include parent representatives in planning next session
	Parents are too busy dealing with basics of life: food, shelter, emotional stability	Work with support agencies to keep them informed, offer transportation. Provide written information.

(Continued)

(Continued)

4. Feeling function:

- Identify statements that capture the new narrative the school will develop regarding parents. These statements will describe both parents' motivations and their value to the school.
- Note that some leaders will want to skip right to this step. (Or if they can't find evidence to support what they believe the current view to be, it may reflect their own biases or stereotypes of teachers or parents.) However, without first identifying the current view and possible steps to take to overcome this view, participants may not understand the magnitude of change needed.

5. Develop at least two action steps: These will move the school toward the new vision. One of the action steps should be to determine how to include parents in conversations on parent involvement.

Use the ideas you generated in Step 4, taking into account which issues are of most concern in your school:

- Are different parent groups perceived in different ways? Are there conflicts between them?
- Are communication channels open? Do parents feel welcome in classrooms and meetings to which they are invited?
- Do parents and staff communicate about hopes and concerns for children? Chevalier (2000) asked parents, representatives from community organizations, law enforcement personnel, and key executives from a large local employer to develop survey questions to unearth common concerns. Their parent survey included questions such as "What kinds of support did they need for their children? What did they think about homework? What did they want for their children's futures? What were they afraid might happen to their kids?" (p. 491). Not only were the questions different from what the school would have generated, but the results were used by the other stakeholders. For example, the sheriff changed community-policing policies.

Inviting Parental Involvement

How opportunities for parental involvement are communicated is every bit as important as the actual opportunities available. Several studies have concluded that parents respond when schools invite them to be involved (Pena, 2000; Fields-Smith, 2005; Tam & Heng, 2005).

However, we've already seen ways that communications can go awry:

- **Differences in the information that Sensing types and Intuitive types need** (as shown in Chapter 5): For example, an Intuitive teacher might say, "More independent reading at home helps," speaking of children in general. The Sensing parent might hear, "Your child isn't reading independently enough," which may or may not be true.
- **Cultural differences:** For example, when one school held an African American Parent Day, some parents felt it was singling them out. Other

parents said they came specifically because they were singled out. Further, parents from other cultures had differing reactions, both favorable and negative.

- **Language differences:** Again, input from parents or students might be the best way to overcome these barriers.
- **Technology differences:** Most schools already use various means of communication—e-mail, paper announcements, phone calls, etc.—to account for different family circumstances and preferences.

A few universal suggestions can improve how families perceive invitations for involvement.

Be specific. General invitations to volunteer are not as effective as specific volunteer lists. With a general survey, we found that parents respond in one of four ways:

1. "Yes, here is what I will volunteer for." These parents use the form as intended.

2. "Call me when you need something." Many of these parents really will help out, but often schools don't have good mechanisms for following through.

3. "I can help with these kinds of events, so call me when needed." The faster the school can get these events on the parent's calendar, the better their actual response rate will be.

4. No response. They may not have time, they may be hesitant because of the barriers listed above, or they may not see things on the list they want to do.

If your school already has volunteer lists, consider how people with different type preferences might view the options. Just like students, teachers, and administrators, parents have personality preferences that influence the tasks they like and do well. Use Chart 9.2 to

- Evaluate whether your school offers a full range of appealing options.
- Consider how to recruit parents for certain roles by using some of the language in the chart to make a position or initiative appealing to them.
- If you've introduced type concepts to parents (see below, "Partnering with Parents to Help Their Children Succeed"), have them use the chart to identify possible volunteer positions that they'd find most meaningful.
- Help teachers understand the wide variety of ways in which parents might choose to volunteer.

Communicate often and in multiple ways. Even the best-planned communications can go astray—we've certainly missed events at our own children's schools because announcements were lost in the bottom of overflowing backpacks, accidentally erased from answering machines, omitted from an e-mail list—or transcribed incorrectly to our calendars. Lam (2004) reported that for his fourth-grade class

Chart 9.2   Typical Preferences in Volunteer Tasks

ISTJ	ISFJ	INFJ	INTJ
• Individual, behind-the-scenes, hands-on assignments or tasks • Administrative areas, especially organizational, financial, record keeping • Oversee or perform routine maintenance responsibilities	• Office administration, financial and other record keeping • Health issues—screening for hearing problems, etc. • Tutoring, one-on-one opportunities	• Direct, creative involvement in student learning—arts or science enrichment, small groups, etc. • Creating or advising school communication, student publications, etc. • Task forces focused on what could be	• Long-range planning and strategy development • Direct, creative involvement in student learning—arts or science enrichment, small groups, etc. • Research
ISTP	**ISFP**	**INFP**	**INTP**
• Student arts or crafts projects that use the parent's talents • Transportation, repairs, maintenance, technology, etc. • Hands-on, physical venues—camp, sports	• Child care • Craft and artistic endeavors • Teacher material preparation, repairs, organizing or administrative tasks	• One-on-one tutoring or coaching • Deep, solo work on a cause or vision they believe in • Involvement in efforts to fashion or uphold school or community values	• Conceptual and analytical projects • Long-range planning, strategy development • Research into new approaches or school strategies
ESTP	**ESFP**	**ENFP**	**ENTP**
• Activity-oriented programs, with any age group • Hands-on projects: production, construction • Efforts where people they know invited them to participate	• Tangible tasks: food preparation, transportation, child care, etc. • Greeting, visiting, serving people • Event planning for community-building celebrations or gatherings	• Networking among organizations/groups, especially those with a creative focus • Music, drama, public speaking, promoting • Leadership at the start of new efforts	• Networking among groups or organizations, especially those with a novel or global focus • Drama, music, public speaking • Marketing, fundraising
ESTJ	**ESFJ**	**ENFJ**	**ENTJ**
• Organizing people and community projects • Direct, tangible, need-related efforts • Financial management	• Management or administrative roles directly related to serving people or the community • Event planning—family oriented, social, or educational events • Organizing medical or social services—food shelves, day care, shelters, recovery groups, etc.	• Structuring projects or tasks to target major needs • Leadership, public speaking, or teaching for adults or children • Planning activities that provide a sense of harmony and fun	• Leadership, long-range planning, strategic alignment, visioning • Fundraising, legal or personnel matters, project evaluation, organizational development • Adult education

at a high-poverty school, the following communication efforts resulted in 22 of 26 families attending a session on helping their children prepare for the state literacy test, and 23 of 26 attend a similar session on the math literacy test:

> On Curriculum Night in October, when I lay out the classroom goals and general curricular themes, I mention the dates of the two upcoming high-stakes tests and explain that I will hold two family test preparation workshops—one in English language arts and one in math—to help ensure student success. I remind parents once again about the workshops during the November parent-teacher conferences. To help ensure high participation in the workshops, I send numerous reminder letters home and offer extra credit to students to encourage their attendance. Most important, I call every family a day or two before the workshop for final confirmation. (p. 45)

In the workshops, parents review work portfolios with their children, walk through the test format, watch as their children complete sample test questions, learn test strategies, and practice games they can play at home to improve skills. Whereas only three students had passed the math and reading tests the year before, 57 percent passed the reading test the year of the study, and 74 percent passed the math test. Over 80 percent of the class reported that their families had helped with homework in the weeks leading up to the test. Further, parents used test language in seeking help for their students, making comments like "Antonio is still having trouble with sequencing" (p. 46). In other words, not only did parents attend, but they increased knowledge they needed to help their students. And the students' results reflected that help—26 percent said that their parents were the biggest factor in their improved performance.

Other ways to communicate, including those listed by Lam, are

- Set firm dates for important events early in the year and send frequent reminders.
- Have teachers telephone parents.
- Consider extra credit for students when parents attend or RSVP.
- Hand out date reminders at conferences.
- Turn invitations into parent-child activities, such as deciphering a coded message or visiting a teacher's Web site to find a message.
- Have students prepare communications. These could be in their native language, take the form of party invitations, or be class-generated, David Letterman-like "Top 10 Reasons to Be There."

Partnering With Parents to Help Their Children Succeed

Schools have multiple opportunities to partner with parents to help students succeed. One way personality type can be used is to help parents understand very real differences between how they learn and how their child learns—parents and children seldom hold the same four preferences. Further, spouses often differ on preferences, leading to tug-of-wars over the "right" way to do homework, which class to take, or the best afterschool activity to pursue. Consider using type to help parents understand their child, navigate homework issues, and plan for productive conferences.

Understanding Type Differences. If students have learned about personality type (see Resource C), engage them in explaining their preferences to their parents. They might share the journal entries they've created, giving examples of how they determined which preferences best describe them. We've had students write letters to their parents—or to next year's teacher—explaining how they learn best.

Chart 9.3, Type Preferences and Learning Styles, may help parents think through how they and their children are the same and different.

For one-on-one conferences when students are struggling academically, Chart 9.4 can be used to help parents consider different approaches to helping their child. To use the chart, consider which preference pair might be causing difficulties.

Homework Success

Note that many of the conflicts above help parents deal with homework dilemmas. Specifically, schools might help

- Extraverted parents understand why interruptions cause frustrations for their Introverted child
- Introverted parents understand why their Extraverted child is on the phone while doing homework
- Sensing parents understand why their Intuitive child balks at structured assignments
- Intuitive parents understand why their Sensing child seems to lack imagination or their definition of creativity
- Thinking parents understand why their Feeling child is upset when they provide suggestions for improving projects or assignments
- Feeling parents understand why their Thinking child balks at new challenges
- Perceiving parents understand why their Judging child resents any changes in schedules that interfere with homework plans
- Judging parents understand why their Perceiving child needs different strategies, such as planning backward, to succeed

However, when some parents come to understand how their children learn best, they may still struggle to see how to provide help at home. Ideally, homework avoids situations where students are learning new skills; instead, students are applying skills they have been taught, practiced in class, and are

Chart 9.3 Type Preferences and Learning Styles

Extraversion	Introversion
• Talks to think things through • Likes to work in groups • Wants to experience something before hearing the theory • Gets ideas from what's happening in the world • Would rather speak or demonstrate than read or write	• Needs quiet to think things through • Likes to work alone or with a student they know well • More interested in theory than trying things out • Gets ideas from inner thoughts • Would rather read or write than speak
Sensing	**Intuition**
• Likes to work with facts, concrete things • Wants a practical reason for assignments • Pays attention to the details, specifics • Wants to know exactly what's expected in an assignment • Likes to finish one project, then start another	• Likes to work with imagination, hunches, symbols • Likes to explore possibilities for change • Pays attention to the "big picture," general concepts • Seeks freedom to learn • Likes to have a number of projects underway
Thinking	**Feeling**
• Likes to ask and answer, "Why?" • Likes to solve problems, look at data • Wants feedback that shows specific achievement • Responds best when things are logical, clear • Wants to be competent, in charge	• Looks for ways to give personal meaning to assignments • Likes assignments where others are helped • Responds best to personal encouragement, validation • Needs warm, friendly classrooms • Seeks harmony when working with others
Judging	**Perceiving**
• Plans and organizes to meet deadlines • Prefers clear goals • Seeks to complete tasks • Does best work when things are predictable, orderly • Likes milestones, completion points	• Energized at last minute before a deadline • Likes to follow curiosity, define task as it goes along • Resists completing a task if there is more to explore • Works best when it feels like play • Works best when a genuine choice in assignments is given

Chart 9.4   Type Preferences and Student Needs

Type Preference	Explanation/Suggestion
Extraversion: Parents and teachers may worry if these students • Chat, move about, have TV or radio on during study time • Seldom read for pleasure • Answer back	• The preference describes how people get their energy—these students need action or interaction to have the energy to do schoolwork. • Reading is an Introverted activity. Parent and child might sit together, reading silently. Offer sources for high-interest reading materials. • Extraverts say what they're thinking. Ask, "Is that what you meant to say?" giving a second chance before assuming the worst.
Introversion: Parents and teachers may worry if these students • Respond slowly to questions • Withdraw or play alone • Refrain from giving opinions or sharing feelings	• Introverted students need more wait time. Count to at least 10 before expecting an answer. • Explain that Introverts need alone time to build up energy; school is draining for them. Parents might ask the child how much downtime he or she would like after school. • Introverts often don't share unless asked directly. Allow them time to think through their feelings before having to respond.
Sensing: Parents and teachers may worry about these students if they • Ask too many questions, seeming insecure about learning or inattentive to directions • Pick up concepts slowly • Complain that they'll never use what they're learning	• Sensing students want information sequentially and prefer not to proceed until directions are clear. • Sensing types learn step-by-step, through practice. Find ways to provide immediate feedback to build confidence. • Help make valid, real-world connections.
Intuition: Parents and teachers may worry about these students if they • Lose things, forget details • Rush through skills practice, perform poorly • Fail to follow directions	• Intuitive children may not be aware of physical details, such as whether they wore a jacket to school. Provide routines or reminders. • Intuitive children lose interest in repetitive tasks. Find ways to add variety when they need to practice. • Intuitive students are drawn to ideas, not directions. Write down directions they need to follow.

Type Preference	Explanation/Suggestion
Thinking: Parents and teachers may worry about these students if they • Complain or argue • Shut down, claiming a task is stupid instead of trying, or are overly competitive • Are insensitive	 • Thinking students see the flaw first and enjoy debate. Don't engage if rules are firm. • Thinking students need to show competency and avoid chances for publicly falling short. Offer private chances to build skills. Channel competition into beating personal bests. • Thinking students may not be aware of impact on others. Get them involved in solutions ("What's your plan for fixing this?")
Feeling: Parents and teachers may worry about these students if they • Are disinterested in math or science • Seek too much personal feedback • Shut down at any constructive criticism	 • Feeling students prefer subjects involving people or relationships. Help them find a friend to study with, or relate the subjects to helping others. • Feeling types need to know they are liked. Help them learn to judge their own work through comparing it to good examples or rubrics • Feeling types often see criticism as evidence that someone dislikes them. Start with the positive.
Judging: Parents and teachers worry about these students if they • Rush through work in order to be done • Work until overly exhausted, holding themselves to strict goals or expectations • React negatively to surprises or schedule changes	 • Judging types find pleasure in finishing. Help them understand quality expectations from the beginning. • Judging types put work before play. Help them avoid overcommitment. • Judging types like certainty. Help them form reasonable expectations—schedules do change!
Perceiving: Parents and teachers worry about these students if they • Take a last-minute approach to assignments • Create crises by not planning ahead for trips to libraries, purchasing supplies, etc. • Work without seeming to accomplish anything	 • Perceiving students often need pressure to become motivated. Help them plan backward to ensure projects will be finished. When do they *really* need to start? • Perceiving students don't naturally plan. To avoid family crises, keep a supply of poster board, glue, report covers, etc. on hand. Or ask for teacher communication. • Perceiving students get caught up in process. Help them set minideadlines, such as showing three completed problems five minutes from now.

now extending at home. Support for learning the skills happens in the class-rooms. Even with practice homework, though, Lapp and Flood (2004) reported

> Many parents pleaded for homework to be done at school, either within the classroom or in homework study clubs after school. They explained that their homes were often not conducive to doing homework because of large numbers of people in a small environment. They simply did not have the resources to provide a quiet place for their children to perform the tasks that the homework required. Furthermore, they stated that they did not feel equipped to help their children with the homework that the teacher required. (p. 69)

Clearly, then, schools need to think about the needs of students with all preferences. Do they have what they need to complete the homework? Beyond the environmental needs described above, consider the following:

- How do Sensing students get their questions answered? How can Thinking students be assured that their results are correct?
  - Are clear examples, rubrics, answer keys, Web sites, or phone numbers for help and other explicit information provided? Are expectations clear?
  - Do they have time while still at school to begin the homework to see if they have questions?
- Is homework meaningful for Intuitive students?
  - Does homework go beyond practice problems, or are there choices of which problems to do?
  - Are there options for creativity?
- Are there avenues for Feeling students to get personal help?
  - If different teachers run homework centers each day, how do they build relationships with students?
  - Do teachers have strategies for praising Feeling students even when they're struggling ("You are working so hard at this, aren't you?" "It is so easy to help you because I can read your handwriting," "Look, you've figured out the first part," or "I bet you'll be ready to read this to your sister tonight.")
- Is additional time provided without penalty for students to finish class work?

While students can't expect to have their learning style needs met at all times, the above questions are designed to build support nets where it counts most—during homework, when students are to be working independently. What better way to build confidence than to work to ensure that they have what they need to complete the assigned tasks?

Mediating Between Parents and School Staff When Conflicts Arise

Parents want schools to care as much about their children as they do. However, their actions may not be perceived that way, especially if schools hold a deficit or in loco parentis view of parents. Johnye Ballenger, who works as a pediatrician at a community clinic in Boston, described her role in helping other staff members deal with parents:

> I was able . . . to sort of mediate the explosions of affect and anger that tended to be read as threatening and inappropriate by the professionals. . . . I have never met a parent who was mean, evil or didn't care about her child. Maybe they don't parent very well, but they do love their kids . . . all of them do . . . and I've known lots of parents as young as thirteen and as old as in their fifties . . . and they generally do the best they can with the resources they have. (Lawrence-Lightfoot, 2000, p. 81)

Many parents did not have positive experiences in schools themselves—they were judged as behavior problems or written off academically. They may believe the same thing is happening to their own child when behavior or academic problems arise. The best way to begin in conflict situations is with statements that show the parent you share the same goal: school success for the child. As one principal called parents to inform them of their student not doing class work or making a poor behavior choice, she always began with, "I know your child is capable of doing great work and making better decisions because I've seen it happen. Today, however, they made a poor choice [or they let up on effort.]" When the principal starts with the positive (not fluffy feedback but detailed information on actual observations of good work), the parent unites with her on solving the problem.

While many principles for conflict resolution are universal, as we saw in Chapter 5, people with different type preferences actually differ in what they consider conflict, how they react, and how they deal with it. In truth, you can only control your own behavior, although you can do your best to meet the needs of people with different preferences.

Chapter 8 describes a process for working through disciplinary incidents with students; this process can also be used during parent meetings.

When parent meetings are about academic concerns, Chart 9.5, Communication Styles and Interacting With Parents, can help you think through whether your processes take into account the needs of the different preferences. Do parents get the information they need about their students? Is it delivered in a way that addresses their particular interests and concerns?

Conferences

As important as conferences are to parents' involvement in their children's education, time is always a factor.

Chart 9.5   Communication Styles and Interacting With Parents

Sensing and Thinking types (ST) tend to focus on	**Remember to include**
• Facts—grades, test scores, rules, adherence to policies • Weaknesses—where the child needs to improve • Logic—"If your child would ___ then___."	• Values—is the student caring, funny, conscientious, etc.? • What strengths can the student build on? Where is progress being made? • Parent input—"What motivates or interests your child?"
Sensing and Feeling types (SF) tend to focus on	**Remember to include**
• Facts—details about organization, neatness, grades • The child's contribution to classroom harmony • Values—how the child exhibits values in the classroom	• Future potential—evidence of creativity, leadership, special interests • Where the child benefits from competitive attitudes, even if it's competing for personal bests • Strengths—how this child excels compared to peers
Intuitive and Feeling types (NF) tend to focus on	**Remember to include**
• The potential they see in the child • Samples of creative work that demonstrate the child's unique talents • All-class creative efforts for conferences	• Proficiencies—parents want evidence of math facts, reading improvement, etc. • Evidence of progress toward standards • Portfolio of individual work
Intuitive and Thinking types (NT) tend to focus on	**Remember to include**
• Systems—grading, homework, instructional theories, curriculum • Data—grades, test scores • Concerns and solutions	• The child—personal effort, interests, and successes • Stories of their child in the classroom that show student achievement • Future potential and ways to involve the parent

All parents can react negatively to anything concerning their own child; both Thinking and Feeling parents may be angry with a school when their child isn't doing well. Type theory, though, would predict that Thinking parents, naturally inclined to critique first, might be more likely to criticize their child when the student is present. Certain procedures can help minimize that anger *and* protect the child.

Set up the rules of the conference from the start. Appeal to their need for fairness, order, and logic. *Act confident.* If they start to criticize the school or the student, try some statements (designed to appeal to logic, fairness, and problem solving), such as:

- I'm here to look for solutions with you.
- Here's what's worked before in similar cases [I'd like to present what we've tried . . .].
- When [the student's] done, let's brainstorm some possibilities for that.
- With all due respect, we're here to . . .
- What's the fair/logical way to address this?
- I understand your viewpoint, but we're going to hear from both sides.

The other extreme is parents who are too soft on their children—who don't share the school's high expectations for behavior or academics. Often, they point to home situations, the child's busy schedule, or other excuses. They may even admit they're worn down and not willing to press the child. In this case, an administrator might appeal to the facts:

- The standards the child is expected to learn—the same as every other child in the class
- The school's view of the connection between effort, ability, and achievement
- The ways the school is supporting effort-based ability
- Goals for this student
- A contract with the parent and student for meeting those goals.

Again, the Problem-Solving Model (Resource B) may be the best approach to discussion from the school's standpoint. Parents who do not trust the school, though, may view it as a mechanism to control them. Using it implicitly is often more productive:

- Make sure everyone is clear on the facts, including your school's belief in the child's ability to learn and what has been tried (Sensing)
- List possibilities, including soliciting ideas from the parents (Intuition)
- Discuss the pros, cons, and workability of the various ideas (Thinking)
- Check for buy-in. Does it fit within school parameters? Can the parents uphold their part? Does the child agree to put forth his or her best effort in trying the ideas? Are resources available to monitor or enact the plan? (Feeling)

Chapter Summary

Using type as a model to look at parental involvement allows schools to

- Examine the facts (Sensing) about their parents
- Develop alternative explanations for parent behaviors or involvement levels; develop ideas for parental involvement (Intuition)
- Analyze events, such as open houses, including logistics and outcomes (Thinking)
- Seek out the personal stories of each family (Feeling).

Using type as a framework also helps schools work with parents in other ways. The framework informs us for what tasks parents will readily volunteer, given their personality preferences. This understanding compels staff to think and provide multiple points of access to the school community. In addition, type cues leaders to parental concerns via the kinds of things they communicate to teachers or administrators. Finally, school leaders can help parents increase their understanding of how their student learns, "normalizing" differences between parents and their children.

Reflection

- What one step could you take immediately to increase parent involvement in activities that affect student achievement? With whom could you partner in taking that step?
- Most of the suggestions in this chapter may fit in with your school's current practices. Review your practices, though, with type in mind. Are any steps missing or being slighted?
- Recall a recent interaction with a parent that didn't go well. What might the parent have needed that he or she didn't receive?

10

Strategies for Coping With the Stress of School Leadership

There are many problems for these teachers which arise from the intensification of their work. They are harassed by the burdens of time with insufficient time to complete all of their work tasks in ways that give satisfaction. They have to cut corners in their work by doing essential things first, including a host of administrative and other non-teaching duties, at the expense of creative work like lesson preparation. . . . They become socially and professionally isolated as a result of lack of time and opportunity for relaxed interaction with work peers. . . . They face a host of emotional and physical symptoms of stress, including anxiety, guilt and constant tiredness from the persistent presence of unmet needs in their working lives. (Smyth et al., 2000, p. 144)

Jane, whose preferences are Introversion, Intuition, Feeling, and Judging (INFJ), was planning team-building sessions for an organization when a colleague e-mailed her, "Who should we bring in to cover the team building? Who has the expertise?" When Jane responded that she had the expertise, the colleague reiterated that they needed outside help. The response, and the other suggestions it included, kept Jane awake for hours. Did the colleague not understand her background in management interventions? Or view her as a know-it-all? Finally Jane got up, headed to her computer, and spent three hours crafting a short response. The colleague promptly called with an apology, they resolved the misunderstanding, and Jane continued her planning for the intervention.

Here's a description of what stresses INFJs:

> You experience stress when it appears to you that no one is listening to your foresights. You take your unique and intuitive abilities seriously and when others are inattentive and/or dismissive, you can experience significant degrees of tension and anxiety. In such situations, you perceive your very authenticity as being brought into question and cast in doubt. With a keen focus on possibilities coupled with trusting your intuitions, you can become deeply disillusioned whenever an organizational environment doesn't support your vision. (Berens et al., 2001, p. 33)

That description accurately captures exactly why Jane lost so much sleep over what many other people would have resolved with a quick phone call or stated course of action.

Who You Are Is How You're Stressed

Type theory describes definite patterns in what creates and heightens stress in people with different personality preferences. Think about it:

- Type describes natural preferences for what we do well. Stress is heightened when, as in Jane's case above, others ignore or deny what we see as our core selves.
- We develop skills with the other preferences, but they always remain less developed than our natural preferences—we use more energy when operating out of our preferences, a guaranteed cause of stress.
- As described in Chapter 2, one preference function is our *dominant* function (Sensing, Intuition, Thinking, or Feeling), our best path for motivation and success. In Chart 2.1, the dominant function, denoted by *D*, is listed first under the four-letter type code, as highlighted in Picture 10.1 for ISTJ.
- The opposite function, labeled *I* for each type as shown in Chart 2.1, is the inferior function, the one that develops last and is hardest to use. In Picture 10.1, the inferior function for ISTJ is Intuition.
  - Dominant Sensing types struggle with Intuition—brainstorming and imagining future possibilities.
  - Dominant Intuitive types struggle with Sensing—details and describing present reality.
  - Dominant Thinking types struggle with Feeling—stepping into the shoes of others.
  - Dominant Feeling types struggle with Thinking—being logical, objective.

Picture 10.1   Order of Function Development for ISTJ
ISTJ
D: Sensing
A: Thinking
T: Feeling
I: Intuition

Refer to your type in Chart 2.1. Isn't using the function labeled *I* stressful for you? And if we're already stressed by conflict, deadlines, work overload, family situations, illness, fatigue, or any of a host of other stressors, being called on to use that inferior function can just about send us out of control.

Quenk (1993) described what happens under extreme stress as "in the grip" experiences. We actually become trapped in our inferior function, lose our sense of humor, find ourselves making all-or-none statements, and view reality with tunnel vision, ignoring vital information in our temporarily narrowed perspective.

Few professions offer as many opportunities for stress as school leadership. Remember that the overall culture of school administration is Thinking and Judging; 70 percent of school principals share those preferences. And in general, TJs can get over most conflict with a good night's sleep. *If your preferences are not Thinking and Judging, the inherent structure of the job may be more stressful for you than for your colleagues.* Their views of success, competency, and conflict may differ considerably from your own.

For example, compare how Thinking and Feeling types deal with angry parents. If a parent is angry or confrontational, Thinking and Feeling school leaders usually can rely on their training in conflict resolution to deescalate the problem, but what happens afterward?

- Educators with a preference for Thinking often report that after a quick reflection on whether they followed proper procedures (Thinking/Perceiving) or brought things to a logical closure (Thinking/Judging), they put the problem aside. If they've done their best, they can get over things with a good night's sleep.
- Educators with a preference for Feeling often replay the events in their mind, wondering if they handled things correctly, how angry the other party might still be, and what the future fallout might entail, thus often staying emotionally involved with the conflict for quite some time.

Thus while *all* of us are stressed by illness, change, conflict, overwork, etc., what makes the situation even worse varies from person to person. Educational leadership in schools or districts is stressful due to the complexity of the job and the wide number of constituencies. In this chapter, we'll examine what heightens stress for each personality type, strategies for decreasing stress, and how to get "out of the grip" when circumstances are overwhelming.

Day-to-Day Ways to Cope

For many of us, day-to-day reality means operating out of our preferences. Perhaps it's the demands of your job, or maybe you're "odd type out" at work. The following suggestions might provide help in those circumstances.

If you're an Extravert in an Introverted world . . .

- School leadership can be isolating. Make sure you find a confidante or mentor outside of your school district with whom you can safely talk through issues and frustrations.
- When possible, find a partner for solo tasks such as budgeting or data review.

- Don't let the urgent—phone calls, e-mails, unexpected paperwork details—trap you in your office too much. You thrive on being out and about, interacting with staff and students. Set a goal of being in classrooms each day. Design opportunities to meet with students, such as having a Principal Advisory group, meeting with various focus groups, or leading an extracurricular activity.
- If your leadership team is mostly Introverted, give them your new idea and set a time for getting feedback. Ask again if you don't hear from them.

If you're an Introvert in an Extraverted world . . .

- Your job is most likely fraught with interruptions, naturally frustrating for Introverts. Arrive early to accomplish must-dos without interruptions, but find ways to leave on time.
- Take the long way home. Avoid cell phone conversations at all costs and instead listen to favorite music or an escapist audio book so you have some energy when you arrive.
- Identify at least three ways to get 15 minutes of downtime when high demands for interaction drain you of energy. Ask your support staff or assistant to handle student discipline matters for a quarter of an hour while you recharge. Quietly observe the classroom of an Introverted teacher, where the relative quiet will be relaxing. If all else fails, retreat to the restroom.
- Reserve the right to respond to requests or ideas later—but state when you'll be ready to share your opinion.

If you're a Sensing type in an Intuitive world . . .

- Find a metaphor or analogy that describes a dilemma you face at work. What new insights does such thinking provide?
- Engage in a tangible project when strategic planning or generating options becomes frustrating—read to a class, make your own copies, scrub a few desks, or decorate a bulletin board to accomplish one tangible task.
- Work with an Intuitive to think out five years and escape the moment. What do you want your school to be like? Where do you want to be?
- Encourage your team to use the Problem-Solving Model (Resource B) so that discussions and decisions are grounded in factual reality.

If you're an Intuitive type in a Sensing world . . .

- Find at least one regular outlet for creativity. Write humor pieces for the staff newsletter. Help a teacher generate new lesson plans. Devise unusual treats for team meetings. Find creative outlets after work. Anything.
- On communications of importance, run a draft of your details and procedures by someone else, preferably someone who has developed skills with recognizing whether the Sensing need for detail is satisfied.
- Before suggesting a change, reflect on current traditions and what aspects of the status quo are working well.
- Keep a copy of the Problem-Solving Model, Chart B.1, in front of you to anticipate your colleagues' concerns with your ideas.

If you're a Thinking type in a Feeling world . . .

- Identify at least three logical or objective tasks in which you can engage when frustrated by the emotional outbursts or needs of others. You might save data analysis, critiquing curriculum, scheduling, or reviewing action plans for such occasions.
- Practice emphasizing points of agreement before offering counterarguments.
- Remember that the culture of most elementary schools is Feeling. Start with the positive, find ways to recognize individual contributions and strengths, and spend time on activities that build community.
- Find a confidante or mentor outside of the district with whom you can share your frustrations regarding the illogical behavior of the adults in your building.

If you're a Feeling type in a Thinking world . . .

- Remember, those around you may not value how others feel. Be logical in how you champion the values and needs of various stakeholders: "If we take that position, then students could very well . . .", "You're setting a precedent for . . .", or "You'll please those parents. But have you considered. . . ."
- Consider finding a kindred spirit at work who can voice privately to you what you are doing well; you might not hear much from others! Use the critiques from everyone else to improve your professionalism.
- Use logic to set boundaries. Devise an objective framework to determine the responsibilities you'll undertake. Determine criteria: available time, whether it serves your top values or mission, whether others would benefit from carrying it out if you say no, etc.
- "Office politics" is usually not a forte for Feeling types, who tend to forget that not everyone values harmony. Find an objective person to serve as a sounding board. What motivations, not in your best interest, could others have? How can you minimize the risk of being backstabbed?

If you're a Judging type in a Perceiving world . . .

- Grab solo assignments or projects where you can control the project and, therefore, meet the deadline without undue stress from waiting for others to complete their tasks.
- Practice voicing alternatives instead of your first choice, even if you've already evaluated which option is best.
- Negotiate in advance how others will make your deadline. Help them plan backward. For example, if a grant is due October 1 and you need input from colleagues, make it clear that their deadline is September 15 to give you time to write. What else is on their calendars that might prevent them from meeting that deadline? Do they need to meet with you on September 7 to clarify needs? Do they need to be done before school starts?
- If others arrive late for meetings, lower your frustration by planning for it. Bring a book to read or e-mails to answer. If you're in charge, start with

important topics so there is incentive to arrive on time (often, people assume you'll wait until everyone is there) and have someone record important information on a whiteboard for late arrivals to copy.

If you're a Perceiving type in a Judging world . . .

- Plan backward anytime that someone else is depending on you and will be stressed if you miss a deadline. Get advice on how long the task will take. Sit down with your calendar and determine when you realistically need to start, accounting for other meetings, family commitments, and other deadlines.
- Take responsibility for areas where the process is just as important as the outcome, such as working with the student council or increasing family involvement.
- Set "false deadlines." Commit to meeting with someone two days early to discuss your written draft of a new policy. Practice giving a presentation to your leadership team the week before you're presenting to the school board.
- Schedule at least a half hour between meetings; they always run over. Avoid the temptation to return just one phone call or glance through your correspondence when you've "got at least five minutes."

When Events Spiral Down . . .

We can't avoid stress completely, especially as school leaders. By recognizing what stresses us the most and making room for activities that bring some rest *before* we explode, we can work to minimize the worst episodes. Carl Jung, the Swiss psychiatrist who was one of the originators of type theory, wrote about the inferior function:

> And it is a fact that it has the strongest tendency to be infantile, banal, primitive and archaic. Anybody who has a high opinion of himself will do well to guard against letting it make a fool of him. (1969, p. 165)

However, "grip" experiences happen, by definition, because we lose control. Sometimes, no matter how hard we try, we get caught in a downward spiral of emotions, doom and gloom, and self-pity. Even as we speak or act, we're thinking, "This isn't me. What's wrong?" We're caught in the grip of our inferior function—not only did we get up on the wrong side of the bed, but we fell right through a hole in the floor.

- Dominant Sensing types (ESTP, ESFP, ISTJ, ISFJ) spiral into negative visions of the future—they'll be transferred to the worst school in the state, or the "wrong" parent will file a lawsuit—as their inferior Intuitive function grips their minds.
- Dominant Intuitive types (ENFP, ENTP, INFJ, INTJ) suddenly find only misery—they're sure they have an incurable disease, they exercise or eat excessively, or find they can't eat a thing—as reality becomes their enemy in the grip of their inferior Sensing function.

- Dominant Thinking types (ESTJ, ENTJ, ISTP, INTP) are sure everyone hates them or they are solely at fault, and they may uncharacteristically give into displays of emotions as their inferior Feeling function takes control.
- Dominant Feeling types (ESFJ, ENFJ, ISFP, INFP) find criticism and bossiness coming out of their mouths, or they use faulty logic to come to paralyzing conclusions. They refuse to listen to others when their inferior Thinking function rules their behavior.

These behaviors aren't pathological but are instead predictable patterns under stress. They are, however, undesirable. Jung (1966) clarified:

To have overwhelming emotions is not in itself pathological, it is merely undesirable. We need not invent such a word as *pathological* for an undesirable thing, because there are other undesirable things in the world which are not pathological, for instance, tax collectors. (p. 24)

However, leaders who assume they can stay under control may not pay enough attention to growing levels of stress. For example, an Intuitive school leader, who prided herself on emotional control and long-range thinking, didn't acknowledge her growing frustration with the school board—until in the midst of a meeting, her inferior Sensing function erupted and she laid out the facts that proved their incompetence on a decision. She never regained their trust. Note that *dominant* Sensing types are skilled in using that function—they would only have shared *appropriate* facts. The dominant Intuitive experienced how our inferior function can make fools of us.

Interestingly, though, the inferior function is often our best path for getting "out of the grip." Why? Because using it gives our dominant function a chance to rest and recover. Think about it practically:

- You can't see the trees (Sensing) and the forest (Intuition) at the same time.
- You can't be objective (Thinking) and subjective (Feeling) at the same time.

Therefore, using the inferior function actually shuts down the dominant function.

For example, an Intuitive and Feeling assistant principal was charged with practically hand-scheduling 900 middle-schoolers; the technology system had so many bugs in it that the automated processes were of minimal help. Further, server problems caused two-day delays in getting feedback. She presented her frustrations to the district superintendent, who nodded and said, "But why was the process so late?" not having heard a word of her concerns. Her direct supervisor told her, "No one at the district cares about how you *feel* about what happened. They want the facts."

Note that the hand scheduling used this administrator's *inferior* function, Sensing. What would have been stressful anyway because of the problems became a nightmare as she overused her weakest function. The strangest thing, though, about our inferior function is that while it can cause stress, we can also use it *to get out of the grip.*

In this case, the next year brought the same problems; the technology system was still full of bugs. The assistant principal, though, kept track of the *facts* of every delay—why, how long, which equipment broke down, time between system communications, the amount of time the server was down, and so on. When she again spoke with the superintendent, this time armed with facts instead of feelings, the superintendent listened and heard. To paraphrase his response, "Well, why didn't you say there was a problem?"

Thus, she not only communicated in terms that the superintendent understood but also focused on Sensing—the details kept her out of the grip.

Grip experiences actually have two root causes: overusing our dominant *or* inferior functions. Think of using these as an exercise in lifting weights. If you're used to bench-pressing 200 pounds, just as your strengths lie with your dominant function, you can still injure yourself if you try lifting 300 pounds. Similarly, there comes a point where you can overuse your dominant function and lose perspective. At the other extreme, using the inferior function is similar to those first days at the gym—without careful concentration and technique, it is easy to cause injury, just as we struggle to use our inferior function well without skills and techniques. Too much weight—or too much of the inferior function—will quickly cause stress.

Table 10.1, Sources of Stress for Each Type, summarizes the most stressful circumstances or activities for each type.

Charts 10.1–10.8 provide more detailed information on stress for the extraverted and introverted forms of each dominant function, what triggers "grip" experiences, and pathways out. Note that these pages pair off the 16 personality types. If you examine Chart 2.1, you'll see that two Extraverted types have Sensing listed as the dominant function, ESTP and ESFP—these are the Extraverted Sensing types. Similarly, look at INFJ and INTJ; both have Intuition listed as the dominant function and are the Introverted Intuitive types. The paired functions also share the same inferior, since it is opposite their dominant; for example, ESTP and ESFP share Intuition as their inferior while INFJ and INTJ share Sensing.

Activity 10.1
Helping Teachers Deal With Stress

Acknowledge to your teaching staff that their lives are stressful. The best description we've heard of being an elementary teacher is, "It's like holding a birthday party for your eight-year-old, only there's 30 of them, with no other adult helpers. And they stay for six hours. And come back for 180 days straight."

The following exercise may help your staff find ways to deal with stress if they already know their personality types:

- Table 10.1 contains a summary of what causes stress in each of the 16 types. Use this as an opening handout so that teachers understand that while all types are stressed by overwork, illness, conflict, and so on, different extenuating circumstances make it even worse for each type.
- Get teachers into type-alike groups by the eight dominant functions:
  o Extraverted Sensing (ESTP and ESFP)
  o Introverted Sensing (ISTJ and ISFJ)

o Extraverted Intuition (ENTP and ENFP)
o Introverted Intuition (INTJ and INFJ)
o Extraverted Thinking (ESTJ and ENTJ)
o Introverted Thinking (ISTP and INTP)
o Extraverted Feeling (ESFJ and ENFJ)
o Introverted Feeling (ISFP and INFP)

Provide them with the chart (pages 159–166) for their dominant function. Ask them to read the information silently and quick-write about the following two questions:

1. Does this information bring to mind any specific times when I felt out of control or "in the grip?" Are there any stories I would feel comfortable sharing with my colleagues? For example, sharing a stressful incident from college might be safer than sharing one from work.

2. Do the suggested pathways to relieve stress bring to mind other activities or techniques that work for me? What might I share with the group?

- After about five minutes of reflection/writing time, let them process in their small groups and brainstorm how, both in and out of school, they can use the suggested strategies. What do they already do? What adjustments might they make?

Chapter Summary

Type theory describes definite patterns in what creates and heightens stress in people with different personality preferences. By understanding one's behavior, one is more adept at identifying stressful situations and responding to them. The job of school leadership is complex—multiple demands, constituencies, interests, and surprises. Each of us responds in different ways to perceived stress. The chapter provides concrete information to help school leaders understand what situations or events can trigger heightened stress for people with their personality preferences *and* strategies for coping. This information is key for avoiding exhaustion, emotional outbursts, and the harmful physical toll of stress.

Reflection

- Reflect on any policies or procedures that your staff complains about regularly. Do these produce undue stress for teachers with particular preferences?
- Think back through an experience when you felt out of control. Do the type concepts presented in this chapter provide any insights into why that particular set of circumstances was so stressful? What might you do next time in a similar situation?
- Reflect on a teacher who seems to be experiencing unusual levels of stress. While it is never a good idea to tell someone, "You seem to be in the grip of your inferior function," do the person's personality preferences suggest any particular reasons for stress? Could that type information provide you with strategies for helping the person? Ways to prevent a clash?
- How might you use this information with students? For example, could parts of it be used with seniors as they work through the college search process?

Table 10.1   Sources of Stress for Each Type (Hirsh & Kise, 2006a)

ISTJ	ISFJ	INFJ	INTJ
• Uncertainty, changes without clear logic or support • When something goes wrong despite tremendous effort • Not being respected for hard work • When others ignore reality	• Changes imposed without clear direction • Overextending in service to others • When others ignore traditions or common sense • When their efforts are unappreciated	• Crises with no time for reflection • Extensive attention to details • Cynicism, conflict from others • When their ideas are ignored or change proceeds without their input	• Change without sufficient planning • Lack of autonomy • Planning carefully yet getting poor results because of outside factors • Feeling they've lost control of an event or situation

ISTP	ISFP	INFP	INTP
• Changes not grounded in logic • Imposed rules, lack of autonomy • Too little introverted time • Emotional outbursts	• Disharmony, values conflicts • Rules or policies that don't take into account individual differences • Lack of concrete direction during change • Being pressured to make decisions quickly	• Conflicts over values • Injustices • When personal expression is discouraged or concerns are dismissed • Lack of time to explore ideas or alternatives	• When others doubt their competency • Emotional outbursts • Lack of autonomy • Changes without clear logic or rationale

ESTP	ESFP	ENFP	ENTP
• Long-range planning • Too many restrictions or rules • Changes that jettison what clearly works • Being rushed to make decisions	• Critique without support • Speculation, planning without concrete parameters • Not having resources to meet expectations • When relationships are threatened	• Details, procedures, structures • Changes that threaten relationships • Overextending themselves • Lack of options	• Paperwork, details, routines • Restrictions: procedures, mandates, rules • Dilemmas without options • When others misjudge them or question their competency

ESTJ	ESFJ	ENFJ	ENTJ
• Changes that go against their principles • When careful planning doesn't bring results • Dealing with emotions • Not being recognized for competency	• Being caught in the middle of disputes • Changes that seem to compromise values • Lack of emotional support • When personal strengths and contributions aren't recognized	• Failed relationships • Negative atmospheres • When values are ignored • When they believe conflict or failure is their fault	• Feeling powerless or being ignored • Bureaucracies, paperwork, procedures • Inefficiencies or illogical changes • Being accused of treating people as objects

Chart 10.1: Stress and the Extraverted Sensing Types (ESTP and ESFP)

When life is going right, Extraverted Sensing types are fully engaged in the present, encouraging the rest of us to make the most of each day. They're positive, fun loving, and full of energy.

The following circumstances increase stress for ESTPs and ESFPs:

- They're forced to overuse Intuition, for instance by having to do too much strategic planning or speculating more than a year into the future, especially if district leadership or others are forcing quick decisions.
- Illness, disabilities, or damaged relationships make the present moment lose its joy.
- Circumstances impose too much structure. This could be a continuous stream of doctor's appointments, tight deadlines, or agendas and schedules over which they have no say.

Often as circumstances overwhelm them, the Extraverted Sensing types bury themselves in a flurry of activity to deal with the stress. If their inferior function, Intuition, takes over, everything becomes negative. Symptoms of a true "grip" experience include:

- Withdrawal, pondering disastrous visions of the future ("I'll lose my job," or "I'll lose all my friends.")
- Neglecting to engage in their favorite activities
- Hypersensitivity and misery

Pathways that help ESTPs and ESFPs regain control allow for the productive use of Intuition. Following are some suggestions:

- Ponder the worst that can happen. Develop a contingency plan to deal with that. Often this concrete view of the future cuts off the negative thinking.
- Plan something you can control and would enjoy. Redecorate your bathroom or plan for new garage shelving. Explore a graduate school program for yourself or schooling options for your child. Pick up vacation brochures and dream of a weekend at a restful place.
- Find a creative outlet—woodworking, poetry, reading science fiction (no reality there!), artistic painting (not window trim), or anything else that uses your imagination.

Chart 10.2: Stress and the Introverted Sensing Types (ISTJ, ISFJ)

When life is going right, Introverted Sensing types are organized and disciplined. They remind others of the worth of time-tested traditions and are acutely aware of the moment. The following circumstances increase stress for ISTJs and ISFJs:

- Normal routines and schedules are disrupted, or they can't use the methods or curriculum they know will work.
- They're asked to create something entirely new, and little specific guidance is given or available—especially if the changes defy common sense or no one explains why the new will be better than the status quo (as often happens with curriculum changes or new school initiatives).
- Present circumstances point to an unpleasant future, such as when events seem out of their control, others aren't being practical about costs and time frames, or others offer nonspecific suggestions.

Often as circumstances overwhelm them, the ISTJs and ISFJs put their noses to the grindstone, as if sheer effort will prevail, doing more and more of what isn't working. Symptoms of a true "grip" experience include

- Uncharacteristic trouble with handling details
- Impulsive behaviors
- Excessive worrying about the future

Pathways that help ISTJs and ISFJs regain control allow for the productive use of Intuition. Following are some suggestions:

- Concentrate on the big picture. What will really matter five years from now? What is the overall goal, not the details? Think of three positives that could come from a negative situation and how they might improve future options.
- Join with others in a creative endeavor. Try a theater group (even if you build sets), a creative cooking class with friends, a group tour of a local tourist site, or a community center class on a totally new subject, such as conversational Norwegian, the art of Venice, karate, or wardrobe strategies.
- Plan step-by-step how you'd handle the worst the future could bring, or talk through alternative ways to think about the situation with someone else.

Chart 10.3: Stress and the Extraverted Intuitive Types (ENTP and ENFP)

When life is going right, the Extraverted Intuitive types put their creative energy into solving problems and finding ways to get the rest of us excited about new ideas and possibilities. They're curious, enthusiastic, and energetic.

The following circumstances increase stress for ENTPs and ENFPs:

- Their core motivation is threatened or integrity is challenged. For ENTPs, it's when others question their competency. For ENFPs, it's when relationships are at risk or they're forced to face a dilemma alone.
- There are restraints. Perhaps others erect unnecessary barriers, they can't find partners in their efforts, or policies get in the way of their values or principles.
- They are forced to deal with details and facts to such an extent that they lose track of what really matters.

Often as circumstances overwhelm them, the Extraverted Intuitive types obsess on finding more options, no matter how crazy they may seem, until there are no more options and they spiral into the grip. Symptoms of a true "grip" experience include

- Overindulging in the senses, perhaps mindlessly watching television or, eating, sleeping, or exercising too much or too little
- Obsessing over physical symptoms, imagining grave diseases
- Resisting any call to reexamine facts *or* obsessing on unimportant details

Pathways that help ENTPs and ENFPs regain control allow for more productive use of Sensing. Following are some suggestions:

- Find a solitary pursuit that uses the five senses, such as contemplation in nature, walking or biking, yoga, or journaling about specific events.
- Take care of yourself. Establish a healthy exercise routine, schedule a massage, make time for a relaxing bath or sauna, or find another way to focus on tangible physical needs. Go to bed early. Simplify, simplify, simplify!
- Concentrate on the facts of a situation and the bottom-line outcome you desire. What really happened? How might others define the problem? What was the toll on emotions, fatigue, and so on? What realistic steps can you take to avoid similar situations?

Chart 10.4: Stress and the Introverted Intuitive Types (INTJ, INFJ)

When life is going right, Introverted Intuitive types are imaginative, pursuing creative and intellectual endeavors. They are optimistic, thorough in their pursuit of understanding, and insightful.

The following circumstances increase stress for INTJs and INFJs:

- They're forced to extravert too much. They lose confidence and energy when robbed of reflective time.
- Their carefully crafted plans are derailed by the actions of others.
- They have to work with too many details and start making mistakes. By nature, they are perfectionists, but details can be their nemesis—a recipe for stress.

Often as circumstances overwhelm them, the Introverted Intuitive types withdraw further, trying to solve the situation on their own. If their inferior function, Sensing, takes over, they become convinced that the whole world is against them. Symptoms of a true "grip" experience include

- Engaging in mindless activities, such as shopping, watching television, overeating, or excessive exercise
- Exhibiting unnatural pessimism
- Cutting off normal interactions, perhaps skipping regular forays with friends or ignoring outside advice or points of view

Pathways that help INTJs and INFJs regain control allow for the productive use of Sensing. Following are some suggestions:

- Engage in detailed crafts or activities where following directions is essential. Needlework, practicing a musical instrument, organizing files or finances, jigsaw puzzles, or woodworking are a few examples.
- Pursue a physical activity outside, such as hiking, biking, or rowing, emphasizing technique and an awareness of the here and now.
- Concentrate on reality. Taking time to contemplate a sunrise or sunset, watch the waves roll in, or sit on the front steps and listen to the crickets can bring rest. So can dwelling on the facts. How have you misinterpreted what happened?

Chart 10.5: Stress and the Extraverted Thinking Types (ESTJ and ENTJ)

When life is going right, Extraverted Thinking types are planning, organizing, and solving problems for the rest of us. They're logical, analytical, and objective.

The following circumstances increase stress for ESTJs and ENTJs:

- They begin to doubt they can prevail over a situation, especially if they thought they had things under control. When conflicts erupt among teachers, Extraverted Thinking types can be especially frustrated because it's a roadblock to progress they can't control.
- A deeply held principle is violated. School leaders have often developed their own systemic model of what will work, and they struggle when what they are being asked to do goes against that model.
- They unintentionally hurt someone, especially if they thought their actions were in the best interests of all involved.

Often as circumstances overwhelm them, they become rigid, intent on carrying out their plans and closed to new information or ideas. If their inferior function, Feeling, takes over, they may lose control of their emotions. Symptoms of a true "grip" experience include

- Extreme task orientation, acting coldly toward all involved
- Hypersensitivity or emotionalism
- Self-pity or uncharacteristic illogic

Pathways that help ESTJs and ENTJs regain control involve productive use of Feeling. Following are some suggestions:

- Step back and talk with someone about how different courses of action will be interpreted by other stakeholders. You might also take inventory of your own emotional state.
- Complete a values clarification exercise to determine what matters to you personally. What 5–10 values are most important to you?
- Find a recreational activity that allows you to access inner feelings, values, or motivations. Consider painting, journaling, reading literature, or engaging in spiritual direction exercises.

Chart 10.6: Stress and the Introverted Thinking Types (ISTP, INTP)

When life is going right, Introverted Thinking types are on a lifelong search for reason, underlying principles of action, and truth. They're curious, observant, and deliberate in how they choose to engage with others.

The following circumstances increase stress for ISTPs and INTPs:

- Crises require too many activities and interactions. A lack of introverted time means they lose their autonomy to make sense of situations.
- Situations defy their logical view of what should happen. Emotional outbursts, from students, teachers, or others, are especially disturbing.
- Others fail to grasp their analysis of a situation, ignore their ideas, or somehow block their implementation of the smooth, logical solutions that are their forte. Curriculum and instructional mandates are especially frustrating if they know what they are doing is working.

Often as circumstances overwhelm them, the Introverted Thinking types pour their efforts into logical analysis. If their inferior function, Feeling, takes over, they overreact to comments and emotions. Symptoms of a true "grip" experience include

- Obsessing over minor inconsistencies or critiques
- Closing themselves off even further from those closest to them
- Uncharacteristically displaying emotions

Pathways that help ISTPs and INTPs regain control allow for productive use of Feeling. Following are some suggestions:

- Focus on relationships and values. What is personally meaningful, and what do others need? Introverted Thinking types may find it easier to talk through issues with a total stranger (the person next to them on an airplane).
- Join with others for social pursuits, such as pick-up basketball, wine club, a neighborhood woodcutting gathering, or volunteering at a food shelf.
- Clarifying what brings meaning to your life. Family? Learning? Bringing order? Authenticity? The individual students you've helped? (List them.) How should these priorities be figured into decisions?

Chart 10.7: Stress and the Extraverted Feeling Types (ESFJ and ENFJ)

When life is going right, Extraverted Feeling types are engaged in motivating and helping others and upholding community values. They're encouraging, friendly, and caring, and ready to take leadership roles.

The following circumstances increase stress for ESFJs and ENFJs:

- They are asked to compromise their values, especially if others misconstrue their motivations.
- Conflict erupts or others are hurt, especially if the Extraverted Feeling type believes it is his or her fault.
- They're doing their best and no one is providing emotional support, especially if they feel belittled, misunderstood, or patronized.

Often as circumstances overwhelm them, the Extraverted Feeling types put all their efforts into re-establishing harmony, perhaps taking on even more tasks to try to keep everyone happy. If their inferior function, Thinking, takes over, they may become uncharacteristically harsh. Symptoms of a true "grip" experience include

- Avoiding their usual interests
- Excessive self-criticism, overanalyzing any little remark from others, and questioning even the strengths others appreciate in them
- Faulty logic: "If that's what they think, then . . ."

Pathways that help ESFJs and ENFJs regain control allow for productive use of Thinking. Following are some suggestions:

- Find an objective third party to generate possible solutions and then work through a logical analysis of the pros and cons of each idea and its possible consequences.
- Engage in leisure pursuits that require logic, such as reading mysteries, playing chess, or solving puzzles. Watching movies or reading novels, then analyzing how the characters were logical or illogical, can also be restful.
- Apply logic to setting boundaries. Use a matrix. What are your priorities? What criteria should you be using to say yes and no to the requests of others? Family time? The amount of energy you'll expend? The networking you can do? Be specific.

Chart 10.8: Stress and the Introverted Feeling Types (ISFP and INFP)

When life is going right, Introverted Feeling types are intensely focused on meaning and values, quietly assisting others and reminding them of what is important. They are easygoing and flexible but willing to lead when doing so will further their beliefs or causes. The following circumstances increase stress for ISFPs and INFPs:

- Harmony is lost or relationships are threatened, among adults or students.
- Others ask them to compromise their values or act in ways that don't feel authentic to the Introverted Feeling type.
- Others rush them to make important decisions or fail to provide necessary information so that they can thoroughly contemplate possible implications.

Often as circumstances overwhelm them, the Introverted Feeling types lock into their own beliefs, viewpoints, or chosen course of action, sure that they alone understand what is important. If their inferior function, Thinking, takes over, they find fault with everything. Symptoms of a true "grip" experience include

- Becoming overly bossy, suddenly barking orders at students or coworkers
- Refusing to listen to new information or perspectives, not considering whether they themselves may have formed an incorrect opinion of what has happened
- Verbalizing criticism loudly and harshly, especially if the remarks don't seem to fit with reality

Pathways that help ISFPs and INFPs regain control allow for productive use of Thinking. Following are some suggestions:

- Step back from a situation and review it logically. What was really said and done? What were the natural consequences? What universal truths were violated?
- Organize something tangible, such as your CD collection, office files, bookshelves, or anything else that would benefit from logical analysis of the best system.
- Find a leisure activity that employs logic, perhaps playing bridge, chess, or Risk; solving mystery or logic puzzles; or taking a philosophy or accounting class.

Resource A: Descriptions of Leadership Styles for the 16 Types

ISTJ

Main leadership roles: Administrative, Systemic Instructional Leadership

Management style: ISTJs excel when they can establish procedures and protocols, guide others in following them, organize for efficiency, and proceed with implementing plans, working to meet all designated objectives. They are decisive, dependable, and expect the same from others.

General Strengths

- Working with details—schedules, documents, regulations, data
- Using past experience and accurate facts to draw conclusions
- Keeping daily activities running smoothly
- Solving immediate problems
- Carrying through on commitments

At Their Best as Leaders

- Implementing plans and monitoring change efforts
- Taking a commonsense approach to solving problems
- Running a team where all are treated fairly
- Modeling efficiency and reliability
- Effectively using hierarchies, traditions, and structures for stability

Typical Areas for Growth as a Leader

- Exploring impact of logical choices on people
- Planning the big picture, three to five years out
- Being flexible
- Considering change if the status quo is okay, being overly cautious
- Offering praise and recognition
- Delegating tasks

Collaboration Style

- Naturally organize everything and everyone
- Take task-oriented, time-saving approach
- Provide pressure toward closure, limiting options
- *May* irritate others by waiting too long to contribute ideas while pondering them

Communication Style

- Reflective time before answering
- Factual, down-to-earth, businesslike approach
- Sequential, detailed communication of events and plans
- *May* come across as inflexible or uncaring.

Practical Next Steps

- Ask a trusted team member for feedback on how decisions, communications are being perceived. Factor in the problem-solving Feeling prompts (p. 188).
- Bring others into the process. Get concrete about what needs to be different in three to five years. Then identify what needs to change.
- Limit nonnegotiables where possible. Allow for reflection before deciding whether exceptions could be made.
- List out what you value most. What might still be made better? Where could change be advantageous?
- Praise can be factual, which often seems more sincere to ISTJs. Conveying praise through notes may be easier than in person.
- Ask how else you could spend your time for the greatest impact. Who would benefit from learning new tasks or perspectives?

Type

ISTJ	ISFJ	INFJ	INTJ
ISTP	ISFP	INFP	INTP
ESTP	ESFP	ENFP	ENTP
ESTJ	ESFJ	ENFJ	ENTJ

Function: ST

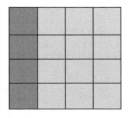

Order of Preferences
1. Sensing
2. Thinking
3. Feeling
4. Intuition

STs seek honesty:
- Be brief and specific
- Be sequential

ISTP

Main leadership roles: Administrative, Systemic Instructional Leadership

Management style: ISTPs excel in action-oriented leadership environments, taking a concrete, linear approach to finding novel and efficient solutions to problems. Their flexible, easygoing style lets them work within working systems yet challenge inefficiencies and perfect new, effective approaches.

General Strengths:

- Taking on challenges, solving problems, fixing situations
- Working independently on what needs to be done
- Being objective, unbiased, realistic
- Accepting and dealing with risks
- Working effectively in crisis situations

At Their Best as Leaders

- Troubleshooting while shooting from the hip
- Developing practical, efficient routines or methods
- Influencing by having all necessary information
- Cutting red tape to address the situation at hand
- Expecting only the best from everyone

Typical Areas for Growth as a Leader

- Developing relationships with people on a personal level

- Working with ambiguity

- Setting long-term goals, both personal and organizational

- Being aware of the individual needs and motivations of others

- Having unrealistic expectations of others

- Factoring in how others view actions

Collaboration Style:

- Quietly expect each team member to contribute
- Complete their share of tasks on their own
- Provide relevant information and examples of what works
- *May* irritate others by being too set on their own efficient, logical approaches to tasks

Communication Style

- Communicate through action more than words
- Emphasis is on concrete terms, realistic images, and specific examples
- Prefer giving feedback after time for reflection
- *May* come across as rigid because they tend to only voice ideas after forming conclusions

Practical Next Steps

- Talk with a school leader who prefers Feeling. What community-building activities does his or her staff appreciate most? What specific benefits result? Try one with your staff.
- When you're trying new solutions and can't predict results, list possible outcomes and what actions you could take.
- Use the planning process in Chapter 4, Activity 4.5, to set organizational goals. Then consider what personal goals might help you move that plan forward. Choose one and write an action plan.
- Read through the Feeling styles for communication (p. 72), collaboration (p. 89), and conflict (p. 88). What do you need to remember? What two steps could you take to meet their needs?
- Remember that people and the systems they create aren't always logical. Consciously disregard how you would carry out a task and go with the flow, ignoring all but the end result.
- Understand the political nature of your work environment and the interconnectedness of your position. On whose good graces does your ability to be effective depend? Draw a cause/effect map.

Type

ISTJ	ISFJ	INFJ	INTJ
ISTP	ISFP	INFP	INTP
ESTP	ESFP	ENFP	ENTP
ESTJ	ESFJ	ENFJ	ENTJ

Function: ST

Order of Preferences

1. Thinking
2. Sensing
3. Intuition
4. Feeling

STs seek honesty:

- Be brief and specific
- Be sequential

ESTP

Main leadership roles: Administrative, Systemic Instructional Leadership

Management style: ESTPs excel at making things happen in practical, expedient, and pragmatic ways. They focus on the here-and-now aspects of getting the job done while keeping the work environment enjoyable for all. Their can-do attitude keeps others focused on what is or isn't working and who is taking action.

General Strengths

- Being adaptable, observant, and realistic
- Meeting practical needs in the most efficient way
- Reminding others of the joys of this life, this *present* time
- Solving problems in a straightforward, logical manner
- Taking on challenges that need fixing now

At Their Best as Leaders

- Negotiating and selling ideas
- Guiding others in crisis situations, staying effective
- Tackling tasks in efficient, expedient ways
- Procuring what others need to get the job done
- Adding fun or excitement to work and routines

Typical Areas for Growth as a Leader

- Setting priorities and following through

- Being sensitive to the emotional needs of others

- Examining personal as well as external factors when problems arise

- Embracing new strategies or methods with which they have no experience

- Taking time for reflection

- Mapping out long-range plans and goals

Collaboration Style

- Help things happen because they believe nothing is impossible
- Focus energy on resolving issues rather than processing theories or possible scenarios
- Need to see the practical benefits of team efforts
- *May* irritate others by ignoring protocols or procedures

Communication Style

- Concentrate on accuracy and practicality
- Straightforward about the positive and the negative
- Prefer sequential communications, immediate answers to questions
- *May* come across as confrontational when they are merely seeking clarity

Practical Next Steps

- List your current responsibilities and goals. Ponder what will happen if you fail to meet them. Use that information to set priorities and meet them. Use backward planning.
- Look at the Feeling prompts in Chart C.1, Problem-Solving Model. Use them to think through others' needs or perspectives.
- The next time things don't go as planned, make a T-chart, listing on one side the ways others or outside factors contributed to the problem, on the other side how you may have contributed.
- Use your networking skills to find out who is using it. Call or visit to gain firsthand experience—seeing it may help you gain motivation to learn more.
- Work through the reflection questions for each chapter in this book. Jot down notes or discuss them with another administrator.
- Ponder your goals for the next year, for five years from now. Then plan backward. What do you need to be doing now?

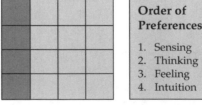

Type

ISTJ	ISFJ	INFJ	INTJ
ISTP	ISFP	INFP	INTP
ESTP	ESFP	ENFP	ENTP
ESTJ	ESFJ	ENFJ	ENTJ

Function: ST

Order of Preferences

1. Sensing
2. Thinking
3. Feeling
4. Intuition

STs seek honesty:

- Be brief and specific
- Be sequential

ESTJ

Main leadership roles: Administrative, Systemic Instructional Leadership

Management style: ESTJs excel at expecting results and working to get systems in place that are efficient, logical, and goal oriented. They expect others to work as hard as they themselves do, look for action as proof of accountability, and are predictable in their behaviors, beliefs, and expectations of others.

General Strengths

- Organizing and supervising
- Taking action and getting results
- Separating facts from emotions
- Valuing rituals, traditions, and celebrations to foster belonging
- Tracking details and following rules and procedures

At Their Best as Leaders

- Making things secure, stable, and predictable
- Using standards and data to move toward desired results
- Focusing on practical, real-world relevance and results
- Using facts and past experiences to make decisions
- Developing orderly, efficient environments with procedures, expectations, and controls

Typical Areas for Growth as a Leader

- Developing flexibility in thinking and adapting actions
- Delegating leadership responsibilities
- Dealing with change and disruptions in plans
- Focusing on the human elements of leadership
- Allowing for flexibility in how others reach goals
- Making exceptions when circumstances warrant them

Collaboration Style

- Take charge but also take responsibility
- Organized and task oriented
- Push to clarify goals, responsibilities, time lines, standards, etc
- *May* irritate others by proceeding independently

Communication Style

- Direct, realistic, matter-of-fact, efficient
- Provide detailed instructions to others, trying to eliminate room for error
- Use logic to persuade others
- *May* come across as narrow-minded if they efficiently assume they have enough information

Practical Next Steps

- Use the Problem-Solving Model, Appendix B, on your own. Require yourself to concentrate on the Intuitive and Feeling steps.
- Complete Activity 4.1, Leadership Roles Reflection, and begin by delegating your "Quadrant IV" responsibilities. Ask those who take the roles to explain how they will report progress.
- Practice by having an "open door policy" at least one day a week where everything that comes to your attention (or door) is addressed.
- Revisit Chart 3.1, What Each Preference Needs During Change. How might meeting these needs increase efficiency and effectiveness?
- Set a clear expectation for final results, but let each person write their own action plan, using the process on p. 63, to demonstrate how they will meet it.
- While setting precedents is a valid concern, before saying no, allow time for reflection. In this case, will it really make a difference?

Type   Function: ST

ISTJ	ISFJ	INFJ	INTJ
ISTP	ISFP	INFP	INTP
ESTP	ESFP	ENFP	ENTP
ESTJ	ESFJ	ENFJ	ENTJ

Order of Preferences
1. Thinking
2. Sensing
3. Intuition
4. Feeling

STs seek honesty:
- Be brief and specific
- Be sequential

ISFJ

Main leadership roles: Administrative, Community Instructional Leadership

Management style: ISFJs excel at setting clear expectations so people know where they stand and what needs to happen. People feel cared for through the ISFJ management style. The focus is on achieving results through positive relationships. They respect bureaucracies, systems, and procedures and expect others do so as well.

General Strengths

- Tirelessly working to get the job done
- Keeping and enjoying traditions
- Providing stability, improving efficiency
- Offering sensible and matter-of-fact attention to the daily concerns of people
- Dutifully learning about new ideas or methods

At Their Best as Leaders

- Taking care of details so others can be successful
- Valuing and honoring contractual commitments
- Motivating others through kindness and cooperation
- Encouraging others to do their best
- Organizing through administrative systems, structures, and rules

Typical Areas for Growth as a Leader

- Letting go of traditions if progress requires it
- Making room for one's own needs
- Understanding constructivist and inquiry-based instruction
- Being direct with others when necessary
- Setting priorities
- Requiring others to follow through

Collaboration Style

- Willing to work hard, expecting the same of others
- Prefer groups that value relationships
- May provide ideas and resources but prefer to let others decide whether or not to use them
- *May* irritate others by not being forthcoming with opinions or preferences

Communication Style

- Good listening skills
- May communicate their opinions or wishes indirectly
- Accurately recall specific details of conversations and situations
- *May* come across as passive-aggressive to those who readily speak their minds

Practical Next Steps

- Meet with others in the same position and get their input on what needs to change.
- Set up a personal and professional calendar. Make time for friends and interests—and stick to it.
- Use a learning styles framework when working with adults or students. Are a variety of learning opportunities offered in your building?
- Study the Intuition/Thinking communication style on p. 72. Which elements might you use to clarify your messages?
- List criteria for setting priorities: deadlines, school goals, teacher needs, etc. Then prioritize your tasks accordingly.
- Remember that requiring others to complete their duties helps them grow and allows you to concentrate on the work that best uses your strengths.

Type

ISTJ	ISFJ	INFJ	INTJ
ISTP	ISFP	INFP	INTP
ESTP	ESFP	ENFP	ENTP
ESTJ	ESFJ	ENFJ	ENTJ

Function: SF

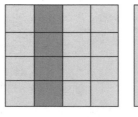

Order of Preferences

1. Sensing
2. Feeling
3. Thinking
4. Intuition

SFs seek to know you:

- Listen carefully
- Be practical

ISFP

Main leadership roles: Administrative, Community Instructional Leadership

Management style: ISFPs are perfectionists and lead others to have the same high expectations for themselves, providing for autonomy for results-oriented staff. They work to establish a harmonious, enjoyable work environment. While they work well in crises, they prefer to avoid confrontations and negative emotional outbursts.

General Strengths

- Working invisibly to meet others' needs
- Showing sensitivity and loyalty
- Recognizing others' strengths and contributions
- Preserving tradition and community values
- Providing direct, personal, caring assistance

At Their Best as Leaders

- Encouraging all to uphold mission and values
- Conscientiously organizing to accomplish tasks
- Enrolling people in practical, kind, and cooperative ways
- Staying flexible when problems or ambiguities arise
- Working within systems, structures, and rules

Typical Areas for Growth as a Leader

- Dealing with conflict

- Changing the status quo

- Thinking strategically, broadening possibilities

- Taking a tough stance

- Establishing authority

- Taking credit for accomplishments

Collaboration Style

- Work to establish harmony
- Prefer win-win approach to problems
- Loyal to group, processes, and traditions
- *May* irritate others by avoiding conflict

Communication Style

- Speak louder through actions than words
- May not offer opinions readily—*unless* values are violated
- Concentrate on practical matters, facts, details
- *May* come across as illogical or emotional if group dynamics seldom allow them to be heard

Practical Next Steps

- Seek out classes in conflict resolution, ideally ones that use type concepts. Facing personal conflict helps develop skills for working with staff to resolve interpersonal conflicts.
- Work with a colleague who thinks very differently from you. Look at your strategic plan. What won't come to pass three years from now if you don't change curriculum, team structures, or other "givens"?
- Practice thinking "outside the box" with a colleague who prefers Intuition. Choose an issue with long-range (three to five years) implications. Use the Problem-Solving Model to examine possibilities.
- Your preferred path is empathizing when others fall short. When others need corrective feedback to advance school or district goals, work out in advance what you will say and require.
- Some ISFPs benefit from "assertiveness training." When would a direct leadership approach be more effective than your usual plea to values and priorities?
- Remember that educational leadership has its political side. Think of taking credit as a pathway for obtaining resources others need.

Type   **Function: SF**

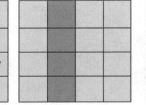

ISTJ	ISFJ	INFJ	INTJ
ISTP	ISFP	INFP	INTP
ESTP	ESFP	ENFP	ENTP
ESTJ	ESFJ	ENFJ	ENTJ

Order of Preferences

1. Feeling
2. Sensing
3. Intuition
4. Thinking

SFs seek to know you:

- Listen carefully
- Be practical

ESFP

Main leadership roles: Administrative, Community Instructional Leadership

Management style: ESFPs excel at engaging and motivating others through an easygoing management style that mobilizes people to get the job done. They value their position of authority and use that to influence others. They are team players who enlist the help of others to keep track of ongoing details and follow-through.

General Strengths

- Troubleshooting in the moment
- Tackling nuts-and-bolts of organization
- Being generous with time and talents
- Negotiating and communicating warmth, excitement, and acceptance
- Approaching work flexibly; easygoing yet realistic

At Their Best as Leaders

- Mobilizing others to take action
- Viewing each person as important, keeping work fun
- Responding to opportunities, problems
- Sensing and responding to an organization's overall sense of well-being

Typical Areas for Growth as a Leader

- Setting and sticking to firm limits

- Understanding the big picture

- Long-term planning

- Separating the important from the urgent, setting priorities

- Following organizational procedures

- Exploring theories and models

Collaboration Style

- Work to make collaboration fun, harmonious
- Need input, feedback, and encouragement
- Prefer short-term projects with assistance on follow-through
- *May irritate others by socializing too much*

Communication Style

- Positive, humorous communicators
- Enjoy conversations, focus on people's needs and emotions
- May avoid conflict, stay silent instead
- *May come across as unbusinesslike*

Practical Next Steps

- Use Thinking skills. What precedents might you be setting? What are logical consequences, and how might they help others learn? How does the limit create trust or other values?
- Take time to reflect on how your actions connect to student achievement and other overall goals. Look for patterns in data and ask, "What does this add up to?"
- Work with someone else so you don't get bogged down in the details. Use your values to set goals and then plan backward. What should you be doing now?
- Ask yourself, "Of all my tasks, which address my biggest priorities?" Rank them. Can some be done later, allowing you to concentrate on roles that affect student achievement?
- Review organizational policies that affect your work. Talk with someone who can explain the rationale.
- Identify two or three educational models being used by colleagues. Ask them what practical benefits they are seeing and use these as motivation to learn more.

Type   Function: SF

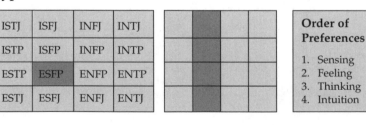

ISTJ	ISFJ	INFJ	INTJ
ISTP	ISFP	INFP	INTP
ESTP	**ESFP**	ENFP	ENTP
ESTJ	ESFJ	ENFJ	ENTJ

Order of Preferences

1. Sensing
2. Feeling
3. Thinking
4. Intuition

SFs seek to know you:

- Listen carefully
- Be practical

ESFJ

Main leadership roles: Administrative, Community Instructional Leadership

Management style: ESFJs excel at leading by meeting staff needs, providing support and necessary resources, often through the networks of people they've established over time. They handle tasks efficiently and predictably, enjoying the authority to make things happen. They respect and expect others to work within hierarchies.

General Strengths

- Being organized, prompt, and accurate
- Knowing what matters for people and organizations
- Encouraging others and motivating them
- Planning to meet the physical, social, and emotional needs of others
- Working with data to pinpoint where others need help

At Their Best as Leaders

- Encouraging others in their roles
- Structuring the work environment to allow everyone to show their best selves
- Providing support and assistance
- Understanding the impact of demands on people and trying to compensate
- Organizing for people so all needs are met

Typical Areas for Growth as a Leader

- Setting limits to meet own needs

- Setting boundaries so as not to seem meddlesome

- Focusing on strategies as well as relationships

- Planning for change

- Being businesslike

- Using logic to persuade others

Collaboration Style

- Active team player, ready to do his or her part
- Cooperative, seeking group harmony
- Adept at keeping team on task
- *May* irritate others by making decisions too quickly

Communication Style

- Warm and caring, people-centered
- Seek others' opinions, thrive on conversation.
- Concentrate on details important to those they know
- *May* come across as opinionated in their drive to get things done

Practical Next Steps

- Work with someone who prefers Thinking to set logical criteria. Will the task further your top priorities? Would someone benefit from learning how? Will it keep you from using your strengths?
- Monitor others' views of your interventions. Before you help, ask what the person needs or whether they want help at all.
- Look at workplace goals with your values in mind. What strategies will bring those values to reality? Make action plans.
- Ask who benefits most from the status quo. Use your values as motivation to seek change. Who will be helped?
- Remember that most school leaders prefer Thinking and put business before relationships. Practice concise communication and getting right down to business.
- Especially in conflict situations, think through if-then, cause-effect, and natural consequences. Ignore how you feel.

Type

ISTJ	ISFJ	INFJ	INTJ
ISTP	ISFP	INFP	INTP
ESTP	ESFP	ENFP	ENTP
ESTJ	**ESFJ**	ENFJ	ENTJ

Function: SF

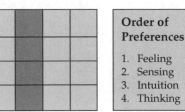

Order of Preferences

1. Feeling
2. Sensing
3. Intuition
4. Thinking

STs seek to know you:

- Listen carefully
- Be practical

INFJ

Main leadership roles: Visionary, Community Instructional Leadership

Management style: INFJs excel at leadership through strong, authentic values. They inspire others to work toward a cause or purpose, such as educating all students regardless of circumstances. They are adept at providing specific feedback to help others support that purpose, accommodating personal needs unless they go against the common good.

General Strengths

- Providing insights, especially about what matters to people
- Dealing with complex issues
- Developing others, unearthing their potential
- Being organized to reach goals
- Adding creativity

At Their Best as Leaders

- Actively and accurately anticipating how relationships and events will play out
- Developing long-range goals and an organizational sense of vision and purpose
- Using their understanding of others to motivate them toward common goals
- Building consensus, promoting understanding, winning cooperation
- Providing freedom and autonomy

Typical Areas for Growth as a Leader

- Backing vision with concrete data, goals, measurable steps
- Sharing corrections, engaging in necessary confrontation
- Recognizing and dealing with organizational politics
- Working solo too long on ideas before seeking input
- Paying attention to reality, what *is*
- Adding logic, if-then, cause-effect to communication

Collaboration Style

- Help others bridge differences, emphasizing empathy and harmony
- Perform solo tasks that contribute to group goals
- Prefer small, efficient teams
- *May* irritate others by going too far on their own before getting input

Communication Style

- Quiet enthusiasm
- Concentrate on values, creativity, and possibilities
- Like time for reflection or writing to think through ideas—want time before articulating orally
- *May* irritate others by reading between the lines, finishing their thoughts for them

Practical Next Steps

- Ask for specific critique on plans from people involved in the implementation.
- Frame feedback in terms of what will help the person grow, resolving conflict as the route to productive future relationships.
- Talk with an objective outsider about "What's in it for them," *them* being the other players. Explore possible motivations.
- At each step ask yourself, "Are there interested parties who will want a say? Can I increase buy-in for the final product by getting their input now?"
- List what you value in the present moment, including your personal life. Evaluate whether you have time for the things you value.
- Develop a specific set of Thinking questions to think through your arguments.

Type   Function: NF

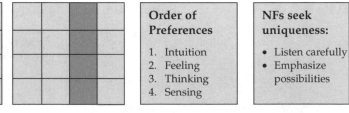

ISTJ	ISFJ	INFJ	INTJ
ISTP	ISFP	INFP	INTP
ESTP	ESFP	ENFP	ENTP
ESTJ	ESFJ	ENFJ	ENTJ

Order of Preferences

1. Intuition
2. Feeling
3. Thinking
4. Sensing

NFs seek uniqueness:

- Listen carefully
- Emphasize possibilities

INFP

Main leadership roles: Visionary, Community Instructional Leadership

Management style: INFPs excel at leading through their values concerning education. They are committed to helping their staff grow in their positions and abilities and make decisions based on the needs of others. Profoundly democratic, they manage in a low-key fashion, avoiding fanfare and sidestepping the negative assumptions of others.

General Strengths

- Upholding values and ideas
- Focusing on what is compassionate and caring
- Modeling honesty and hard work
- Adding a spirit of harmony and peace
- Tirelessly working for causes they value

At Their Best as Leaders

- Inspiring others with creative visions of what could be
- Building an environment where all feel valued
- Motivating others to work toward a positive vision of the future
- Facilitating people and processes democratically
- Overseeing complex projects from start to finish, ensuring the overall purpose is met

Typical Areas for Growth as a Leader

- Dealing with conflict

- Working the system, understanding politics

- Meeting deadlines by avoiding perfection

- Considering values of others

- Being realistic

- Setting clear expectations

Collaboration Style

- Prefer to work alone or with a small, creative team
- Facilitate group harmony
- Agreeable—unless values are violated
- *May* irritate others by "lone wolf" behavior, but they need to process before sharing ideas

Communication Style

- Persuading through values, emotions, strength of ideas
- Strong nonverbal language
- Stories or images to convey ideas
- *May* come across as stubborn because they hold thoughts until they are convictions

Practical Next Steps

- Seek specific training in conflict management. Practice using logic, the language of most school leaders, and a method for keeping emotions at bay.
- Map out allegiances within your organization and the roles each "player" fills. What do you need to remember so that your ideas and projects are supported?
- Identify when timeliness is more important than perfection. Act accordingly. Schedule time for detailed paperwork—and ask a colleague to hold you accountable.
- Evaluate whether others' values are as appropriate to their situations, position, or vision as yours are to your goals.
- Remember that reaching a vision requires dealing with reality. How might you use the Sensing and Thinking needs during change (p. 41) to plan for what might actually happen?
- Develop an appreciation for structure and order. Consider the ST communication style. What does this require of you as a leader?

Type

Function: NF

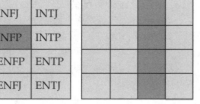

ISTJ	ISFJ	INFJ	INTJ
ISTP	ISFP	INFP	INTP
ESTP	ESFP	ENFP	ENTP
ESTJ	ESFJ	ENFJ	ENTJ

Order of Preferences

1. Feeling
2. Intuition
3. Sensing
4. Thinking

NFs seek uniqueness:

- Listen carefully
- Emphasize possibilities

ENFP

Main leadership roles: Visionary, Community Instructional Leadership

Management style: ENFPs excel at ethical, caring leadership, empowering others to reach their full potential as a pathway to more happiness and satisfaction. Relationships are key to how they lead; they easily identify others' thoughts and feelings. They know how to motivate others to embrace new ideas and innovative strategies.

General Strengths

- Bringing energy, enthusiasm, and ideas to any endeavor
- Influencing and persuading others
- Pursuing new possibilities
- Celebrating and appreciating others
- Finding creative solutions

At Their Best as Leaders

- Energizing others through the strength of their ideas
- Guiding others toward change
- Creating a catalytic vision of what could be
- Adapting quickly to changing situations and new directions
- Working from inspiration, flexible plans

Typical Areas for Growth as a Leader

- Promoting too many new ideas or initiatives

- Underestimating physical, mental, and time limitations

- Confronting difficult people or dealing with office politics

- Setting clear expectations and guidelines for others

- Spending time in reflective practice

- Administrative tasks—schedules, budgets, etc.

Collaboration Style

- Strive for diversity
- Network, building synergistic coalitions
- Hub of helping all get along
- Build relationships with each team member
- *May* irritate team members by expanding agendas or trying to pursue too many priorities at once

Communication Style

- Focus on the big picture of possibilities and human potential
- Affirm others and in turn appreciate feedback
- Concentrate on values, impact on people
- *May* be seen as "all ideas" without supporting facts, details, or logic

Practical Next Steps

- Chart out your initiatives and rank them according to your values. Which have the most impact? Which get in the way of others?
- Use reflective time to evaluate the cost of overcommitment. What are the facts? Late nights? Missed appointments or deadlines? Missed personal commitments or opportunities?
- In conversation with a trusted other, use logic, cause-effect, and if-then reasoning to determine the costs or benefits of confrontation and then determine a course of action.
- *Ask* your staff for examples of what they want and don't usually receive from you. Have another leadership team member provide suggestions. Look at examples from other schools.
- Schedule reflective time into your week—a set time at a coffee shop or a solo exercise period—to think through a recent situation or decision.
- Look for systems that work for you, other members of your team who enjoy detailed work, or . . .

Type

ISTJ	ISFJ	INFJ	INTJ
ISTP	ISFP	INFP	INTP
ESTP	ESFP	**ENFP**	ENTP
ESTJ	ESFJ	ENFJ	ENTJ

Function: NF

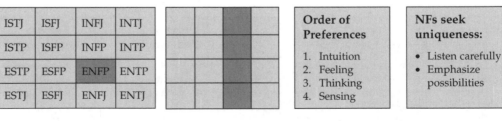

Order of Preferences
1. Intuition
2. Feeling
3. Thinking
4. Sensing

NFs seek uniqueness:
• Listen carefully
• Emphasize possibilities

ENFJ

Main leadership roles: Visionary, Community Instructional Leadership

Management style: ENFJs excel at knowing their staff personally, giving responsibilities to the individuals who can best carry them out, and minimizing office politics. They believe that people make things happen and work to preserve relationships, managing with a sense of humor and good-natured fun.

General Strengths

- Tirelessly pursuing endeavors they believe in
- Being responsive and responsible
- Articulating needed messages
- Motivating people to work toward goals
- Building relationships and community

At Their Best as Leaders

- Bringing energy and enthusiasm to activities and organizations
- Creating harmonious environments
- Mentoring, communicating confidence in others
- Organizing small and large undertakings
- Planning yet allowing people autonomy

Typical Areas for Growth as a Leader

- Being objective and logical

- Accepting criticism, not taking it personally

- Understanding organizational politics and those who don't look for "win-win"

- Dealing with "win-lose" players or situations

- Caring for self as well as others

- Limiting the number of interests and initiatives

Collaboration Style

- Relationships and harmony come first
- Value everyone's opinions and ideas
- Focus on improving things for the common good
- *May* irritate others by hesitating to challenge others when challenge is needed

Communication Style

- Natural communicators, connecting emotionally
- Listen well and hear what is being said
- May avoid delivering tough messages
- *May* come across as bossy as deadlines approach

Practical Next Steps

- Use the Problem-Solving Model to form arguments. Concentrate on facts and Thinking criteria.
- Brace yourself to hear flaws first and remember that Thinking types show care by helping others improve. Ask how a sensible person would regard the critique.
- Know that one can be political while acting with integrity. Get an organization chart. Label who knows whom, friendships, what other positions they've held, and who gets things done regardless of title.
- Before and after meetings, question others' motives. What do they have to win/lose from outcomes? Develop a checklist of factors that motivate people to operate this way. Use it to evaluate the "game."
- Practice detachment and let others sometimes help themselves. Take care of yourself, too. Get away from work; pursue social friendships and other favorite diversions.
- Determine priorities for each quarter of the year and stick to them. Set up implementation plans, including details and dates. Make details fun—tie out budgets with someone, use colored folders, etc.

Type

ISTJ	ISFJ	INFJ	INTJ
ISTP	ISFP	INFP	INTP
ESTP	ESFP	ENFP	ENTP
ESTJ	ESFJ	ENFJ	ENTJ

Function: NF

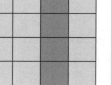

Order of Preferences

1. Feeling
2. Intuition
3. Sensing
4. Thinking

NFs seek uniqueness:

- Listen carefully
- Emphasize possibilities

INTJ

Main leadership roles: Visionary, Systemic Instructional Leadership

Management style: INTJs excel at laying out clear, logical plans and expectations. Their questioning style motivates others to be ready with answers and in-depth understanding of the strategies and actions under their direction. They enjoy the autonomy and authority leadership provides, using it to make the vision become reality.

General Strengths

- Envisioning how to change things, shift paradigms, break new ground
- Analyzing, contrasting, categorizing
- Setting priorities and establishing plans
- Using logic, clarifying concepts
- Thinking and acting independently

At Their Best as Leaders

- Long-range planning for school improvement, including goals and time lines
- Challenging the system with sincere questions
- Providing autonomy to competent colleagues
- Making complex decisions while accounting for details
- Setting a vision, fostering coherence of purpose, and following through

Typical Areas for Growth as a Leader

- Adding details to vision

- Being patient with "slower minds"

- Enjoying the present moment

- Taking time to train and develop others

- Being aware of the impact of critique and skepticism

- Listening to others' input and ideas

Collaboration Style

- Challenge group consensus with alternatives that bring new perspectives
- Autonomous roles that contribute to group tasks
- Small teams where each person counts
- *May* irritate others by proceeding without them

Communication Style

- Straightforward, terse, single-minded
- Critique readily to improve or change ideas and plans brought to them
- Emphasize outside-the-box perspectives
- *May* come across as overly critical or arrogant

Practical Next Steps

- Look at Sensing needs during change (p. 41) and include them in planning. Collaborate with someone who has those skills.
- When others don't "see" your vision, think about what will capture their attention. Look at Sensing/Feeling communication needs (p. 72) to understand what you might be leaving out
- Schedule time for friendships and interests outside of work. Ride a bike, watch the sunset, savor a leisurely meal, pursue a hobby.
- Use Chapter 4 to delegate tasks, training those who need help. Realize that the net outcome is more time for envisioning.
- Practice voicing positives first and showing appreciation. Look at Chart 5.1 to understand Feeling needs in communication. Where can you be more intentional in changing the impression you make?
- Write down others' ideas and ponder their merit. Ask for input *before* you've worked out your full vision.

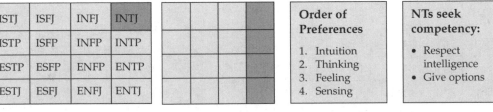

Type

ISTJ	ISFJ	INFJ	INTJ
ISTP	ISFP	INFP	INTP
ESTP	ESFP	ENFP	ENTP
ESTJ	ESFJ	ENFJ	ENTJ

Function: NT

Order of Preferences

1. Intuition
2. Thinking
3. Feeling
4. Sensing

NTs seek competency:

- Respect intelligence
- Give options

INTP

Main leadership roles: Visionary, Systemic Instructional Leadership

Management style: INTPs excel at envisioning new systems, analyzing situations, and easily identifying different aspects and viewpoints. They motivate others via the clear excellence of their ideas, adopting a hands-off style and expecting that others will resolve their own conflicts and work toward the presented vision.

General Strengths

- Conceptualizing systems, structures, programs
- Finding unique solutions to complex problems
- Theorizing, contributing intellectual insights
- Pointing out logical errors or long-term consequences of courses of action
- Providing clear analytical frameworks for understanding

At Their Best as Leaders

- Setting the vision and letting others work in their own style to get there
- Holding everyone to high achievement standards, then raising the bar
- Influencing through depth of knowledge, power of ideas
- Developing frameworks that organize priorities, actions
- Focusing on key factors that lead to continuous improvement

Typical Areas for Growth as a Leader

- Learning to delegate

- Handling project details

- Giving positive feedback and praise

- Recognizing how one's style affects others

- "Translating" complex ideas

- Accepting other styles of excellence

Collaboration Style

- Work independently on tasks for the group
- Appreciate intellectual "equals"
- Minimal meeting time for working on clear goals that require group input
- *May* irritate others by holding ideas until they're polished

Communication Style

- Are terse and precise in word choice
- Prefer writing over verbal communication
- Can use language skills to gain power, position
- *May* come across as too intellectual to be useful to others

Practical Next Steps

- Use Chapter 4 to delegate. Monitor what happens when people use their strengths. Do you have more time for your ideal tasks?
- Look at Sensing and Feeling needs during change (p. 41) and for communication (p. 72). Let someone with these skills review plans.
- Practice first through written communication. Focusing on specifics is fine.
- Remember that engaging others through Feeling skills may ultimately provide you with more resources or support.
- Practice explaining your thoughts in three to five easily understandable points. Not everyone relates to conceptual models.
- Study other types of intelligence—interpersonal, intrapersonal, and emotional. Where might you receive "low marks"?

Type

Function: NT

ISTJ	ISFJ	INFJ	INTJ
ISTP	ISFP	INFP	INTP
ESTP	ESFP	ENFP	ENTP
ESTJ	ESFJ	ENFJ	ENTJ

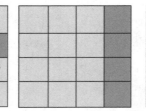

Order of Preferences

1. Thinking
2. Intuition
3. Sensing
4. Feeling

NTs seek competency:

- Respect intelligence
- Give options

ENTP

Main leadership roles: Visionary, Systemic Instructional Leadership

Management style: ENTPs excel at enthusiastic, principle-centered leadership of the projects, initiatives, and events that interest them, motivating others to join in. They have a systemic view of leadership, expecting staff to work efficiently and autonomously on the implementation details that will bring the leadership vision to fruition.

General Strengths

- Envisioning new ideas and embracing theories
- Adding both energy and insights to endeavors
- Exhibiting resourcefulness in dire or complicated situations
- Meeting challenges proactively
- Solving complex problems, thinking creatively

At Their Best as Leaders

- Fearlessly tackling new endeavors, engaging others through the power of their vision
- Setting high standards for self and others while organizing to meet them
- Dealing with multiple multifaceted issues and situations
- Seeking new ideas, models, and logical systems
- Constantly improving what is in place

Typical Areas for Growth as a Leader

- Staying open to others' ideas

- Recognizing the role of emotions and values

- Avoiding overcommitment of time and resources

- Working with details, nuts-and-bolts of implementation

- Acknowledging others' contributions

- Following procedures, processes, rules

Collaboration Style

- Offer new ideas, multiple approaches
- Work best with competitive, competent coworkers
- Need freedom to pursue goals, support for ideas to generate more
- *May* irritate colleagues by taking center stage

Communication Style

- Focus on models, theories, and ideas
- Enjoy intellectual banter and debate
- Actively seek other opinions, ideas, and feedback, offering logical critiques
- *May* come across as challenging or dismissive of others' ideas

Practical Next Steps

- Ask questions such as "Tell me more," "Can you give an example?" "What have others thought?" Listen and reflect before critiquing.
- Get to know your staff and their personalities so that your decisions include some understanding of the impact on others.
- Partner with a "realist," prioritize organizational goals, and focus resources. What can actually be done in three months? Six months?
- Work with someone strong with details. Look at Sensing and Judging needs during change (p. 41) and plan for meeting them.
- Reflect, listing the contributions of your staff or team that lead to your overall effectiveness and that of the organization. Start specifically acknowledging their value.
- Note actual results of bending rules or seeking loopholes. Who was inconvenienced or saw it as unfair or a burden on them? What might they not do for you later?

Type

ISTJ	ISFJ	INFJ	INTJ
ISTP	ISFP	INFP	INTP
ESTP	ESFP	ENFP	**ENTP**
ESTJ	ESFJ	ENFJ	ENTJ

Function: NT

Order of Preferences

1. Intuition
2. Thinking
3. Feeling
4. Sensing

NTs seek competency:

- Respect intelligence
- Give options

ENTJ

Main leadership roles: Visionary, Systemic Instructional Leadership

Management style: ENTJs excel at taking charge, solving problems, and marshalling others to work toward goals, yet allowing people flexibility in how they meet them. They are efficient and expect others to comply with efficient routines, yet prefer working with the strategic aspects of leadership over day-to-day details.

General Strengths

- Organizing systems, structures, and people
- Tirelessly working to solve complex problems
- Making efficient use of time and resources
- Pursuing depth of knowledge and theoretical understanding
- Thinking on their feet, being decisive

At Their Best as Leaders

- Motivating others through dynamic, forward-thinking visions
- Charting how and then achieving high goals
- Using logic and conceptual thinking
- Providing strong, standards-based leadership
- Staying rational, focused, and effective throughout change efforts

Typical Areas for Growth as a Leader

- Patience

- Appreciating different styles, points of view

- Meeting the emotional and physical needs of self and others

- Sharing leadership, mentoring potential leaders

- Structuring the details of plans and initiatives

- Rethinking current course of action, models, or methods

Collaboration Style

- Goal-oriented, businesslike approach
- Engage as long as collaboration is efficient and effective, meeting goals and objectives
- Work best with confident, tough-minded, dedicated colleagues
- *May* irritate others because they can't *not* lead

Communication Style

- Analytical, direct, efficient
- May employ conceptual models
- Enjoy task-oriented relationships and conversation
- *May* come across as driven, missing emotional cues or needs of others

Practical Next Steps

- Get logical. Step into the shoes of others and consider their needs. Consider how patience might foster smoother plan implementation, especially if you allow for others' input.
- Study the value of "soft skills." Read the ISFP leadership style page. How might it motivate people whose competency you question?
- Use Chapter 10. How can you reduce organizational stress? Pay special attention to the needs of Extraverted and Introverted Feeling types. What accommodations could you make?
- Develop and coach leadership in others so you have more time for even bigger endeavors. Use Chapter 4 to identify ideal roles.
- Read through Sensing and Feeling needs during change (p. 41). Work with someone to add steps to your strategies to help them keep moving as fast as you want them to.
- Find the person most likely to challenge your plans or actions—and listen to what they tell you!

Type

ISTJ	ISFJ	INFJ	INTJ
ISTP	ISFP	INFP	INTP
ESTP	ESFP	ENFP	ENTP
ESTJ	ESFJ	ENFJ	ENTJ

Function: NT

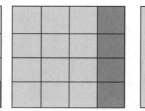

Order of Preferences

1. Thinking
2. Intuition
3. Sensing
4. Feeling

NTs seek competency:

- Respect intelligence
- Give options

Resource B: Problem-Solving, or Z, Model

The framework of personality type provides an excellent, *balanced* process for

- Making decisions
- Solving problems
- Resolving conflict

Individuals and teams can use this process to include the strengths and key input from each of the functions: the facts and history (Sensing), possibilities (Intuition), logical ramifications of each option (Thinking), and community values and commitment (Feeling).

Without a guided process, most people spend too much or too little time on one aspect of decision making. For example, when we use the "S'mores Dilemma" scenario described below with teams to illustrate the process, the dominant Intuitives in the room jump right to generating new ideas, without taking the time to define the real problem. In many businesses, decisions are made based on Thinking criteria (cost, schedules, efficiencies) with almost no attention paid to Feeling criteria (who is committed, how various individuals might be affected). Or a group goes with the solution that seems obvious without taking enough Intuitive time to generate other options.

For teams to use the model effectively, they need to (a) see evidence of the team's blind spots and how the model helps them compensate and (b) practice. At first, the steps can be time consuming because people with different preferences may disagree about whether the correct input is being given at various stages. (We've had dominant Sensing types reject whole lists of "facts" generated by dominant Intuitives because they were really hunches or extrapolations from the data.) Therefore, we suggest the following process.

Step 1: Practice Problem

The "S'mores Dilemma" below works well for groups to practice solving a problem. Group experiences with a sample scenario usually provide sufficient evidence that the time spent on using the model is worthwhile. You can use a real-life dilemma as well. Chart B.1, the Problem-Solving Model, contains nine different prompt questions for each stage of the process. Choose two to three of the most relevant prompts for the situation.

Have individuals identify their dominant function, using Chart 2.1. Form groups by dominant function. Provide each group with four pieces of flip chart paper and a marker. Have them write Sensing at the top of one paper, Intuition on the second, Thinking on the third, and Feeling on the last.

Read this lighthearted scenario to the team:

> A family camp holds an opening "S'mores Campfire" each session. Campers are asked to give the first s'more they make to another camper as a way to make a new friend. A few adults have complained about this tradition. They don't like the fact that children hand them s'mores with marshmallows that are either barely warm or burnt to a crisp. Further, they'd rather eat s'mores made with dark chocolate—they don't want to waste food, but they also don't want to eat more than one.[1]

Ask every group to concentrate on the Sensing prompts for five minutes. For the "S'mores Dilemma" the Sensing prompts are

- What are the facts of the situation?
- How is the problem best defined?

Ask the Sensing group to report first because this is their strength. Usually the *Sensing* group's list is short and accurate; the dilemma doesn't contain many facts. For contrast, have the Intuitive group go next, and ask the Sensing types to determine the quality of their list. *Intuitives* usually proceed directly to possible solutions, or their lists are full of assumptions that they don't realize they're making. Then have the Feeling and Thinking groups report. *Feeling* types often present opinions as facts. Usually, the *Thinking* group's facts are quite accurate.

Then move to the Intuition step. Again, ask all groups to work on the same prompts, this time writing their ideas on the paper marked Intuition.

- What are possible ways to solve this dilemma?
- Is this problem analogous to other situations you can think of? Does the analogy provide new ways of thinking of solutions?

This time, have the Intuitive group report first since possibilities are their strength, then the Sensing group as this step is the hardest one for them. *Intuitive* groups usually generate the most options; they latch onto a theme like,

---

1. Occasionally a participant won't know that s'mores are "sandwiches" made of graham crackers, milk chocolate squares, and marshmallows that have been roasted over a campfire. A workshop participant from Germany told Jane that the description was enough for him to assume that the concoctions were another invention of the American industrial machine to hook children on sugar-laden products. . . .

"Oh, this is an icebreaker—what other icebreakers could we use. . . ." *Sensing* types usually generate the fewest options and often struggle with analogies. *Thinking* types might put forth one solution and stop, sure that it's the best.

Continue in the same fashion with the Thinking function. The group now has a list of possibilities. How will they decide which is the best? Use the following prompts:

- What criteria should we use in making the decision?
- What precedents might we be setting?

Again, let the group that just used their dominant function report first—this time, the Thinking group. They usually generate clear criteria: cost, counselor time, etc. *Intuitive* and *Feeling* types often struggle to think of criteria; frequently, they ask for examples.

The last step uses the Feeling function. Remind your team that no matter what solution seemed the best using Thinking criteria, they are now to reconsider the list using Feeling criteria. Frequently, the best Thinking choice is eliminated completely once the Feeling criteria are applied. Use the following prompts:

- How do the proposed solutions fit with community values?
- Do we have buy-in to the proposed solutions? Will the staff carry out what we decide?

Often, the *Feeling* group reports out a process for gaining group consensus, even suggesting that adult campers be polled. *Thinking* types may discount this step if they've provided logical criteria and struggle to come up with other ways to judge the options. *Sensing* types may struggle with so much processing time and just want to take action.

Step 2: Work on a Real Problem

In preparing to focus on a real problem, choose two to three prompts for each step of the process from Chart B.1, the Problem-Solving Model.

Once your team has learned to use the model, the whole group can work on the process at the same time. Have the "dominant function" members assess whether a step is complete; for example, the dominant Sensing types on the team would bring closure to the Sensing step.

However, remember that when a type preference is a clear majority, team members with the opposite preference may mask their opinions. Make sure that you seek out the minority opinion. You might do so in any of the following ways:

- Consider allowing two to three minutes of reflection at each stage of the process so that Introverted team members have a chance to form their thoughts. (Also, announcing the topic in advance of the meeting can help them be more prepared.)

Chart B.1   Problem-Solving Model

Sensing

- How is the problem best defined?
- What are the facts? Who? What? When? Where? Why?
- Which facts are verifiable by a clock, a budget, test results, survey, etc.
- How did we get into this situation?
- What have you or others done to resolve this or similar problems?
- What already exists and works?
- What has already been tried or done? By whom?
- How would a nonbiased individual view the situation?
- What resources are available?

Thinking

- List objective criteria that need to be satisfied.
- Weigh practicality of alternatives.
- What are the pros and cons of each possibility?
- What are the logical consequences of the options?
- What are the costs of each alternative?
- What is the most reasonable course of action?
- Would this option apply equally and fairly to everyone?
- What are the consequences of not deciding and acting?
- What impact would pursuing each option have on other priorities?

Intuition

- What are the connections to larger issues or other people?
- What other ways are there to look at this?
- List the possible solutions or ways to approach the problem.
- What insights and hunches do you have?
- What is this problem analogous to?
- What other directions can be explored?
- What would be other possibilities if there were no restrictions?
- What do the data imply?
- What theories address this kind of problem?

Feeling

- Determine "fit" with personal and organizational values.
- How will the outcome affect the people, process, or organization?
- How will each option contribute to harmony and positive interactions?
- What are the underlying values involved in each choice?
- What are your personal reactions (likes and dislikes) to each alternative?
- How will others respond?
- Who is committed to carrying out the solution?
- How will people be supported if this decision is made?
- How will this affect my own priorities?

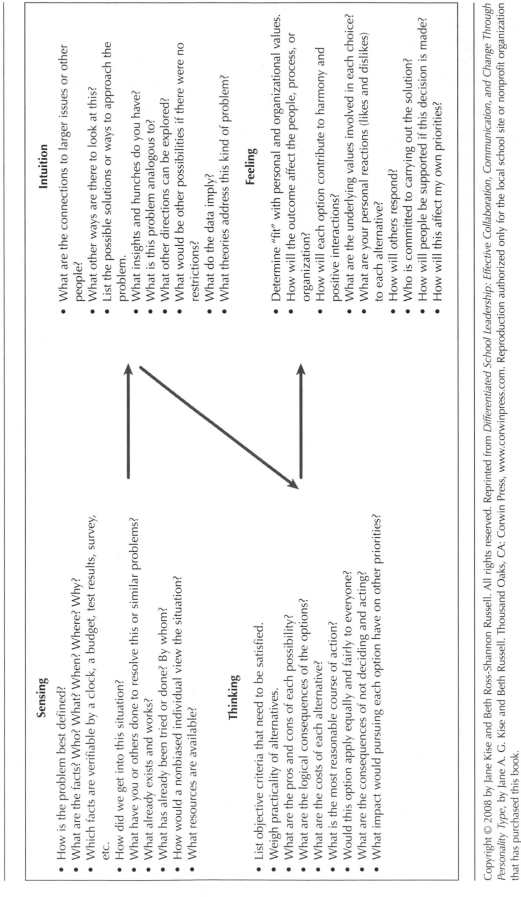

- Use the "dominant group" process described in the "S'more Dilemma" example. While this takes more time, when working alone, the groups often do a better job of contributing through their strengths.
- Formalize the process of checking the reactions of the team members with preferences least like the "team type," perhaps providing extra time for them to prepare a response.

Several ways to use this model are given throughout this book, including

- Leadership team building (page 64)
- Creating school vision (page 92)
- Defining a vision of parent involvement (page 134)
- Student discipline (page 123)
- Parent conferencing (page 147)

Resource C: Making Type a Schoolwide Language

In many of our examples, everyone in the school understands their own personality type. You can use these pages in many ways:

- At a personal level, to reflect on your own leadership and communication style, working to build on strengths and compensate for weaknesses
- To form an effective leadership team and develop team skills in communication, collaboration, and problem solving
- To help teachers form learning communities capable of deep collaboration that affects student achievement
- To work with students on understanding their learning styles, resolving conflict, and motivating them for high achievement

Obviously, the type knowledge needed increases at each level of use. *Differentiation Through Personality Types* (Kise, 2007) provides a workshop for introducing type to students. Below are strategies for increasing teacher knowledge of type so that they can

- Improve team collaboration, recognizing and benefiting from each other's strengths and suggestions
- Use the concepts to adjust their classrooms to meet the needs of all students. Evidence changes beliefs. Having teachers try type techniques in their classrooms convinces them that students have different learning needs.
- Accurately explain type concepts to students. When students also know about type
  - They can learn to recognize when work, instead of being "too hard," is outside of their learning style, then apply strategies to do it.

    o Teachers can use the concepts for classroom management and understanding.

    o Type can serve as a neutral language in discipline (see Chapter 9).

    o The concepts can be used to help them develop as independent learners.

Staff Development Exercises That Help Teachers Understand Type Differences

Page 60 lists options for helping teachers identify their own personality types. The following exercises help them internalize what the preferences mean in the classroom.

Extraversion and Introversion

For Staff. The goal of this exercise is to help teachers see the different amounts of wait time people with preferences for Extraversion and Introversion need before they are ready to speak. During a staff development session, provide everyone with a card that is red on one side and green on the other; coloring circles on each side of an index card is sufficient. Pose a question for them to consider:

- Their response to a film clip you've shown
- Their reaction to a new process you're introducing
- A short case study on student behavior. What action would they take?
- What one book do they wish everyone in the room would read? Or what movie would they like everyone to see?

Tell them to start with "red side up." When they are ready to talk about their response, even if they haven't formulated the whole answer, they are to turn their card to the green side.

Usually a few people turn their cards over to green right away. A few take three or four minutes. The rest are somewhere in the middle. Ask the group the following questions:

- What was it like to have "wait time" before the discussion started? Some of the Extraverts report that they almost had to get up and pace, the silence was so frustrating. Some of the Introverts will say, "We took how long? It only seemed like a moment." They often savor the time. Others will report that it gave them time to recall a specific book's title, although they could have remembered it more quickly if they could have conversed with someone about it.
- At what point did they want to talk? When they had a full answer? To bounce ideas off others? To clarify something? Many Extraverts are ready before they have a final answer; they think through conversation. Many Introverts want to have an answer ready before voicing an opinion.

Have teachers do a quick-write on what it means in their classrooms.

For Students. Ask all teachers to try a similar exercise with their students so they can see the results. Easy ways include the following:

- Pose a math question and asking students to raise their hands if they know the answer. Then pose another and have students think for at least a full minute before raising their hands. How many more go up?
- Use the exercise the same way it was used with teachers.
- Use the cards for "all-respond" discussions. Have all students turn the green side up. Begin a discussion, letting students know that everyone will need to participate out loud. When they have contributed a thought, they are to turn "red side up." Often, some of the more Introverted students will respond quickly, to get it over with. Some of the Extraverted students will struggle to stay silent, glancing around the room to see how many more cards need to turn over before they can speak again.

One teacher reported that in an honors social studies class, 10 minutes passed before all students were ready to discuss a substantive topic. "But," she said, "then it was the best discussion we'd ever had. Every student was prepared to answer and wanted to be called on."

The teachers can then discuss "fair classrooms" with students. Extraversion and Introversion is about having the energy to learn, so classrooms need both interactive and reflective time.

Sensing and Intuition

For Staff. Ask all teachers to write about a snowman for two minutes. They can't ask questions.

After they are finished, display the definition of Sensing and Intuition (page 7). Ask for volunteers to read what they wrote and have the group guess whether the response is more Sensing or Intuitive. (Note that this is *not* a definitive way to determine each person's preference. They may have been second-guessing what was wanted, wondered what this was for and not really engaged, and so on.) Emphasize that Sensing and Intuition are unconscious processes; we naturally pay attention to information through one of the processes first. If asked, everyone in the room could have produced a Sensing response, such as directions for building a snowman or a description of a snowman. If asked, everyone in the room could also have written an Intuitive response, such as a fictional story, poem, analogy, or philosophical statement about snowmen.

Sample responses from middle-school students are given in Table C.1, Student Snowman Descriptions. Make copies of the descriptions, cut them apart, and shuffle them. Instruct teachers to work in groups to sort the descriptions into Sensing, Intuitive, or unsure. This gives them practice before using the exercise with students.

For Students. Have teachers use the same exercise with students. The way we debrief this exercise is typical of how we prevent labeling or stereotyping. The

Table C.1   Student Snowman Descriptions

Sensing	Intuition
A snowman is tall, and it has three circles stacked on top of each other. There is a big circle on the bottom and a medium-sized one in the middle. Then there is a small one on the top, and a snowman is cold. You can only make a snowman in the winter. A snowman has a hat on its head, and its nose is made of a carrot. Then in the middle of the snowman are three charcoal balls lined up on it. Then you put a scarf around its neck. Then you put two charcoal balls for his eyes. Then you're done.	Once upon a time there was a snow-woman. She was the best snowman there was. And so one day she saw a boy snowman and then she fell in love, and so she told her snow-woman friends that she fell in love. Her friends were like, "With who?" and she said, "The boy who just moved next door to me." And so then she said, "He is so fine." So the snowman and her friends and she went out with him, and her snowfriends tried to get with him, and she was like, "This is my man. You'll better back up." So they were like, "Who you think you talkin' to?"
It's white and has two gumball eyes. It has three sections, head, body and bottom. Also, it has a scarf. Me and my friends built it at school the other day. We spent 30 minutes before lunch working on it. We tried making the balls frozen so if someone was to try to destroy it they would get hurt. The snowman stands six feet tall and has stick arms. If you wanted to see the snowman, here it is [picture included].	A long time ago in the northern part of Alaska, a young kid found a bottle filled with something blue in it. He ran to go show it to his mom, but he slipped on some ice. The bottle fell and cracked. The blue stuff poured into the snow, it made . . .
A snowman is made of snow, and sometimes he has raisins as eyes and a carrot nose. People make snowmen in their yard on a snowy day or a nice winter day. There can be snowmen, women, or angels. A snowman is always white, unless you see a couple of yellow spots. People build snowmen to just knock down, to talk to, or they're bored. People also use a scarf, mittens, even twigs for their arms. People can also use snowmen to use as plays or stuff like that. Making snowmen is what a lot of people do for fun in the winter. It's like a tradition. Snowmen also melt when it starts to get warm outside.	Once upon a time there was a snowman. He lived in the North Pole and he loved it. He could slide down icy slopes or ski on icicles. He would eat snowballs with snocones for dessert. He was so happy. Until that fateful day when global warming melted away the region he lived in. He ran from the heat, but it only created more heat that melted him faster. He found a passing iceberg and jumped on. He floated as far as Florida where it was hot all the time. He ran as fast as he could to the nearest supermarket where he went straight to the frozen food section. He opened the door of an ice freezer and jumped in. He was frozen once again! The end.
A snowman is made of snow obviously. He usually consists of three or more balls of snow for the body. The stereotypical way to dress him up is a top hat on the snowman's head, a carrot for his nose, lumps of coal for his mouth and for buttons, and two sticks for arms. I always thought it was fun to run and tackle the snowman, but that's just me.	Once there was a snowman that was all alone and had no friends. He always played hide-and-go-seek with squirrels. One day a bunny came by and the snowman bent down and petted the bunny. Next think you know, the bunny bit the snowman's carrot nose off.

Sensing	Intuition
Snowmen are cool. You make them during winter. When I was little, we made one every year. We used food items, hats, and fake jewelry. Our snowman had a lot of snow always. The height of them would be somewhere around five feet, and then when it got warm, we took off all the stuff and ruined it. Now we don't make them because no one cares about them like we used to.	There was once a snowman named Cheesecake because that was all he ate. One day Cheesecake went to buy a cheesecake for his birthday, but to his horror when he got there it was on fire. "Save the cheesecakes?" he yelled. Then he started to run to save the cheesecakes. When something stopped him: "I'm your fairy God squirrel. My name is Shminda," it said. Then it gave him a magic potion, and Cheesecake saved the cheesecakes (after drinking the potion). The end.
A snowman has three parts to make a body. A snowman's hands are sticks. A snowman has no legs. A snowman's nose is a carrot. A snowman is made out of snow. A snowman can't move. A snowman does not have daring. A snowman can't feel. A snowman's eyes are not real.	The snowman is a real man who lives with his son, his wife, and his pet dog, and he is a musician and is always on field trips and promises his son that he will be at his hockey game and never does, and the night that he came back he brought his son a harmonica. And he says, "It's a magical harmonica," and he takes it to school and at school there is a bully who always picks on him and he takes the harmonica away and on the next trip that his father goes on he dies in a car accident and two years later in the winter his father's spirit comes back but he goes into a snowman and he helps his son a lot. He helps him beat the bully and his son is the only one who knows about him and when it starts to be summer his son takes him to the mountains so he can live always.
You roll a big snowball for the bottom, then you make a medium snow ball for his body. Then you roll a small snowball for its head. Put some buttons in its body. After that, get a hat and put it on the top of his head. Also, grab a carrot for its nose. Get some sticks and put them at the middle so that you could build his own hand and put a mitten on it. Put some food on it.	There once was a snowman, and he really liked cheese. One day, he ate a piece of radioactive cheese. This cheese turned him more and more into a radioactive animal cracker with each bite. Once he had swallowed it, he was a radioactive animal cracker that was shaped like a snowman. As a radioactive animal cracker (called r-aac from here on out) he still really liked cheese . . .

teachers tell students that they might really be an N even though they wrote an S example, perhaps because they were second-guessing what the teacher wanted. Or an S might have written an N example because he or she loves telling stories. We also ask, "If we'd asked you to write about how to build a snowman, could you have done so? If we'd said to write a fiction story about a snowman, could you have done so?" All heads nod at both questions.

So that students internalize the difference, teachers might extend the exercise by choosing another object, such as a two-liter pop bottle, a pop can, or a bag of cookies. Have students work in pairs to

- Use the Sensing preference to generate a list of 20 facts about the object
- Use the Intuitive preference to generate a list of 20 ways to use the object (other than its intended use)

Talk with the students about which list was easiest for them. Often, they agree that they struggled more with one than the other.

In both cases, the exercises build staff awareness of the differences in how their colleagues and their students learn. Have them discuss their classroom experiences in their learning communities:

- Have them bring samples of student work. What did they notice? How did students react?
- What did they learn about their own classroom biases?

Random Puzzlers: Helping Teachers and Students Understand Their Learning Needs

Again, this exercise can be used with both staff and students, adjusting the questions for student ability levels.

For Staff.

1. Duplicate Table C.2 and cut apart the problems, so that you have enough separate problems for each participant to have one, plus a few extra.

2. Fold the strips and place them in a basket or other attractive container.

3. Tell participants, "You'll each be drawing a 'puzzler,' a problem to solve, from this basket. There are eight different problems that require different skills. Please don't look at your problem until everyone has theirs. Then, we will all work on our problems in silence. This is an Introverted activity. If you finish while others are still working, please come up and draw another activity from the basket and begin working on that one."

4. Circulate among participants to check on progress. Often, people who receive problems that match their personality preferences are done in no time but then get one that doesn't match. A few people really struggle.

Table C.2

1. Generate a list of 20 things associated with the word *signal* (e.g., fire alarm).

2. List 10 things that become smaller as they age (e.g., oranges shrink as they dehydrate).

3. A PALINDROME is a word or number that reads the same forward or backward. The year 1991 and the word *level* are good examples. Your challenge is to determine how many whole numbers between 100 and 1,000 are palindromes.

4. A group of friends walked to school, each knowing a special secret. Each told one more person the "SECRET" during math class. During music class, everyone who knew told two people. By the end of the lunch hour, 48 people knew the "SECRET." How many people started the day walking to school knowing the secret?

5. If three times a number is increased by 12, the result is the same as when twice the number is increased by 24. And the lucky number is . . . ?

6. Printed below are code words for various VEGETABLES. When you have identified one of the words, use the letters in that word to help you decode the rest of the words.
   GCOOSVR   RNLQCGM   NSVCVSFR
   GFJFOZ   SQLSQR

7. Create a rhyming poem of at least four lines about SPAGHETTI.

8. Generate a list describing 20 uses for old, worn shoes (e.g., a flower planter).

5. After five minutes or so, have participants do one of the following. Note that either of these steps allow participants to get up and move around—Extraversion—after the experience of Introverted problem solving.

   - Form problem groups—those working on the same problem gather to help each other solve it. Emphasize giving hints rather than providing answers. What help can you offer that allows the person to keep thinking?

   - *Or* go immediately to analysis. Have participants rate their experience with their problem and line up on a continuum by posting the following signs:
     o I *hate* doing this kind of problem.
     o Neutral—neither fun nor frustrating
     o I *loved* my problem.

     Then ask for comments from each end of the continuum about why they're standing where they are. What was the experience like? Common comments include, "I wanted to talk with someone to see if I was on track," "I would have done better if I'd known what the other problems were," "I got the *wrong* one for me and felt stupid when I saw others going up to get a second one when I'd barely started," and "It was so nice to have it quiet so I could work!"

6. Hand out Table C.3—all of the problems, answers, and the type preference they fit best.

7. Have group participants discuss the following questions. Depending on the number of groups, you might have all groups discuss questions 1–3, then assign questions 4, 5, or 6 to different groups.

   - On a scale of 1 (anxiety producing) to 10 (enjoyable), what was your experience in working on the puzzler you received?

   - Did your puzzler match your learning style? Did the match or lack of match affect your response to the problem?

   - What little changes could be made to the activity to make it more enjoyable? (Note: This asks how to adjust the puzzlers for other learning styles.) Possible responses include
     o If I could have worked with a partner . . . (Extraversion)
     o If I could have talked it through with someone . . . (Extraversion)
     o If I'd just known what others were working on . . . (Extraversion)
     o If I could have had more examples . . . (Sensing)
     o If I'd had one of the other puzzlers . . . (Often Feeling, since they can struggle with the logic required in so many)
     o If I could have written about a food of my choice . . . (Feeling)

   - Few puzzlers tap into the Feeling preference. Examples include
     o Generate a list of 10 words that describe the feeling or texture of sadness.
     o Write a rhyming poem about your best friend (favorite food, etc.).
     o Generate a list of 20 ways a book might be helpful to someone. Include uses beyond reading, such as pressing flowers!

     Ask the Feeling types in your group about their experiences with logic problems. While many Feeling types excel at math, those who

Table C.3   Random Puzzlers

1. Generate a list of 20 things associated with the word *signal* (e.g., fire alarm).	*Intuition—making connections.* *Sample answers: stopwatch, signal gun, wink, hand clap, bugle, etc.*
2. List 10 things that become smaller as they age (e.g., oranges shrink as they dehydrate).	*Intuition—making connections.* *Sample answers: people, flowers, people's egos, etc.*
3. A PALINDROME is a word or number that reads the same forward or backward. The year 1991 and the word level are good examples. Your challenge is to determine how many whole numbers between 100 and 1,000 are palindromes.	*Thinking—looking at patterns, ordering the world.* *Answer: 90. There is a pattern, 10 for each number beginning and ending with 1, 2, 3, 4, . . . 9, 101, 111, 121 . . .*
4. A group of friends walked to school, each knowing a special secret. Each told one more person the "SECRET" during math class. During music class, everyone who knew told two people. By the end of the lunch hour, 48 people knew the "SECRET." How many people started the day walking to school knowing the secret?	*Thinking—using logic.* *Answer: Eight people.*
5. If three times a number is increased by 12, the result is the same as when twice the number is increased by 24. And the lucky number is . . . ?	*Sensing—using procedures to solve a problem.* $3X + 12 = 2X + 24. \ X = 12$
6. Printed below are code words for various VEGETABLES. When you have identified one of the words, use the letters in that word to help you decode the rest of the words. GCOOSVR RNLQCGM NSVCVSFR GFJFOZ SQLSQR	*Thinking—finding patterns.* *Carrots, celery, spinach, onions, potatoes.*
7. Create a rhyming poem of at least four lines about SPAGHETTI.	*Intuition—creating something new.*
8. Generate a list describing 20 uses for old, worn shoes (e.g., a flower planter).	*Intuition—brainstorming.* *Sample answers: doorstop, pencil holder, insect cruncher, etc.*

do usually had strong, favorite teachers or also consider themselves good at procedures or Intuition. Empirically, Sensing/Feeling types most often claim to have math anxiety.

- Look back at the puzzlers. How might some of them be changed to meet the needs of more of the preferences?
  o Example: for the SECRET, it might start with a note on how harmful gossip can be. Feeling types might then be more motivated to calculate how quickly gossip spreads.
- How could this activity be adapted for use with students to help them learn that effort creates ability?
- Have each group share their major conclusions with the whole group.
- Have participants quick-write on one of the following prompts: "I can use what I learned through this exercise with my students by. . . ." or "I can reach more students if I. . . ."

For Students. Students can work on the same problems, adjusted for ability levels. When they've completed them, ask them what would have made it easier? Goals with students are

- Help them understand that their struggles were related to learning styles, not ability. What would have helped them put in extra effort to achieve? Their responses will be similar to those of the adults.
- Have them consider what this means for future assignments that require them to work out of their learning style. How can they adjust? What help will they need?

Differentiation Case Study

Set up a station-based lesson, one station for each of the four learning styles as described in *Differentiation Through Personality Types* (Kise, 2006). A sample of differentiated assessment choices for the novel *The Skin I'm In* (Flake, 1998) is included in Chart C.1.

Note that this exercise is an example of embedded staff development. At one school, all teachers had read the book so that we could discuss what we learned about our students' lives and how we might use the text with our students. However, we also made use of a chance to model how to differentiate.

- Enlarge to poster size the activities for each quadrant, each on a separate sheet of paper. Set one at each station.
- Place blank poster paper and markers at each station. Note: for groups larger than 10, set up two sets of stations. One set should illustrate a social studies or language arts unit and the other a math or science unit.
- Ask participants to walk around silently and review the different stations. They should write their responses to the following prompts on the flip chart paper provided without discussing their reactions with anyone. When they have finished, they can return to their seats and talk quietly with others who are done.

- Then have participants meet in learning styles groups (Introversion/ Sensing, Introversion/Intuition, Extraversion/Sensing, Extraversion/ Intuition) and discuss their reactions to the way the exercise was structured. What did they like and dislike about how the lessons were communicated to them? Note that the exercise actually meets *no one's* learning style. Extraverts want to discuss their reactions as they occur; Introverts want the whole lesson on one piece of paper so they can examine it while sitting down.

Note: The learning style framework involves the *quadrants* of the type table so that students have the *energy* and *information* to learn.

Type table quadrants

Introversion Sensing	Introversion Intuition
Extraversion Sensing	Extraversion Intuition

Thinking and Feeling also play a role in learning, but the quadrants of the type table provide a better four-part framework for initial differentiation of learning styles; conflicts in learning styles are often most acute when Introverted teachers have Extraverted students and vice versa.

For communication and leadership, though, the function pairs are the best way to examine differences.

Function Pairs

Sensing Thinking	Sensing Feeling	Intuition Feeling	Intuition Thinking

Chart C.1   *The Skin I'm In:* "Assessment Activities" for Teachers

Choose one of the following ways to share with other teachers your experiences with reading *The Skin I'm In*.

Introversion and Sensing	Introversion and Intuition
• Prepare a flow map of about 10 key events in the book. By each event, write your reaction to that event or why you think it was important to the story. • As you read, keep a list of events in the book that remind you of events or students in your own classroom.	• Think of three to five questions you would like to ask the character in your book. Imagine that you are the character and answer the questions. • Brainstorm how you might use the book, or an excerpt from it, with your students. What would you have them do? What would be your essential question?
Motivating words for IS learners: Read, identify, list, label, name, notice, observe, apply, analyze, graph, examine, work, prepare, do, organize, complete, answer, listen	**Motivating words for IN learners**: Read, think, consider, design, evaluate, clarify, speculate, dream, envision, paraphrase, brainstorm, create, elaborate, illustrate, write, reflect, chew on, make connections, compare, contrast
Extraversion and Sensing	**Extraversion and Intuition**
• Make a tree map of two or three major themes of your book and the events that explore those themes. Use the map to tell your group what you learned from the book. • Make a "Hall of Fame/Hall of Shame" poster of characters in the book, using your own drawings, clip art, or magazine photos. Under each picture write why your character deserves his or her placing.	• Collaborate with another teacher to act out a dialogue based on a scene in the book. However, change the ending to reflect a better choice a character could have made. • Design your own method to communicate to other teachers your reactions to or learnings from the novel you read.
Motivating words for ES learners: Build, show, assemble, tell, discover, make, demonstrate, figure out, touch, design, suggest, solve, choose, construct, examine, explore, discuss	**Motivating words for EN learners**: Create, solve, discover, pretend, design, synthesize, collaborate, find a new . . . , generate, visualize, evaluate, develop, problem solve, experiment, discuss

Resource D: Further Reading on Personality Type

Hirsh, S. K., & Kise, J. A. G. (2006a). *SoulTypes: Matching your personality and spiritual path.* Minneapolis, MN: Augsburg Books.

Hirsh, S. K., & Kise, J. A. G. (2006b). *Work it out: Using personality type to improve team performance* (Rev. ed.). Mountain View, CA: Davies-Black.

Hirsh, S. K., & Kummerow, J. M. (1989). *LifeTypes.* New York: Warner Books.

Kise, J. A. G. (2006). *Differentiated coaching: A framework for helping teachers change.* Thousand Oaks, CA: Corwin Press.

Kise, J. A. G. (2007). *Differentiation through personality types: A framework for instruction, assessment, and classroom management.* Thousand Oaks, CA: Corwin Press.

Murphy, E. (1992). *The developing child.* Mountain View, CA: Davies-Black.

Pajak, E. (2003). *Honoring diverse teaching styles: A guide for supervisors.* Alexandria, VA: Association for Supervision and Curriculum Development.

Payne, D., & van Sandt, S. (2007). *Psychological type in schools: Applications for educators* (2nd ed.). Gainesville, FL: Center for Applications of Psychological Type.

Quenk, N. L. (2002). *Was that really me? How everyday stress brings out our hidden personality.* Mountain View, CA: CPP, Inc.

References

Acheson, K. A., & Gall, M. D. (1980). *Techniques in the clinical supervision of teachers.* White Plains, NY: Longman.

Andrews, D., & Lewis, M. (2002). The experience of a professional community: Teachers developing a new image of themselves and their workplace. *Educational Research, 44*(3), 237–254.

Annenberg Institute for School Reform, Brown University (2005). *Professional development strategies that improve instruction: Professional learning communities.* Providence, RI: Author. Retrieved February 7, 2005, from www.annenberginstitute.org.

Aram, J. D. (1990). Appreciative interchange: The force that makes cooperation possible. In S. Srivasta, D. L. Cooperrider, & Associates (Eds.), *Appreciative management and leadership* (pp. 175–204). San Francisco: Jossey-Bass.

Barger, N. J., & Kirby, L. K. (1995). *The challenge of change in organizations: Helping employees thrive in the new frontier.* Palo Alto, CA: Consulting Psychologists Press.

Barth, R. S. (2005). Turning book burners into lifelong learners. In DuFour, R., Eaker, R., & DuFour, R. (Eds.), *On common ground: The power of professional learning communities* (pp. 114–133). Bloomington, IN: National Educational Service.

Berens, L. V., Cooper, S. A., Ernst, L. K., Martin, C. R., Myers, S., Nardi, D., et al. (2001). *Quick guide to the 16 personality types in organizations: Understanding personality differences in the workplace.* Huntington Beach, CA: Telos Publications.

Block, P. (2002). *The answer to how is yes: Acting on what matters.* San Francisco: Barrett-Koehler Publishers, Inc.

Blumburg, A. (1974). *Supervisors and teachers: A private cold war.* Berkeley, CA: McCutchan.

Bridges, W. (2000). *The character of organization: Using personality type in organization development* (updated ed.). Mountain View, CA: Davies-Black.

Brock, S. A. (1997). Strategies for using psychological type to enhance leaders' communication. In Fitzgerald, C. R., & Kirby, L. K. (Eds.), *Developing leaders: Research and applications in psychological type and leadership development* (pp. 465–486). Palo Alto, CA: Davies-Black Publishing.

Chavkin, N. F., & Gonzalez, D. L. (1995). *Forging partnerships between Mexican American parents and the schools* (Report No. EDO-RC-95-8). Washington, DC: Office of Educational Research and Improvement. (ERIC Document Reproduction Service No. ED388489)

Checkley, K. (2004). A is for audacity: Lessons in leadership from Lorraine Monroe. *Educational Leadership, 61*(7), 8–13.

Chevalier, R. (2000). The community engagement process at St. Martin's Parish. In Senge, P., Cambron-McCabe, N., Lucas, T., Smith, B., Dutton, J., & Kleiner, A. *Schools that learn* (pp. 489–495). New York: Doubleday.

Clancy, S. G. (1997). STJs and change: Resistance, reaction, or misunderstanding? In Fitzgerald, C. & Kirby, L. K. (Eds.), *Developing leaders: Research and applications in psychological type and leadership development* (pp. 415–438). Palo Alto, CA: Consulting Psychologists Press.

Cogan, M. L. (1973). *Clinical supervision.* Boston: Houghton Mifflin.

Costa, A. L., & Garmston, R. J. (1994). *Cognitive coaching: A foundation for Renaissance Schools.* Norwood, MA: Christopher-Gordon.

Costa, A. L., & Kallick, B. (2000). *Discovering and exploring habits of mind.* Alexandria, VA: Association for Supervision and Curriculum Development.

Cotton, K. (2003). *Principals and student achievement: What the research says.* Alexandria, VA: Association for Supervision and Curriculum Development.

Danielson, C. (2002). *Enhancing student achievement: A framework for school improvement.* Alexandria, VA: Association for Supervision and Curriculum Development.

Davis, S., Jenkins, G., Hunt, R., & Draper, S. M. (2005). *The pact: How three young men make a promise and fulfill a dream.* New York: Dutton.

Delpit, L. (1995). *Other people's children: Cultural conflict in the classroom.* New York: The New Press.

Dewey, J. (1910). *How we think.* Minneola, NY: Dover Publications, Inc.

Drummond, K. V., & Stipek, D. (2004). Low-income parents' beliefs about their role in children's academic learning. *The Elementary School Journal, 104*(3), 197–213.

DuFour, R. (2004a). Are you looking out the window or in a mirror? *Journal of Staff Development, 25*(3), 63–64.

DuFour, R. (2004b). What is a "professional learning community"? *Educational Leadership, 61*(8), 6–11.

Dutton, N., Quantz, R., & Dutton, N. (2000). The great game of high school. In Senge, P., Cambron-McCabe, N., Lucas, T., Smith, B., Dutton, J., & Kleiner, A., *Schools that learn* (pp. 370–377). New York: Doubleday.

Eckert, P. (2000). Interview quoted in Kleiner, A., Communities of practice. In Senge, P., Cambron-McCabe, N., Lucas, T., Smith, B., Dutton, J., & Kleiner, A., *Schools that learn* pp. 377–380). New York: Doubleday.

The Efficacy Institute (2006). About our approach. Retrieved March 23, 2007, from www.efficacy.org.

Eisner, E. W. (1979). *The educational imagination: On the design and evaluation of educational programs.* New York: Macmillan.

Epstein, J. L. (2002). *School, family and community partnerships: Your handbook for action* (2nd ed.). Thousand Oaks, CA: Corwin Press.

Epstein, J. L., & Jansorn, N. R. (2004). School, family, and community partnerships link the plan. *Education Digest, 69*(6), 19–23.

Euvrard, G. (2006). The values manifesto project. *Educational Leadership, 63*(7), 43–46.

Felder, R. M. (2002). The effects of personality type on engineering student performance and attitudes. *Journal of Engineering Education, 19*(1), 3–17.

Fields-Smith, C. (2005). African American parents before and after *Brown. Journal of Curriculum and Supervision, 20*(2), 129–135.

Fink, E., & Resnick, L. B. (2001). Developing principals as instructional leaders. *Phi Delta Kappan, 82*(8), 598–626.

Fitzgerald, C. (1997). The MBTI and leadership development. In Fitzgerald, C., & Kirby, L. (Eds.), *Developing leaders: Research and applications in psychological type and leadership development* (pp. 33–59). Palo Alto, CA: Davies-Black.

Flake, S. G. (1998). *The skin I'm in.* New York: Hyperion.

Fullan, M. (1993). *Change Forces: Probing the depths of educational reform.* London: The Falmer Press.

Fullan, M. (2001). *The NEW meaning of educational change* (3rd ed.). New York: Teachers College Press.

Giles, H. C. (2005). Three narratives of parent-educator relationships: Toward counselor repertoires for bridging the urban parent-school divide. *Professional School Counseling, 8*(3), 228–236. Retrieved March 23, 2007, from http://schooled.brooklyn.cuny.edu/Giles-narratives.pdf.

Goldhammer, R. (1969). *Clinical supervision: Special methods for the supervision of teachers.* New York: Holt, Reinhart & Winston.

Goodwin, D. R. (2006). *Team of rivals: The political genius of Abraham Lincoln.* New York: Simon & Schuster.

Haley, C. V., & Pimi, R. (1994). Blazing international trails in strategic decision-making research. In *Proceedings of the Myers-Briggs Type Indicator and Leadership: An International Research Conference* (pp. 19–29). College Park, MD: National Leadership Institute.

Hammer, A. E. (Ed.). (1996). *MBTI applications: A decade of research on the Myers-Briggs Type Indicator®.* Palo Alto, CA: Consulting Psychologists Press.

Hargreaves, A. (1994) *Changing teachers, changing times: Teachers' work and culture in the postmodern age.* New York: Teachers College Press.

Hargreaves, A. (2002). Teaching and betrayal. *Teachers and teaching: Theory and practice, 8*(3/4), 394–407.

Hargreaves, A., & Fink, D. (2004). The seven principles of sustainable leadership. *Educational Leadership, 61*(7), 8–13.

Heifetz, R. A., & Linsky, M. (2004). When leadership spells danger. *Educational Leadership, 61*(7), 33–37.

Hirsh, S. K., & Kise, J. A. G. (2000). *Introduction to type and coaching.* Mountain View, CA: Consulting Psychologists Press.

Hirsh, S. K., & Kise, J. A. G. (2001). *Using the MBTI tool in organizations* (3rd ed.). Mountain View, CA: Consulting Psychologists Press.

Hirsh, S. K., & Kise, J. A. G. (2006a). *SoulTypes: Matching your personality and spiritual path* (2nd ed.). Minneapolis, MN: Augsburg Fortress.

Hirsh, S. K., & Kise, J. A. G. (2006b). *Work it out: Using personality type to improve team performance* (rev. ed.). Mountain View, CA: Davies-Black.

Huelsman III, C. B. (2002). *Mathematics anxiety: An interdisciplinary approach.* Updated unpublished master's thesis, Marylhurst University, Marylhurst, OR.

Hunter, M. (1984). Knowing, teaching and supervising. In P. L. Holford (Ed.), *Using what we know about teaching.* Alexandria, VA: Association for Supervision and Curriculum Development.

Jensen, E. (1998). *Teaching with the brain in mind.* Alexandria, VA: Association for Supervision and Curriculum Development.

Johnson, D. A. (1992). Predicting promotion to management in the wholesale grocery industry using the type differentiation indicator. *Journal of Psychological Type, 23,* 51–59.

Jones, S. (2006, July 13). We have to stop the slide among black students. *StarTribune* (Minneapolis, MN), p. A15.

Joyce, B. (2004). How are professional learning communities created? *Phi Delta Kappan, 86*(1), 76–83.

Jung, C. G. (1966). Two essays on analytical psychology. In R. F. C. Hull (Trans.), *Collected works* (Vol. 7). Princeton, NJ: Princeton University Press.

Jung, C. G. (1969). Psychology and religion: West and East. In R. F. C. Hull (Trans.), *Collected works* (Vol. 11). Princeton, NJ: Princeton University Press.

Killen, D., & Murphy, D. (2003). *Introduction to type and conflict.* Mountain View, CA: CPP, Inc.

Kirby, L. (1997). Introduction: Psychological type and the Myers-Briggs Type Indicator. In Fitzgerald, C. & Kirby, L. (Eds.), *Developing leaders: Research and applications in psychological type and leadership development* (pp. 3–31). Palo Alto, CA: Davies-Black.

Kise, J. A. G. (2002, September). [Classroom observation field notes]. Unpublished raw data.

Kise, J. A. G. (2003). [Dissertation journal notes]. Unpublished raw data.

Kise, J. A. G. (2004). *Long underwear in the tropics: A study of a team of teachers, reflective practice, learning styles, and classroom climates.* Unpublished doctoral dissertation, University of St. Thomas, St. Paul, MN. (UMI No. 3126503)

Kise, J. A. G. (2005). Coaching teachers for change: Using the concepts of psychological type to reframe teacher resistance. *Journal of Psychological Type, 65*(6), 47–58.

Kise, J. A. G. (2006). *Differentiated coaching: A framework for helping teachers change.* Thousand Oaks, CA: Corwin Press.

Kise, J. A. G. (2007). *Differentiation through personality types.* Thousand Oaks, CA: Corwin Press.

Kleiner, A. (2000). Communities of practice. In Senge, P., Cambron-McCabe, N., Lucas, T., Smith, B., Dutton, J., & Kleiner, A., *Schools that learn* (pp. 377–380). New York: Doubleday.

Lam, L. T. (2004). Test success, family style. *Educational Leadership, 61*(8), 44–47.

Lapp, D., & Flood, J. (2004). No parent left behind. In Lapp, D., Block, C. C., Cooper, E. J., Flood, J., Roser, N., & Tinajero, J. V. (Eds.), *Teaching all the children: Strategies for developing literacy in an urban setting* (pp. 63–72). New York: The Guilford Press.

Lawrence, G. (1993). *People types and tiger stripes* (3rd ed.). Gainesville, FL: Center for Applications of Psychological Type.

Lawrence-Lightfoot, S. (2000). *Respect: An exploration.* Cambridge, Massachusetts, Perseus Books.

Leonard, P. E., & Leonard, L. J. (2001). The collaborative prescription: Remedy or reverie? *International Journal of Leadership in Education, 4*(4), 383–399.

Lewis, A. E., & Forman, T. A. (2002). Contestation or collaboration? A comparative study of home-school relations. *Anthropology & Education Quarterly, 33*(1), 60–89.

Little, J. W. (1990). The persistence of privacy: Autonomy and initiative in teachers' professional relations. *Teachers College Record, 91*(4). Retrieved November 11, 2004, from http://www.tcrecord.org/Content.asp? ContentId=406

Lortie, D. (1975). *Schoolteacher.* Chicago: University of Chicago Press.

MacDaid, G. P., McCaulley, M. H., & Kainz, R. I. (1991). *Atlas of type tables.* Gainesville, FL: Center for Applications of Psychological Type.

Marzano, R. J. (2003). *What works in schools: Translating research into action.* Alexandria, VA: Association for Supervision and Curriculum Development.

Marzano, R. J., Waters, T., & McNulty, B. A. (2005). *School leadership that works: From research to results.* Alexandria, VA: Association for Supervision and Curriculum Development.

McCaulley, M. H. (1975). How individual differences affect health care teams. *Health Team News, 1*(8), 1–4.

McCaulley, M. H. (1990). The Myers-Briggs Type Indicator and leadership. In K. E. Clark & M. B. Clark (Eds.), *Measures of leadership* (pp. 381–418). West Orange, NJ: Leadership Library of America, Inc.

McNeil, L. M. (2000). *Contradictions of school reform: Educational costs of standardized testing.* New York: Routledge.

Murphy, E. (1992). *The developing child.* Mountain View, CA: Davies-Black.

Myers, I. B., with Myers, P. B. (1993). *Gifts Differing: Understanding personality type.* Palo Alto, CA: Consulting Psychologists Press.

Myers, I. B. (1998). *Introduction to Type®* (6th ed.). Mountain View, CA: Consulting Psychologists Press.

Myers, I. B., McCaulley, M., Quenk, N., & Hammer, A. (1998). *MBTI® manual: A guide to the development and use of the Myers-Briggs Type Indicator®* (3rd ed.). Palo Alto, CA: Consulting Psychologists Press.

Newsweek (2003, April 21). The secret war, *141*(16), 25.

Nichols-Solomon, R. (2001). Barriers to serious parent involvement. *Education Digest, 66*(5), 33–37.

Nuñez, R. (1994). *Schools, parents, and empowerment: An ethnographic study of Mexican-origin parents participation in their children's schools.* Unpublished doctoral dissertation, San Diego State University/Claremont Graduate School, San Diego/Claremont, CA.

Olivos, E. M. (2004). Tensions, contradictions, and resistance: An activist's reflection of the struggles of Latino parents in the public school system. *High School Journal, 87*(4), 25–35. Retrieved September 5, 2006, from http://www.ebscohost.com.

Olweus, D. (2003). A profile of bullying. *Educational Leadership, 60*(6), 12–17.

O'Neill, B. A. (1986). An investigation of the relationship between teacher/student personality type and discipline referrals in two Massachusetts high schools (Doctoral dissertation, Boston University, 1986). *Dissertation Abstracts International, 47/04-A,* 1141.

Pajak, E. (2003). *Honoring diverse teaching styles: A guide for supervisors.* Arlington, VA: Association for Supervision and Curriculum Development.

Pena, D. C. (2000). Parent involvement: Influencing factors and implications. *Journal of Educational Research, 94*(1), 42–54.

Quenk, N. L. (1993). *Beside ourselves: Our hidden personality in everyday life.* Palo Alto, CA: Consulting Psychologists Press.

Reeves, D. B. (2004). *Accountability for learning: How teachers and school leaders can take charge.* Arlington, VA: Association for Supervision and Curriculum Development.

Reeves, D. B. (2005). Putting it all together. In DuFour, R., Eaker, R., & DuFour, R., *On common ground: The power of professional learning communities* (pp. 45–64). Bloomington, IN: National Educational Service.

Reeves, D. B. (2006). *The learning leader: How to focus school improvement for better results.* Alexandria, VA: Association for Supervision and Curriculum Development.

Resnick, L. B. (1999). Making America smarter. *Education Week Century Series, 18*(40), 38–40.

Resnick, L. B. (2005). *Year one: Principles of learning in action.* Instructional leadership workshop materials, Institute for Learning, Pittsburgh, PA.

Resnick, L. B. (2006). *Year two: Learning walks.* Instructional leadership workshop materials, Institute for Learning, Pittsburgh, PA.

Resnick, L. B., & Hall, M. W. (1998). Learning organizations for sustainable reform. *Daedalus: Journal of the American Arts and Sciences, 127*(4), 89–118.

Rushton, S., Knopp, T. Y., & Smith, R. L. (2006). Teacher of the year award recipients' Myers-Briggs personality profiles: Identifying teacher effectiveness profiles toward improved student outcomes. *Journal of Psychological Type, 66*(4), 23–34.

Rytting, M., Ware, R., & Prince, R. A. (1994). Bimodal distributions in a sample of CEOs: Validating evidence for the MBTI. *Journal of Psychological Type, 31*, 32–40.

Saphier, J. (2005). Masters of motivation. In DuFour, R., Eaker, R., & DuFour, R. (Eds.), *On common ground: The power of professional learning communities* (pp. 84–113). Bloomington, IN: National Educational Service.

Schmoker, M. (2006). *Results now: How we can achieve unprecedented improvements in teaching and learning.* Arlington, VA: Association for Supervision and Curriculum Development.

Senge, P. M., Kleiner, A., Roberts, C., Ross, R. B., & Smith, B. J. (1994). *The fifth discipline fieldbook: Strategies and tools for building a learning organization.* New York: Currency Doubleday.

Smyth, J., Dow, A., Hattam, R., Reid, A., & Shacklock, G. (2000). *Teachers' work in a globalizing economy.* London and New York: Falmer Press.

Sparks, D. (2005). *Leading for results: Transforming teaching, learning and relationships in schools.* Joint publication of National Staff Development Council, Corwin Press, and National Association of Secondary School Principals.

Sparks, D. (2006). "Appeal to the heart as well as the head." *Tools for Schools for a Dynamic Community of Learners and Leaders, 9*(4), 1–2.

Strahan, D. (2003). Promoting a collaborative professional culture in three elementary schools that have beaten the odds. *The Elementary School Journal, 104*(2), 127–146.

Suskind, R. (1998). *A hope in the unseen: An American odyssey from the inner city to the Ivy League.* New York: Broadway.

Tam, K. Y., & Heng, M. A. (2005). A case involving culturally and linguistically diverse parents in prereferral intervention. *Intervention in School and Clinic, 40*(4), 222–230.

Thurston, L. P., & Navarrette, L. A. (2003). Rural, poverty-level mothers: A comparative study of those with and without children who have special needs. *Rural Special Education Quarterly, 22*(1), 15–23.

Trueba, H. T., Jacobs, L., & Kirton, E. (1990). *Cultural conflict and adaptation: The case of Hmong children in American society.* New York: The Falmer Press.

Walck, C. L. (1997). Using the MBTI in management and leadership: A review of the literature. In Fitzgerald, C. & Kirby, L. (Eds.), *Developing leaders: Research and applications in psychological type and leadership development* (pp. 33–59). Palo Alto, CA: Davies-Black.

Waters, J. T., Marzano, R. J., & McNulty, B. (2004). Leadership that sparks learning. *Educational Leadership, 61*(7), 48–51.

Wheatley, M. J. (2002). *Turning to one another: Simple conversations to restore hope to the future.* San Francisco: Berrett-Koehler.

White, E. B. (1945). *Stuart Little.* New York: HarperCollins.

Whittaker, T. (2003). *What great principals do differently: Fifteen things that matter most.* Larchmont, NY: Eye on Education.

Wiseman, R. (2002). *Queen bees and wannabes: Helping your daughter survive cliques, gossip, boyfriends & other realities of adolescence.* New York: Three Rivers Press.

Zeman, N. (1991, September 9). Buzzwords. *Newsweek, 118*(11), 9–15.

Index

CORWIN
PRESS

The Corwin Press logo—a raven striding across an open book—represents the union of courage and learning. Corwin Press is committed to improving education for all learners by publishing books and other professional development resources for those serving the field of PreK–12 education. By providing practical, hands-on materials, Corwin Press continues to carry out the promise of its motto: **"Helping Educators Do Their Work Better."**